"[A] wake-up call." —*Spirituality and Health*

"Louv's case for outdoor play is a convincing one, and the possibility of a drug-free 'nature' cure for many modern ills is too tantalizing to ignore." —*Audubon* magazine, Editors' Choice

"A magnificent case for unplugging our kids from the Net and letting them roam free again in the woods."
—Mike Davis, author of *Ecology of Fear*

"Richard Louv's provocative new book about kids' growing 'nature-deficit disorder' . . . is raising debate and tough questions nationwide."
—*Parade* magazine

"*Last Child in the Woods* isn't an exercise in nostalgia. Mr. Louv provides plenty of evidence to back up his core contention."
—*The Wall Street Journal*

"Writing to the heart and intellect with telling anecdotes and pertinent research, Louv gives the reader—parent, educator, scientist—an assessment of the social and ecological consequences of America's divorce from nature and prescribes new paths for reconnecting children with nature, resulting in healthier, better-adjusted kids who will care for our planet."
—Craig Tufts, chief naturalist, National Wildlife Federation

"Startling. . . . Makes a strong argument for the fact that nature helps kids develop their senses, stimulates their imagination and teaches them to take risks." —*The Monroe (LA) News-Star*

"Louv has a wealth of advice for parents, teachers, policy-makers, and urban planners. . . . A must read for those with a keen interest in the subject." —*The Raleigh (NC) News and Observer*

"This book is an eye-opener for adults involved with children and for adults themselves. I hope it becomes the turning point it deserves to be." —Bernice Weissbourd, contributing editor to *Parents* magazine and author of *Putting Families First*

"*Last Child in the Woods* has hopeful things to say, too, citing a growing body of research that indicates that engagement with the natural world may prove a powerful antidote to many of the things that ail kids today. . . . Provides inspiring examples of ways and places where nature is consciously and thoughtfully being brought back into children's lives all over the country." —*The Madison (WI) Capital Times*

"Especially enchanting are Louv's personal experiences as a father of two boys and the love for his children which inspires so much of the narrative." —*In Balance* magazine

"A wake-up call for parents, educators, and anyone who cares about children and the future of our society. . . . This book is bound to get children off the couch and away from the screen, to re-ignite their innate sense of curiosity and awe. . . . *Last Child in the Woods* should be required reading for anyone who lives with or works with children—or anyone who plans to in the future." —Martha Farrell Erickson, Ph.D., co-chair of the Presidential Initiative on Children and founding director of the Children, Youth, and Family Consortium, University of Minnesota

Praise for *Last Child in the Woods*

"One of the most thought-provoking, well-written books I've read in recent memory. It rivals Rachel Carson's *Silent Spring*."
—*The Cincinnati Enquirer*

"Important and original. . . . As Louv so eloquently and urgently shows, our mothers were right when they told us, day after day, 'Go out and play.'"
—*The Christian Science Monitor*

"An eloquent, urgent, and timely book [that] presents important ideas and remedies for parents, schools, and communities."
—Samuel Osherson, Ph.D., author of *Finding Our Fathers*

"This book is an absolute must-read for parents." —*The Boston Globe*

"Nature needs its children: where else will its future stewards come from? Louv's book is a call to action, full of warnings—but also full of ideas for change."
—*Publishers Weekly*

"A single sentence explains why Louv's book is so important: 'Our children,' he writes, 'are the first generation to be raised without meaningful contact with the natural world.' This matters, and *Last Child in the Woods* makes it patently clear why *and* lays out a path back."
—*The Ecologist*

"With this scholarly yet practical book, Louv offers solutions today for a healthier, greener tomorrow."
—*Washington Post Book World*

"One of the best books I've read in years."
—*The Fort Collins Coloradoan*

"The simplest, most profound, and most helpful of any book I have read on the personal and historical situation of our children, and ourselves, as we move into the twenty-first century."
—Thomas Berry, author of *The Dream of the Earth*

"The book is an inch-thick caution against raising the fully automated child." —*The New York Times*

"Our society has been de-natured and few seem aware of how seriously television and the Internet have replaced nature in the lives of our children. This book is essential for the effective prescriptions for the recovery. Every parent should read this book, but equally important, every teacher should take it to heart and take every student into nature." —Paul Dayton, Ph.D., winner of the E. O. Wilson Naturalist Award

"Engrossing. . . . Thrilling to read." —*St. Louis Post-Dispatch*

"Affecting. . . . Has the force of a polemic, but none of the badgering quality; it's delivered with the casual feel of an afternoon hike." —*Austin (TX) American-Statesman*

"I found myself seeing the last chapter through suddenly blurry eyes and wondering, as I reached for the Kleenex, how I could sign on to Richard Louv's team." —*The San Diego Union-Tribune*

"Brilliant, encouraging." —*Healthy Beginnings* magazine

"Our children are part of a truly vast experiment—the first generation to be raised without meaningful contact with the natural world. Richard Louv provides insight on what it's doing to our children, and savvy advice about how to restore the age-old relationship between people and the rest of the planet." —Bill McKibben

"An honest, well-researched and well-written book, among the first to give name to an undeniable problem." —*The Atlanta Journal-Constitution*

LAST CHILD IN THE WOODS

ALSO BY RICHARD LOUV

LAST
CHILD
IN THE
WOODS

Saving Our Children from
Nature-Deficit Disorder

RICHARD LOUV

ALGONQUIN BOOKS OF CHAPEL HILL
2006

Published by
Algonquin Books of Chapel Hill
Post Office Box 2225
Chapel Hill, North Carolina 27515-2225

a division of
Workman Publishing
708 Broadway
New York, New York 10003

The author is grateful to reprint with permission of their authors or publishers excerpts from the following: "New Mexico," from *Phoenix: The Posthumous Papers of D. H. Lawrence*, edited by Edward McDonald, copyright 1936 by Frieda Lawrence, copyright renewed 1964 by the estate of the late Frieda Lawrence Ravagli, used by permission of Viking Penguin, a division of Penguin Group (USA) Inc. "Kiss Nature Goodbye," by John Beardsley. "The Need for Nature: A Childhood Right," by Robin Moore. "Ecstatic Places," by Louise Chawla. "Views of Nature and Self-Discipline: Evidence from Inner City Children" and "Coping with ADD: The Surprising Connection to Green Play Settings," by Andrea Faber Taylor, Frances E. Kuo, and William C. Sullivan. *The Rise of Theodore Roosevelt*, by Edmund C. Morris, copyright Putnam, 1979. The author has made every attempt to obtain permission for additional quoted material.

Library of Congress Cataloging-in-Publication Data
Louv, Richard.
    Last child in the woods : saving our children from nature-deficit disorder /
Richard Louv.—Rev., 1st pbk. ed.
    p. cm.
Includes bibliographical references and index.
    ISBN-13: 978-1-56512-522-3; ISBN-10: 1-56512-522-3 (PB)
    1. Nature—Psychological aspects.   2. Children and the environment.   I. Title.
BF353.5.N37L68 2006
155.4'18—dc22   2005057050

10 9 8 7 6 5 4 3 2 1
First Paperback Edition

For Jason and Matthew

There was a child went forth every day,

And the first object he look'd upon, that object he became,

And that object became part of him for the day or a certain part of the day,

Or for many years or stretching cycles of years.

The early lilacs became part of this child,

And grass and white and red morning glories, and white and red clover,

and the song of the phoebe-bird,

And the Third-month lambs and the sow's pink-faint litter,

and the mare's foal and the cow's calf, . . .

—WALT WHITMAN

I like to play indoors better 'cause that's where all the electrical outlets are.

—A FOURTH-GRADER IN SAN DIEGO

CONTENTS

ACKNOWLEDGMENTS

THIS BOOK, LIKE MOST, was a collective effort. My wife, Kathy Frederick Louv, and sons, Jason and Matthew, provided logistical, emotional, and intellectual support; they lived the research, too.

Publisher Elisabeth Scharlatt and literary agent James Levine made the book possible. Elisabeth's gentle, clear-eyed perspective offered depth for roots and careful pruning of overgrowth. She is a joy to work with. Algonquin's Amy Gash also offered wise and timely support, as did Craig Popelars, Ina Stern, Brunson Hoole, Michael Taeckens, Aimee Bollenbach, Katherine Ward, and the rest of the Algonquin team. Heavy editorial lifting was shared by my talented friend and virtual brother, Dean Stahl. Other invaluable editorial support came from John Shore, Lisa Polikov, and Cheryl Nicchitta. Friends and fellow journalists nurtured this work for a decade. Among them, Helen and David Copley, whose longtime support of my column in the *San Diego Union-Tribune* offered an early home for many of the ideas in this book, and my editors there, over the years, Karin Winner, Bill Osborne, Bernie Jones, Lora Cicalo, Jane Clifford, and Peter Kaye. Providing timely reality checks: John Johns, David Boe, Larry Hinman, Karen Kerchelich, Rosemary Erickson, R. Larry Schmitt, Melissa Baldwin, Jackie Green, John Parr, Marti Erickson, Jon Funabiki, Bill Stothers, Michael Stepner, Susan Bales, Michael Goldstein, Susan White, Bob Laurence, Jeannette De Wyze, Gary Shebler, Anne Pearse Hocker, Janet Fout, Neal Peirce, LaVonne Misner, Melissa Moriarty, the men of DMG, and, especially by example, Michael Louv.

For their patience and support, my gratitude also goes to the Leadership for a Changing World partners: Advocacy Institute, Robert F. Wagner Graduate School of Public Service at New York University, and the Ford Foundation.

While an author traditionally does not thank people quoted in his or her book, accuracy and respect require special thanks to two groups: the teachers, especially John Rick, Brady Kelso, Tina Kafka, David Ward, and Candy Vanderhoff, who encouraged their students to share their thoughts; the students themselves (some of their names have been changed herein); and the hardy band of professors and researchers who have plowed this field in recent years, often without adequate recognition. I am particularly grateful to Louise Chawla, who not only shared her own findings but pointed me to the work of others, whom you will meet along the way. My apologies to those researchers not quoted here, but whose work is invaluable nonetheless.

Finally, I wish to thank Elaine Brooks, who did not live to read the book she helped inspire, but who speaks from these pages.

ONE EVENING WHEN my boys were younger, Matthew, then ten, looked at me from across a restaurant table and said quite seriously, "Dad, how come it was more fun when you were a kid?"

I asked what he meant.

"Well, you're always talking about your woods and tree houses, and how you used to ride that horse down near the swamp."

At first, I thought he was irritated with me. I had, in fact, been telling him what it was like to use string and pieces of liver to catch crawdads in a creek, something I'd be hard-pressed to find a child doing these days. Like many parents, I do tend to romanticize my own childhood — and, I fear, too readily discount my children's experiences of play and adventure. But my son was serious; he felt he had missed out on something important.

He was right. Americans around my age, baby boomers or older, enjoyed a kind of free, natural play that seems, in the era of kid pagers, instant messaging, and Nintendo, like a quaint artifact.

Within the space of a few decades, the way children understand and experience nature has changed radically. The polarity of the relationship has reversed. Today, kids are aware of the global threats to the environment — but their physical contact, their intimacy with nature, is fading. That's exactly the opposite of how it was when I was a child.

As a boy, I was unaware that my woods were ecologically connected with any other forests. Nobody in the 1950s talked about acid rain or holes in the ozone layer or global warming. But I knew my woods and my fields; I knew every bend in the creek and dip in the beaten dirt paths. I wandered those woods even in my dreams. A kid today can likely tell you about the Amazon rain forest — but not about the last time he or she explored the woods in solitude, or lay in a field listening to the wind and watching the clouds move.

This book explores the increasing divide between the young and the natural world, and the environmental, social, psychological, and spiritual implications of that change. It also describes the accumulating research that reveals the necessity of contact with nature for healthy child—and adult—development.

While I pay particular attention to children, my focus is also on those Americans born during the past two to three decades. The shift in our relationship to the natural world is startling, even in settings that one would assume are devoted to nature. Not that long ago, summer camp was a place where you camped, hiked in the woods, learned about plants and animals, or told firelight stories about ghosts or mountain lions. As likely as not today, "summer camp" is a weight-loss camp, or a computer camp. For a new generation, nature is more abstraction than reality. Increasingly, nature is something to watch, to consume, to wear —to ignore. A recent television ad depicts a four-wheel-drive SUV racing along a breathtakingly beautiful mountain stream—while in the backseat two children watch a movie on a flip-down video screen, oblivious to the landscape and water beyond the windows.

A century ago, the historian Frederick Jackson Turner announced that the American frontier had ended. His thesis has been discussed and debated ever since. Today, a similar and more important line is being crossed.

Our society is teaching young people to avoid direct experience in nature. That lesson is delivered in schools, families, even organizations devoted to the outdoors, and codified into the legal and regulatory structures of many of our communities. Our institutions, urban/suburban design, and cultural attitudes unconsciously associate nature with doom—while disassociating the outdoors from joy and solitude. Well-meaning public-school systems, media, and parents are effectively scaring children straight out of the woods and fields. In the patent-or-perish environment of higher education, we see the death of natural history as the more hands-on disciplines, such as zoology, give way to more theoretical and remunerative microbiology and genetic engineering. Rapidly advancing technologies are blurring the lines between humans, other animals, and machines. The postmodern notion that reality is only a construct—that we are what we program—suggests limitless human possibilities; but as the young spend less and less of their lives in natural surroundings, their senses narrow, physiologically and psychologically, and this reduces the richness of human experience.

Yet, at the very moment that the bond is breaking between the young and the natural world, a growing body of research links our mental, physical, and spiritual health directly to our association with nature—in positive ways. Several of these studies suggest that thoughtful exposure of youngsters to nature can even be a powerful form of therapy for attention-deficit disorders and other maladies. As one scientist puts it, we can now assume that just as children need good nutrition and adequate sleep, they may very well need contact with nature.

Reducing that deficit—healing the broken bond between our young and nature—is in our self-interest, not only because aesthetics or justice demands it, but also because our mental, physical, and spiritual health depends upon it. The health of the earth is at stake as well. How the young respond to nature, and how they raise their own children, will shape the configurations and conditions of our cities, homes—our daily lives. The following pages explore an alternative path to the future, including some of the most innovative environment-based school programs; a reimagining and redesign of the urban environment—what one theorist calls the coming "zoopolis"; ways of addressing the challenges besetting environmental groups; and ways that faith-based organizations can help reclaim nature as part of the spiritual development of children. Parents, children, grandparents, teachers, scientists, religious leaders, environmentalists, and researchers from across the nation speak in these pages. They recognize the transformation that is occurring.

Some of them paint another future, in which children and nature are re-united—and the natural world is more deeply valued and protected.

During the research for this book, I was encouraged to find that many people now of college age—those who belong to the first generation to grow up in a largely de-natured environment—have tasted just enough nature to intuitively understand what they have missed. This yearning is a source of power. These young people resist the rapid slide from the real to the virtual, from the mountains to the Matrix. They do not intend to be the last children in the woods.

My sons may yet experience what author Bill McKibben has called "the end of nature," the final sadness of a world where there is no escaping man. But there is another possibility: not the end of nature, but the rebirth of wonder and even joy. Jackson's obituary for the American frontier was only partly accurate: one frontier did disappear, but a second one followed, in which Americans romanticized, exploited, protected, and destroyed nature. Now that frontier—which existed in the family farm, the woods at the end of the road, the national parks, and in our hearts—is itself disappearing or changing beyond recognition.

But, as before, one relationship with nature can evolve into another. This book is about the end of that earlier time, but it is also about a new frontier—a better way to live with nature.

PART I

THE NEW RELATIONSHIP BETWEEN CHILDREN AND NATURE

Here is this vast, savage, howling mother of ours,

Nature, lying all around, with such beauty, and such affection for her children,

as the leopard; and yet we are so early weaned

from her breast to society, to that culture which is exclusively

an interaction of man on man.

—HENRY DAVID THOREAU

1. Gifts of Nature

When I see birches bend to left and right . . .
I like to think some boy's been swinging them.
— ROBERT FROST

IF, WHEN WE WERE YOUNG, we tramped through forests of Nebraska cottonwoods, or raised pigeons on a rooftop in Queens, or fished for Ozark bluegills, or felt the swell of a wave that traveled a thousand miles before lifting our boat, then we were bound to the natural world and remain so today. Nature still informs our years—lifts us, carries us.

For children, nature comes in many forms. A newborn calf; a pet that lives and dies; a worn path through the woods; a fort nested in stinging nettles; a damp, mysterious edge of a vacant lot—whatever shape nature takes, it offers each child an older, larger world separate from parents. Unlike television, nature does not steal time; it amplifies it. Nature offers healing for a child living in a destructive family or neighborhood. It serves as a blank slate upon which a child draws and reinterprets the culture's fantasies. Nature inspires creativity in a child by demanding visualization and the full use of the senses. Given a chance, a child will bring the confusion of the world to the woods, wash it in the creek, turn it over to see what lives on the unseen side of that confusion. Nature can frighten a child, too, and this fright serves a purpose. In nature, a child finds freedom, fantasy, and privacy: a place distant from the adult world, a separate peace.

These are some of the utilitarian values of nature, but at a deeper level, nature gives itself to children—for its own sake, not as a reflection of a culture. At this level, inexplicable nature provokes humility.

As the preeminent nature poet Gary Snyder writes, we attach two meanings to the word nature, which comes from the Latin *natura*—birth, constitution, character, course of things—and beyond natura, *nasci*—to be born. In its broadest interpretation, nature includes the material world and all of its objects and phenomena; by this definition, a machine is part of nature. So is toxic waste. The other meaning is what we call "the outdoors." By this connotation, a man-made thing is not a part of nature, but apart from nature. On its face, New York City may not appear natural, but it does contain all manner of hidden, self-organizing wild places, from the organisms secreted within the humus of Central Park to the hawks that circle above the Bronx. In this sense, a city complies with the broadest laws of nature; it is natural (as a machine is part of nature), but wild in its parts.

When considering children in nature, one hungers for a richer description, a definition with more breathing room—one that does not include *everything* as natural or restrict nature to virgin forest. Snyder is drawn to poet John Milton's phrase, "a wilderness of sweets." "Milton's usage of wilderness catches the very real condition of energy and richness that is so often found in wild systems. A 'wilderness of sweets' is like the billions of herring or mackerel babies in the ocean, the cubic miles of krill, wild prairie grass seed . . . all the incredible fecundity of small animals and plants, feeding the web," he explains. "But from another side, wilderness has implied chaos, eros, the unknown, realms of taboo, the habitat of both the ecstatic and the demonic. In both senses it is a place of archetypal power, teaching, and challenge." When we think of children and the gifts of nature, this third, more bountiful understanding is helpful. For the purpose of this book, when I use the word "nature" in a general way I mean natural wildness: biodiversity, abundance—related loose parts in a backyard or a rugged mountain

ridge. Most of all, nature is reflected in our capacity for wonder. *Nasci.*
To be born.

Though we often see ourselves as separate from nature, humans are
also part of that wildness. My earliest memory of using my senses, and
sensing wonder, came on a cold spring morning in Independence, Missouri. I was perhaps three years old, sitting in a dry field behind my
grandmother's peeling Victorian home. Nearby, my father worked,
planting a garden. He threw down a cigarette—as many were likely to
do in that age, when Midwesterners habitually tossed refuse on the
ground, or launched beer bottles and soda cans and cigarette butts from
their car windows, sparks flying in the wind. The dry grass caught fire.
I remember the exact sound of the flames and smell of the smoke and
the *whoosh* of my father's leg and foot as he stamped and stepped quickly
to chase the fire as it skipped across the field.

In this same field, I would walk around the fallen fruit from a pear
tree, hold my nose and bend at the waist, a careful distance from the
small mounds of ferment, and then experimentally inhale. I would sit
down among the decaying fruit, attracted and repulsed. Fire and fer-
mentation . . .

I spent hours exploring the woods and farmland at the suburban
edge. There were the Osage orange trees, with thorny, unfriendly limbs
that dropped sticky, foul fruit larger than softballs. Those were to be
avoided. But within the windbreaks were trees that we could shinny, the
small branches like the rungs of a ladder. We climbed fifty, sixty feet off
the ground, far above the Osage windbreak, and from that vantage
looked out upon the old blue ridges of Missouri, and the roofs of new
houses in the ever-encroaching suburbs.

Often I climbed alone. Sometimes, lost in wonderment, I'd go deep
into the woods, and imagine myself as Rudyard Kipling's Mowgli, the
boy raised by wolves, and strip off most of my clothes for the ascent. If
I climbed high enough, the branches thinned to the point where, when
the wind came, the world would tip down and up and around and up

and to the side and up. It was frightening and wonderful to surrender to the wind's power. My senses were filled with the sensations of falling, rising, swinging; all around me the leaves snapped like fingers and the wind came in sighs and gruff whispers. The wind carried smells, too, and the tree itself surely released its scents faster in the gusts. Finally, there was only the wind that moved through everything.

Now, my tree-climbing days long behind me, I often think about the lasting value of those early, deliciously idle days. I have come to appreciate the long view afforded by those treetops. The woods were my Ritalin. Nature calmed me, focused me, and yet excited my senses.

"Where All the Electrical Outlets Are"

Many members of my generation grew into adulthood taking nature's gifts for granted; we assumed (when we thought of it at all) that generations to come would also receive these gifts. But something has changed. Now we see the emergence of what I have come to call nature-deficit disorder. This term is by no means a medical diagnosis, but it does offer a way to think about the problem and the possibilities—for children, and for the rest of us as well.

My own awareness of the transformation began in the late 1980s, during research for *Childhood's Future*, a book about the new realities of family life. I interviewed nearly three thousand children and parents across the country, in urban, suburban, and rural areas. In classrooms and living rooms, the topic of the children's relationship with nature sometimes surfaced. I think often of a wonderfully honest comment made by Paul, a fourth-grader in San Diego: "I like to play indoors better, 'cause that's where all the electrical outlets are."

In many classrooms I heard variations on that answer. True, for many children, nature still offers wonder. But for many others, playing in nature seemed so . . . Unproductive. Off-limits. Alien. Cute. Dangerous. Televised.

"It's all this *watching*," said a mother in Swarthmore, Pennsylvania.

"We've become a more sedentary society. When I was a kid growing up in Detroit, we were always outdoors. The kids who stayed indoors were the odd ones. We didn't have any huge wide-open spaces, but we were always outdoors on the streets—in the vacant lots, jumping rope, or playing baseball or hopscotch. We were out there playing even after we got older."

Another Swarthmore parent added, "Something else was different when we were young: our *parents* were outdoors. I'm not saying they were joining health clubs and things of that sort, but they were out of the house, out on the porch, talking to neighbors. As far as physical fitness goes, today's kids are the sorriest generation in the history of the United States. Their parents may be out jogging, but the kids just aren't outside."

This was the mantra among parents, grandparents, uncles, aunts, teachers, and other adults across the country, even in places I would have expected to have a different view. For example, I visited a middle-class neighborhood in suburban Overland Park, Kansas, not far from where I spent my teen years. In the intervening decades, many of the woods and fields had vanished, but enough natural landscape remained to at least provide the opportunity for outside play. Surely kids still played in nature here? Not often, said several parents, who came together in a living room one evening to talk about the new landscape of childhood. Though several lived on the same block, this was the first time that some of these parents had met each other.

"When our kids were in third or fourth grade, we still had a little field behind our place," said one mother. "The kids were complaining about being bored. And I said, 'Okay, you guys are bored? I want you to go out to that field, right there, and spend two hours. Find something to do there. Trust me; just try it one time. You might enjoy yourselves.' So, begrudgingly, they went out to the field. And they didn't come back in two hours—they came back much later. I asked them why, and they said, 'It was so much fun! We never dreamed we could have so much fun!' They climbed trees; they watched things; they chased each other; they played games like we used to do when we were young. So the next day, I said, 'Hey, you guys are bored—why not go out to the field again?' And they answered, 'Nah—we've already done that once.' They weren't willing to let themselves do it again."

"I'm not sure I understand exactly what you're saying," responded a father. "I think that my girls enjoy things like a full moon, or a pretty sunset, or flowers. They enjoy the trees when they turn—that sort of thing."

Another mother in the group shook her head. "Sure, the little things, they notice," she said. "But they're distracted." She described the last time her family had gone skiing, in Colorado. "It was a perfect, quiet day, the kids are skiing down the mountain—and they've got their *headphones* on. They can't enjoy just hearing nature and being out there alone. They can't make their own entertainment. They have to bring something with them."

A quiet father, who had been raised in a farming community, spoke up.

"Where I grew up, a person was just *naturally* outdoors all the time," he said. "No matter which direction you went, you were outdoors— you were in a plowed field, or woods, or streams. We're not like that here. Overland Park is a metropolitan area now. Kids haven't lost anything, because they never had it in the first place. What we're talking about here is a transition made by most of us who grew up surrounded by nature. Now, nature's just not *there* anymore."

The group fell quiet. Yes, much of that once-wild land was being graded and built upon—but I could see woods from the windows of the house in which we were sitting. Nature *was* still out there. There was less of it, to be sure, but it was there just the same.

A day after talking with the Overland Park parents, I drove across the Kansas-Missouri border to Southwood Elementary School in Raytown, Missouri, near Kansas City. I attended grade school at Southwood. To my surprise, the same swings (or so it seemed) still creaked above the hot asphalt; the hallways still shone with the same linoleum tile; the same pint-sized wooden chairs, carved and initialed with black, blue, and red ink, sat waiting in crooked rows.

As the teachers gathered second- through fifth-graders and escorted them into the classroom where I waited, I unpacked my tape recorder and glanced out the window at the blue-green ridge of trees, probably pin oak, maple, cottonwood, or perhaps pecan or honey locust, their limbs shivering and swaying slowly in the spring breeze. How often, as a child, had those very trees inspired my daydreams?

During the next hour, as I asked the young people about their relationship with the outdoors, they described some of the barriers to going outside—lack of time, TV, the usual suspects. But the reality of these barriers did not mean that the children lacked curiosity. In fact, these kids spoke of nature with a strange mixture of puzzlement, detachment, and yearning—and occasional defiance. In the years to come, I would hear this tone often.

"My parents don't feel real safe if I'm going too deep in the woods," said one boy. "I just can't go too far. My parents are always worrying about me. So I'll just go, and usually not tell 'em where I'm going—so that makes 'em mad. But I'll just sit behind a tree or something, or lie in the field with all the rabbits."

One boy said computers were more important than nature, because computers are where the jobs are. Several said they were too busy to go outside. But one girl, a fifth-grader wearing a plain print dress and an intensely serious expression, told me she wanted to be a poet when she grew up.

"When I'm in the woods," she said, "I feel like I'm in my mother's shoes."

She was one of those exceptional children who do still spend time outside, in solitude. In her case nature represented beauty—and refuge. "It's so peaceful out there and the air smells so good. I mean, it's polluted, but not as much as the city air. For me, it's completely different there," she said. "It's like you're free when you go out there. It's your own time. Sometimes I go there when I'm mad—and then, just with the peacefulness, I'm better. I can come back home happy, and my mom doesn't even know why."

Then she described her special part of the woods.

"I had a place. There was a big waterfall and a creek on one side of it. I'd dug a big hole there, and sometimes I'd take a tent back there, or a blanket, and just lie down in the hole, and look up at the trees and sky. Sometimes I'd fall asleep back in there. I just felt free; it was like my place, and I could do what I wanted, with nobody to stop me. I used to go down there almost every day."

The young poet's face flushed. Her voice thickened.

"And then they just cut the woods down. It was like they cut down part of me."

Over time I came to understand some of the complexity represented by the boy who preferred electrical outlets and the poet who had lost her special spot in the woods. I also learned this: Parents, educators, other adults, institutions—the culture itself—may say one thing to children about nature's gifts, but so many of our actions and messages—especially the ones we cannot hear ourselves deliver—are different.

And children hear very well.

2. The Third Frontier

The frontier is a goner. It died with its boots laced.

—M. R. Montgomery

On my bookshelf is a copy of *Shelters, Shacks and Shanties*, written in 1915 by Daniel C. Beard, a civil engineer-turned-artist, best known as one of the founders of the Boy Scouts of America. For half a century, he wrote and illustrated a string of books on the outdoors. *Shelters, Shacks and Shanties* happens to be one of my favorite books because, particularly with his pen and ink drawings, Beard epitomizes a time when a young person's experience of nature was inseparable from the romantic view of the American frontier.

If such books were newly published today, they would be considered quaint and politically incorrect, to say the least. Their target audience was boys. The genre seemed to suggest that no self-respecting boy could enjoy nature without axing as many trees as possible. But what really defines these books, and the age they represented, is the unquestioned belief that being in nature was about *doing* something, about direct experience—and about not being a spectator.

"The smallest boys can build some of the simple shelters and the older boys can build the more difficult ones," Beard wrote, in the forward of *Shelters, Shacks and Shanties*. "The reader may, if he likes, begin with the first [shanty] and graduate by building the log houses; in doing this he will be closely following the history of the human race, because ever since our arboreal ancestors with prehensile toes scampered among the branches of the pre-glacial forests and built nest-like shelters in the trees, men have made themselves shacks for a temporary refuge." He goes on to describe, through words and drawings, how a boy could build some forty types of shelters, including the Tree-top House, the Adirondack, the Wick-Up, the Bark Teepee, the Pioneer, and the Scout. He tells "how to make beaver-mat huts" and "a sod house for the lawn." He teaches "how to split logs, make shakes, splits, or clapboards" and how to make a pole house and secret locks and an underground fort, and, intriguingly, "how to make a concealed log cabin inside of a modern house."

Today's reader would likely be impressed with the level of ingenuity and skill required, and the riskiness of some of the designs, too. In the case of the "original American boy's hogan or underground house," Beard does urge caution. During the creation of such caves, he admits, "there is always serious danger of the roof falling in and smothering the young troglodytes, but a properly built underground hogan is perfectly safe from such accidents."

I love Beard's books because of their charm, the era they conjure, and the lost art they describe. As a boy, I built rudimentary versions of these shelters, shacks, and shanties—including underground forts in the cornfields and elaborate tree houses with secret entrances and a view of what I imagined to be the frontier stretching from Ralston Street beyond the edge of the known suburban world.

Closing One Frontier, Opening Another

In the space of a century, the American experience of nature has gone from direct utilitarianism to romantic attachment to electronic detachment. Americans have passed not through one frontier, but through three; the third frontier—the one that young people are growing up in today—is every bit as much of a venture into the unknown as Daniel Beard experienced in his time.

The passing, and importance, of the first frontier was described in 1893, during Chicago's World's Columbian Exposition—a celebration of the 400th anniversary of Columbus's arrival in the Americas. There, at a meeting of the American Historical Association in Chicago, University of Wisconsin historian Frederick Jackson Turner presented his "frontier thesis." He argued that "the existence of an area of free land, its continuous recession, and the advance of American settlement westward" explained the development of the American nation, history, and character. He linked this pronouncement to results of the 1890 U.S. Census, which revealed the disappearance of a contiguous line of the American frontier—the "closing of the frontier." This was the same year that the superintendent of the census declared the end of the era of "free land," that is, land available to homesteaders for tillage.

Little noted at the time, Jackson's thesis came to be considered one of the most important statements in American history. Jackson argued that every American generation had returned "to primitive conditions on a continually advancing frontier line." He described this frontier as "the meeting point between savagery and civilization." Basic American cultural traits could, he said, be linked to the influence of that frontier, including "that coarseness and strength combined with acuteness and acquisitiveness; that practical inventive turn of mind, quick to find expedients; that masterful grasp of material things . . . that restless, nervous energy; that dominant individualism." Historians still debate Turner's thesis; many, if not most, have rejected the frontier, as Turner saw it, as *the* key to understanding American history and sensibilities. Immigration, the industrial revolution, the Civil War—all had a deep formative influence on our culture. Turner himself later revised his theory to include events that were frontier-like—the oil boom of the 1890s, for example.

Nonetheless, from Teddy Roosevelt to Edward Abbey, Americans continued to think of themselves as frontier explorers. In 1905, at President Roosevelt's inauguration, cowboys rode down Pennsylvania Avenue, the Seventh Cavalry passed for review, and American Indians joined the celebration—including the once-feared Geronimo. The parade, in fact, announced the coming of the second frontier, which existed mainly in the imagination for nearly a century. The second frontier existed in Beard's words and illustrations, and in the family farm, which, though already diminishing in number, continued as an important definer of American culture. Especially in the early decades of the twentieth century, the second frontier also existed in urban America; witness the creation of the great urban parks. The second frontier was a time, too, of suburban manifest destiny, when boys still imagined themselves woodsmen and scouts, and girls still yearned to live in a little house on the prairie, and sometimes built better forts than the boys.

If the first frontier was explored by the acquisitive Lewis and Clark, the second frontier was romanticized by Teddy Roosevelt; if the first frontier was the real Davy Crockett's, the second frontier peaked with Disney's Davy. If the first frontier was a time of struggle, the second frontier was a period of taking stock, of celebration. It brought a new politics of preservation, an immersion of Americans in the domesticated and romanticized fields and streams and woods around them.

Turner's 1893 pronouncement found its counterpart in 1993. His statement was based on the results of the 1890 Census; the new demarcation line was drawn from the 1990 Census. Eerily, one hundred years after Turner and the U.S. Census Bureau declared the end of what we usually consider the American frontier, the bureau posted a report that marked the death of the second frontier, and the birth of a third. That year, as the *Washington Post* reported, in "a symbol of massive national transformation," the federal government dropped its long-standing annual survey of farm residents. Farm population had dwindled so much—from 40 percent of U.S. households in 1900 to just 1.9 percent in 1990—that the farm resident survey was irrelevant. The 1993 report was surely as important as the census evidence that led to Turner's obituary for the frontier. "If sweeping changes can be captured in seemingly trivial benchmarks, the decision to end the annual report is one," reported the *Post.*

This new, symbolic demarcation line suggests that baby boomers—Americans born between 1946 and 1964—may constitute the last generation of Americans to share an intimate, familial attachment to the land and water. Many of us now in our forties or older knew farmland or forests at the suburban rim and had farm-family relatives. Even if we lived in an inner city, we likely had grandparents or other older relatives who farmed or had recently arrived from farm country during the rural-to-urban migration of the first half of the twentieth century. For today's young people, that familial and cultural linkage to farming is disappearing, marking the end of the second frontier.

The third frontier is populated by today's children.

Characteristics of the Third Frontier

In ways that neither Turner nor Beard could have imagined, the third frontier is shaping how the current generation of young Americans, and many to come, will perceive nature.

Not yet fully formed or explored, this new frontier is characterized by at least five trends: a severance of the public and private mind from our food's origins; a disappearing line between machines, humans, and other animals; an increased intellectual understanding of our relationship with other animals; the invasion of our cities by wild animals (even as urban/suburban designers replace wildness with synthetic nature); and the rise of a new kind of suburban form. Most characteristics of the third frontier can be found in other technologically advanced countries, but these changes are particularly evident in the United States (if only because of the contrast with our frontier self-image). At first glance, these characteristics may not seem to fit together logically, but revolutionary times are seldom logical or linear.

In the third frontier, Beard's romantic images of the outdoor child seem as outdated as nineteenth-century depictions of the Knights of the

Round Table. In the third frontier, heroes previously associated with the outdoors are irrelevant; the real Davy Crockett, who symbolized the first frontier, and even Disney's Davy, from the second frontier, are gone and nearly forgotten. A generation that came of age wearing buckskin jackets and granny dresses is now raising a generation for whom all fashion—piercing, tattoos, and all the rest—is urban.

- *For the young, food is from Venus; farming is from Mars*

My friend Nick Raven, who lives in Puerta de Luna, New Mexico, was a farmer for several years before he became a carpenter and then a teacher at a New Mexico prison. Nick and I have fished together for years, but we are very different men. I have described him as an undoubting nineteenth-century father; I am a doubting twenty-first century dad. Nick believes fish should be caught and eaten; I believe that fish should be caught and, most of the time, released. Nick believes that violence is inevitable, that suffering is redemptive, and that a father must teach his children about the harshness of life by exposing them to that harshness. I believe that, as a parent, it's my job to protect my sons from the brutality of the world for as long as I can.

In an earlier book, *The Web of Life*, I described the relationship that Nick and his children had to animals and food:

> When Nick's children were small and he and his family still lived on their farm down a dirt road in a valley of adobes and cottonwoods and chiles, his daughter came home one day to find her favorite goat (not a pet, really, but one that followed her around) skinned, gutted, and strung up in the barn. This was a time when Nick's family was short on shoes, and the meat they ate was meat that Nick butchered or shot. It was a terrible moment for his daughter.
>
> Nick insists he has no regrets, but he still talks about it. She was hurt, he says, but she knew from that moment on, and will for the rest of her life, where the meat that she eats comes from, and that meat is not born plastic-wrapped. This is not the kind of experience I would have wanted for my children, but I have had a different life.

Few of us miss the more brutal aspects of raising food. For most young people, however, memory supplies no experience for comparison. More young people may be vegetarians or consume food from the health food store, but fewer are likely to raise their own food—especially if the food is an animal. In fewer than a half century, the culture has moved from a time when small family farms dominated the countryside—when Nick's way of understanding food was dominant—to a transitional time when many suburban families' vegetable gardens provided little more than recreation, to the current age of shrink-wrapped, lab-produced food. In one way, young people are more aware of the sources of what they eat. The animal-rights movement has taught them about the conditions within, say, poultry factory farms. It's probably no coincidence high school and college students are adopting vegetarianism in increasing numbers. Such knowledge, however, does not necessarily mean that the young are personally involved with their food sources.

• *The end of biological absolutes. Are we mice or are we men? Or both?*

The young are growing up in an era without biological absolutes. Even the definition of life itself is up for grabs.

One morning in 1997, people around the world opened their news-papers to see a disturbing photograph of a live, hairless mouse with what appeared to be a human ear growing from its back. The creature was the product of a team of researchers from the University of Massachusetts and the Massachusetts Institute of Technology that had introduced human cartilage cells into an earlike scaffold of biodegradable polyester fabric implanted onto the back of the mouse. The scaffold nourished the ersatz ear.

Since then, one headline after another has announced some potential blending of machines, humans, and other animals. The implications have evaded the public for two decades, according to the International Center for Technology Assessment, a nonprofit, bipartisan organization that assesses technological impacts on society. As of 2000, several hundred animals—patented life forms—had already been genetically engineered or altered with human genes. Over twenty-four human genes—including those for human growth and nerves—had been inserted into rats, mice, and primates to create creatures called chimera. These new creatures are to be used primarily for medical research, but some scientists seriously discuss the possibility of chimera someday existing outside the lab.

Think what it means for children to grow up now, and how different their experience of nature and definition of life is, or soon will be, from the experiences of us adults. In our childhood, it was clear enough when a man was a man and a mouse was a mouse. Implicit in some of the newest technologies is the assumption that there's little difference between living and nonliving matter at the atomic and molecular level. Some see this as one more example of turning life into a commodity— the cultural reduction that turns living bodies into machines.

As the twenty-first century dawned, scientists at Cornell University reported building the first true nanomachine—near-microscopic robot—capable of movement; the miniscule robot used a propeller and motor and drew power from organic molecules. This development opened "the door to make machines that live inside the cell," one of the researchers said. "It allows us to merge engineered devices into living systems." At Sandia National Laboratories in Albuquerque, a scientist predicted that a system of "massively distributed intelligence" would vastly increase the nanorobots' ability to organize and communicate. "They will be able to do things collectively that they can't do individually, just like an ant colony," he said. Around the same time, an entomologist in Iowa created a machine combining moth antennae and microprocessors that sent signals of different pitches when the antennae picked up the scent of explosives. Researchers at Northwestern University created a miniature robot equipped with the brain stem of a lamprey eel. And a Rockville, Maryland, company engineered bacteria that could be functionally attached to microchips; the company called this invention "critters on a chip."

We can no longer assume a cultural core belief in the perfection of nature. To previous generations of children, few creations were as perfect or as beautiful as a tree. Now, researchers flood trees with genetic material taken from viruses and bacteria to make them grow faster, to create better wood products, or to enable trees to clean polluted soil. In 2003, the Pentagon's Defense Advanced Research Projects Agency funded researchers to develop a tree capable of changing colors when exposed to a biological or chemical attack. And the University of California promoted "birth control for trees," a genetically engineered method of creating a "eunuch-tree that spends more of its energy making wood and not love."

For baby boomers, such news is fascinating, strange, disturbing. To children growing up in the third frontier, such news is simply more hair on the dog—an assumed complexity.

- *A hyperintellectualized perception of other animals*

Not since the predominance of hunting and gathering have children been taught to see so many similarities between humans and other animals, though now those similarities are viewed in a very different, more intellectualized way.

This new understanding is based on science, rather than myth or religion. For example, recent studies reported in the journal *Science* describe how some nonhuman animals compose music. Analyses of songs of birds and humpback whales show they use some of the same acoustic techniques, and follow the same laws of composition, as those used by human musicians. Whale songs even contain rhyming refrains, and similar intervals, phrases, song durations, and tones. Whales also use rhyme in the way we do, "as a mnemonic device to help them remember complex material," the researchers write. According to their study, whales physiologically have a choice: they could use arrhythmic and nonrepeating tunes, but instead, they sing.

Such information is not a substitute for direct contact with nature, but this kind of knowledge does inspire a certain wonder. My hope is that such research will cause children to be more inclined to cultivate an understanding of their fellow creatures. Sure, romanticized closeness—say, swimming with dolphins at an animal touchy-feely resort—may soften some of our loneliness as a species. On the other hand, nature is not so soft and fuzzy. Fishing and hunting, for example, or the way Nick Raven put meat on his table, are messy—to some, morally messy—but removing all traces of that experience from childhood does neither children nor nature any good.

"You look at these kids [in the animal-rights movement], and you largely see urban, disaffected, but still privileged people," says Mike Two Horses, of Tucson, founder of the Coalition to End Racial Targeting of American Indian Nations. His organization supports native people such as the Northwest's Makah tribe, who are traditionally dependent on whale hunting. "The only animals the young animal rightists have ever known are their pets," he says. "The only ones they've ever seen otherwise are in zoos, Sea World, or on whale-watching [now whale-touching] expeditions. They've disconnected from the sources of their food—even from the sources of the soy and other vegetable proteins they consume."

I see more good in the animal-rights movement than Two Horses does, but his point has merit.

• *Contact with nature: so close, and yet so far*
Even as the definition of life itself is up for grabs, the potential for contact with more common wild animals is *increasing*, despite what Two Horses says. In a number of urban regions, humans and wild critters are coming into contact in ways that have been unfamiliar to Americans for at least a century. For one, the U.S. deer population is the highest it has been in a hundred years.

In *Ecology of Fear: Los Angeles and the Imagination of Disaster*, social historian and urban theorist Mike Davis describes what he calls a new dialectic between the "wild" and the "urban": "Metropolitan Los Angeles, now bordered primarily by mountains and desert rather than by farmland as in the past, has the longest wild edge, abruptly juxtaposing tract houses and wildlife habitat, of any major non-tropical city. . . . Brazen coyotes are now an integral part of the street scene in Hollywood and Toluca Lake." A reporter for the British newspaper the *Observer* writes: "[American] settlers and their descendants went about taming the environment with warlike ferocity. After ethnically cleansing the natives, they set about the extermination of bears, mountain lions, coyotes and wildfowl . . . but mountain lions adapted. Los Angeles may be the only city on earth with mountain lion victim support groups."

At midcentury, millions of Americans migrated to suburbia, following the dream of owning their own homes and a piece of land—their own quarter-acre of the frontier. For a while, space was expansive. Today, sprawl does not guarantee space. The newly dominant type of development—with interchangeable shopping malls, faux nature design, rigid control by community covenants and associations—dominates the bellwether metro regions of Southern California and Florida, but also encircles most of the older urban regions of the nation. These dense donuts of development offer fewer places for natural play than the earlier suburbs. In some cases, they offer even fewer natural play spaces than the centers of the old industrial cities.

In fact, parts of urban Western Europe are greener—in the sense of increasing the amount and quality of natural surroundings within urban regions—than most of urban/suburban America, a land still associated with frontier and open space. "An important lesson from many of these European cities has to do with the very perception we have of cities," writes Timothy Beatley, professor in the Department of Urban and Environmental Planning at the University of Virginia, in *Green Urbanism: Learning from European Cities*. Particularly in Scandinavian cities, where green design is gaining popularity, "there is a sense that cities are and ought to be places where nature occurs. In the United States, a challenge remains to overcome the polar distinction between what is *urban* and what is *natural*. Perhaps because of the expansiveness of our ecological resources and land base, we have tended to see the most significant forms of nature as occurring somewhere else—often hundreds of miles away from where most people actually live—in national parks, national seashores, and wilderness areas."

These are some of the trends that form the American context for a de-natured childhood, something that is perhaps as mysterious as—and certainly less studied than—the march of the nanorobots or the advance of the chimera.

3. The Criminalization of Natural Play

For many years I was self-appointed inspector
of snowstorms and rainstorms . . .
— HENRY DAVID THOREAU

CONSIDER MISTER RICK's neighborhood.

Fifteen years ago, John Rick, a middle-school math teacher, and his family moved to Scripps Ranch because of its child-friendly reputation. Set in a lush old eucalyptus grove in a northern San Diego neighborhood laced with canyons and linked by walking paths, Scripps is one of those rare developments where parents can imagine their children enjoying nature, just as they did. A sign near its entrance reads, "Country Living."

"We have more Scout troops per capita than just about anywhere else in the country," says Rick. "The planners fought to have vast amounts of open space for kids to play in and parks for every neighborhood."

A few years after moving to Scripps Ranch, Rick started reading articles in the community's newsletter about the "illegal use" of open space. "Unlike where we had lived before, kids were actually out there running around in the trees, building forts, and playing with their imaginations," he recalls. "They were putting up bike ramps to make jumps. They were damming up trickles of water to float boats. In other words, they were doing all the things we used to do as kids. They were creating for themselves all those memories that we cherish so fondly." And now it had to stop. "Somehow," says Rick, "that tree house was now a fire hazard. Or the 'dam' might cause severe flooding."

Authoritative adults from the Scripps Ranch Community Association chased kids away from a little pond near the public library, where children had fished for bluegills since Scripps Ranch had been a working cattle spread many decades earlier. In response to the tightened regulations, families erected basketball hoops. Young people moved their skateboard ramps to the foot of their driveways. But the community association reminded the residents that such activities violated the covenants they had signed when they bought their houses.

Down came the ramps and poles; and indoors went the kids.

"Game Boy and Sega became their imagination," Rick says. "Parents became alarmed. Their kids were getting fat. Something had to be done." So the parents supported the creation of a skate park in a more willing neighborhood. That neighborhood was ten miles away.

Rick is free to move to another neighborhood, but in the growing donuts of development surrounding most American cities, such restrictions are becoming the rule. Countless communities have virtually outlawed unstructured outdoor nature play, often because of the threat of lawsuits, but also because of a growing obsession with order. Many parents and kids now believe outdoor play is verboten even when it is not; perception is nine-tenths of the law.

One source of constriction is private government. Most housing tracts, condos, and planned communities constructed in the past two to three decades are controlled by strict covenants that discourage or ban the kind of outdoor play many of us enjoyed as children. Today, 47 million Americans live in homes ruled by condominium, cooperative, and homeowners' associations, according to the Community Associations Institute. The number of community associations burgeoned from 10,000 in 1970 to 231,000 today. These associations impose rules on adults and children (if children are allowed in them at all), ranging from mildly intrusive to draconian. Scripps Ranch is governed by one of the more flexible community associations, but even here official squads of adults regularly tear down forts and tree houses built by kids in the wooded canyons.

Some reasons are understandable: for example, concern about camps of transients or the outbreak of fire. But the unintended consequence is the discouragement of natural play.

Public government also restricts children's access to nature. For the most part the criminalization of natural play is more suggestive than real. However, in some communities, young people who try to re-create their parents' childhoods may face misdemeanor charges or see their parents sued. In Pennsylvania, three brothers, ages eight, ten, and twelve, spent eight months and their own money to build a playhouse in their backyard; the district council ordered the boys to tear the tree house down because they had no building permit. In Clinton, Missis-sippi, a family happily spent four thousand dollars to build an elaborate, two-story, Victorian-style tree house. They asked the city if a permit was necessary, and a city official said no. Five years later, the city plan-ning and zoning department announced that the tree house must be de-molished because it violated an ordinance prohibiting construction of an accessory building in front of a house.

Other stringent restrictions on children's outdoor play spring from our efforts to protect nature from human population pressures. For ex-ample, to protect the endangered Arroyo southwestern toad, 3,000 acres of camping and fishing in Angeles National Forest were closed year-round. At California's Oceano Dunes region, kite-flying has been banned because kites scare off a protected species of shorebird, the snowy plover, which has a limited habitat suitable for nesting. After the ban went into effect, a park ranger told Oceano resident Ambrose Simas he could no longer fly kites (perceived as hawks by the plover) with his great-grandson on the same beach where he had once flown kites with his father and grandfather. In my city, it is illegal to "injure, destroy, cut or remove any tree . . . [or] plant . . . growing in any city-owned park . . .

without written permission from the city manager." But what exactly constitutes "to injure?" Does a child seriously injure a tree by climbing it? Some think so. Another statute makes it illegal to "take, kill, wound, or disturb . . . any bird or animal . . . unless the same shall have been declared noxious by the city manager . . . "

If endangered and threatened species are to coexist with humans, adults and children do need to tread lightly. But poor land-use decisions, which reduce accessible nature in cities, do far more damage to the environment than do children. Two examples: Each year, 53,000 acres of land are developed in the Chesapeake Bay watershed; that's about one acre every ten minutes. At that rate, development will consume more land in the Chesapeake watershed in the next twenty-five years than in the previous three and a half centuries, according to the Alliance for the Chesapeake Bay. Similarly, the Charlotte, North Carolina, region lost 20 percent of its forest cover over the past two decades; between 1982 and 2002, the state lost farmland and forests at the rate of 383 acres a day. The U.S. Department of Agriculture projects forests declining from 767,000 acres in 1982 to 377,000 in 2022. Amazingly, developed land in North Carolina increased at a rate twice that of the state's population growth.

As open space shrinks across America, overuse increases. This is true even in those metropolitan regions considered, by the public, to be more suburban than urban. Ironically, people who move to Sun Belt cities expecting more elbowroom often find less of it. Eight of the nation's ten highest-density metropolitan areas are in the West. In some of those cities, typical development methods favor decapitated hills, artificial landscaping, yards the size of gravesites, and few natural play areas. The disappearance of accessible open space escalates the pressure on those few natural places that remain; local flora is trampled; fauna die or relocate, and nature-hungry people follow in their four-wheel-drive vehicles or on their motorcycles. Meanwhile, the regulatory message is clear: islands of nature that are left by the graders are to be seen, not touched.

The cumulative impact of overdevelopment, multiplying park rules, well-meaning (and usually necessary) environmental regulations, building regulations, community covenants, and fear of litigation sends a chilling message to our children that their free-range play is unwelcome, that organized sports on manicured playing fields is the only officially sanctioned form of outdoor recreation. "We tell our kids that traditional forms of outdoor play are against the rules," says Rick. "Then we get on their backs when they sit in front of the TV—and then we tell them to go outside and play. But where? How? Join another organized sport? Some kids don't want to be organized all the time. They want to let their imaginations run; they want to see where a stream of water takes them."

Not every youngster automatically conforms. When Rick asked his students to write about their experiences in nature, twelve-year-old Lorie described how she loved to climb trees, particularly ones on a patch of land at the end of her street. One day, she and a friend were climbing in those branches and "a guy comes along and yells, 'Get out of those trees!' We were so scared; we ran inside and didn't come out again. That was when I was seven, so that old man seemed pretty frightening. But it happened again last year in my own front lawn—but this time it was someone else, and I decided to ignore him, and so nothing happened." Lorie thinks all of this is pretty stupid, limiting her opportunities to be "free and not have to be clean and act like girls who are afraid of a scratch or mud all the time." She adds, "To me, still being considered a kid, it can't be too much to ask. We should have the same rights as adults did when they were young."

Measuring the De-natured Childhood

Over the past decade, a small group of researchers has begun to document the de-naturing of childhood—its multiple causes, extent, and impact. Much of this is new territory; the criminalization of natural play, for example, which is both a symptom and cause of the transformation, is occurring without much notice. Copious studies show a reduced amount of leisure time experienced by American families, more time in front of the TV and the computer, and growing obesity among adults and children because of diet and sedentary lifestyles. We know these things. But do we know exactly how much less time children spend *specifically in nature?* No. "We also don't know if there is any geographic or class divide, in terms of which kids spend time in nature," says Louise Chawla, a Kentucky State University environmental psychology professor and a tireless champion for increasing children's experiences in nature. Good longitudinal studies that span the decades are missing. "We don't have older data to compare. No one thought to ask these questions thirty or fifty years ago," she says.

Like many of us, too many researchers have taken the child-nature connection for granted. How could something so timeless change in such a short time? Even if some researchers asked that question, others dismissed it as an exercise in nostalgia. One reason is that there's no commercial incentive to ask. For years, James Sallis has been studying why some children and adults are more active than others. He is program director of the Active Living Research Program for the Robert Wood Johnson Foundation, a multi-year effort to discover how to design recreational facilities and whole communities so they stimulate people of all ages to be more active. The studies are focusing on such sites as urban parks, recreation centers, streets, and private homes. "Based on previous studies, we can definitely say that the best predictor of preschool children's physical activity is simply being outdoors," says Sallis, "and that an indoor, sedentary childhood is linked to mental-health problems."

I asked him what he had learned about how children use woods, fields, canyons, and vacant lots—in other words, unstructured natural sites.

"We don't ask about those places," he said.

If the Robert Wood Johnson Foundation isn't collecting such data, it's unlikely that studies funded by commercial interests would finance such research. One of the great benefits of unstructured outdoor recreation is that it doesn't cost anything, Sallis explained. "Because it's free, there's no major economic interest involved. Who's going to fund the research? If kids are out there riding their bikes or walking, they're not burning fossil fuel, they're nobody's captive audience; they're not making money for anybody. . . . Follow the money."

Nonetheless, the circumstantial evidence of a generational break from nature is growing in the United States and elsewhere.

In 1986, Robin Moore, a professor of landscape architecture at North Carolina State, charted the shrinkage of natural play spaces in urban England, a transformation of the landscape of childhood that occurred within a space of fifteen years. In 2002, another British study discovered that the average eight-year-old was better able to identify characters from the Japanese card trading game Pokémon than native species in the community where they lived: Pikachu, Metapod, and Wigglytuff were names more familiar to them than otter, beetle, and oak tree. Similarly, Japan's landscape of childhood, already downsized, grew smaller. For almost two decades the well-known Japanese photographer Keiki Haginoya photographed children's play in the cities of Japan. In recent years, "children have disappeared so rapidly from his viewfinder that he has had to bring this chapter of his work to an end," Moore reports. "Either indoor spaces have become more attractive, or outdoor spaces have become less attractive—or both." Moore, who is president of the International Association for the Child's Right to Play and director of the Natural Learning Initiative, cites such causes as poorly designed outdoor spaces; the rapid growth of domestic air-conditioning since the 1950s; apprehensive parents who keep their children close to home; state-mandated school curricula that do not allow time for study outdoors; and the overly structured lifestyle of many families.

Support for scientific research on this issue is more common overseas than in the United States. Nonetheless, a growing body of evidence indicates that direct exposure to nature is essential for physical and emotional health. For example, new studies suggest that exposure to nature may reduce the symptoms of Attention Deficit Hyperactivity Disorder (ADHD), and that it can improve all children's cognitive abilities and resistance to negative stresses and depression.

Nature-Deficit Disorder

The overarching importance of this research combined with our knowledge of other changes in the culture demands a shorthand description. So, for now, let's call the phenomenon *nature-deficit disorder*. Our culture is so top-heavy with jargon, so dependent on the illness model, that I hesitate to introduce this term. Perhaps a more appropriate definition will emerge as the scientific research continues. And, as mentioned earlier, I am not suggesting that this term represents an existing medical diagnosis. But when I talk about nature-deficit disorder with groups of parents and educators, the meaning of the phrase is clear. Nature-deficit disorder describes the human costs of alienation from nature, among them: diminished use of the senses, attention difficulties, and higher rates of physical and emotional illnesses. The disorder can be detected in individuals, families, and communities. Nature deficit can even change human behavior in cities, which could ultimately affect their design, since long-standing studies show a relationship between the absence, or inaccessibility, of parks and open space with high crime rates, depression, and other urban maladies.

As the following chapters explain, nature-deficit disorder can be recognized and reversed, individually and culturally. But deficit is only one side of the coin. The other is natural abundance. By weighing the consequences of the disorder, we also can become more aware of how blessed our children can be—biologically, cognitively, and spiritually—through positive physical connection to nature. Indeed, the new research focuses not so much on what is lost when nature fades, but on what is gained in the presence of the natural world. "There is a great need to educate parents about this research—to awaken or inspire the parents' pleasure with nature play—as the necessary context for continued nature experiences for their children," says Louise Chawla.

Such knowledge may inspire us to choose a different path, one that leads to a nature-child reunion.

PART II

WHY THE YOUNG (AND THE REST OF US) NEED NATURE

Those who contemplate the beauty of the earth
find reserves of strength that will endure as long as life lasts.

—RACHEL CARSON

From wonder into wonder existence opens.

—LAO-TZU

4. Climbing the Tree of Health

I bet I can live to a hundred if only I can get outdoors again.
—Geraldine Page as Carrie Watts, in *The Trip to Bountiful*

Elaine Brooks's gray hair was wound around her head in a great nest. A pencil was stuck through the bun to hold it up. Climbing a hill, she passed quietly through a stand of native vegetation: black sage, laurel leaf sumac, and wild morning glories. She trailed her fingers through non-native species—exotic invaders, she called them—such as oxalis, with yellow blooms that mirror the sun. She enjoyed a special relationship with this stretch of forgotten land. She brought to mind writer Annie Dillard's words about needing to "explore the neighborhood, view the landscape, to discover at least where it is that we have been so startlingly set down, if we can't learn why."

"You know, in three years coming to this open space, I have never seen kids playing here, except on the bike path," said Brooks. She bent to touch a leaf that looks like the paw of a slender cat. "The native lupine is a nitrogen fixer," she explained. "The roots house their own foreign invader—bacteria—which collect nitrogen from air in the soil and transform it into a modified nitrogen that plants need." Some lichens, a complex organism of symbiotic fungi and algae, also feed nitrogen to their neighbors and can live for more than a century.

When land like this is graded, lupine and lichen are destroyed, along with the ecosystems they support. Plants live together, she said, and they die together.

For years, as a community-college teacher, she brought her students here to expose them to the nature many of them had never experienced. She taught them that land shapes us more than we shape land, until there is no more land to shape.

She haunted these thirty acres of lost La Jolla, and filled fifteen note-books with pressed plants, rainfall measurements, and observations of the species that live here. An island of grass, succulents, and cacti, this is one of the last places in California where true coastal sage and a va-riety of other rare native plants can still be found so close to the ocean. Not that anyone planned it this way. In the early 1900s, a light-rail line ran through the patch of wildness, but its tracks were abandoned and pulled up. The land waited. Then in the late 1950s, the city set the cor-ridor aside, assigning to it the forgettable name of Fay Avenue Exten-sion. The plan was to build a major street through this part of the city. But the idea faded. And for nearly half a century, as the town boomed around it, the parcel was forgotten—except for the creation of an as-phalt bike path that covers the ghost rail line.

Wearing jeans, a frayed flannel shirt, and hiking boots, Brooks stood in a field of wild onions, prickly pear, and native nightshade. The pleas-ant scent of licorice arrived from a patch of Mediterranean fennel, first brought to California by pioneers in the 1800s and used as a condiment. Wild oats, also an exotic, towered over most of the desert-designed na-tive plants, which clung to the earth. If you're a plant in this environ-ment, it's safer to keep your head down. "Look here, at the native blue dicks," she exclaimed, pointing to violet, long-stemmed flowers next to wild chrysanthemums. The last, while not native, are as familiar as grin-ning daisies. It's hard to dislike them.

One wonders: Why would anyone spend so many hours and days in what amounts to a big vacant lot?

One answer is that Brooks was a throwback, a rarity in her profession. In the 1940s and 1950s, the study of natural history—an intimate science predicated on the time-consuming collection and naming of life forms—gave way to microbiology, theoretical and commercial. Much the same thing happened to the conservation movement, which shifted from local preservationists with soil on their shoes to environmental lawyers in Washington, D.C. Brooks was uncomfortable in either environmental camp. For years, she worked at the Scripps Institution of Oceanography as a biologist and oceanographer. She became a plankton expert.

She liked teaching better. She believed—as do many Americans—that she should pass along her love of nature. Plus, teaching at the community-college level afforded her the time she needed to know these hills and fields. No one paid her to study this land; but no one said she couldn't.

Brooks was a throwback in another way, as well. The admirable vogue in ecology is to focus on preserving networks of natural corridors, rather than isolated islands of life, which are usually deemed beyond saving. In principle, she agreed with that philosophy. But as Elaine Brooks believed, isolated patches of wild land are valuable to know, as are isolated people.

These islands of nature are most important for the young who live in surrounding or adjacent neighborhoods. She pointed to the scars of a bulldozer that came through years ago. Despite what developers will tell you about restoration, she said, once a piece of land is graded, the biologic organisms and understructure of the soil are destroyed. "No one knows how to easily re-create that, short of years of hand-weeding. Leaving land alone doesn't work; the natives are overwhelmed by the invaders." Spot bulldozing is common across the county, even on land that is supposedly protected. "Much of this destruction is done out of expediency and ignorance," she said. She believed people are unlikely to value what they cannot name. "One of my students told me that every time she learns the name of a plant, she feels as if she is meeting someone new. Giving a name to something is a way of knowing it."

She trotted down a narrow footpath and then over a rise. A red-tailed hawk circled above. On a slope ahead, rivulets of fire-retardant, non-native ice plant had turned into a flood and would soon cover the hillside. But clusters of native agave—a cactus-like succulent from which tequila is made—made their stand. The agave blooms once in its long life; it grows for two decades or more and then in a final burst of energy shoots up a single, trembling flower stalk that can be up to twenty feet high. At dusk, bats dance in the air around it and carry pollen to other flowering agave.

Brooks stopped below a small hillside covered with original native bunch grass, a species that dates from pre-Spanish California, from a time before cattle were introduced. Just as tall-grass prairie once covered the Great Plains states, bunch grass carpeted much of Southern California. (In the Great Plains, botanists can still encounter remnants of tall-grass prairie in deserted pioneer graveyards.) There is something fine about touching this grass, in knowing it.

The Ghosts of Fay Avenue Extension

As we continued our walk through Fay Avenue Extension, Brooks made her way to the highest knoll. From here she had a view of the Pacific Ocean. She often sat alone on this elevation, inhaling the nature and the long view. "One day I caught a movement out of the corner of my eye. A tiny brown frog was sitting on a bush next to me. I said, 'What are you doing here?'"

Sometimes, as she sat here, she imagined herself as her own distant ancestor: One step ahead of something large and hungry, she had leaped into branches and shinnied up a tall tree. At these times she looked out over the rooftops toward the sea, but did not, she said, see the cityscape. She saw savanna—the rolling, feminine, harsh yet nurturing plains of Africa. She felt her breath slow and her heart ease.

"Once our ancestors climbed high in that tree, there was something about looking out over the land—something that healed us quickly," said Brooks. Resting in those high branches may have provided a rapid comedown from the adrenaline rush of being potential prey.

"Biologically, we have not changed. We are still programmed to fight or flee large animals. Genetically, we are essentially the same creatures as we were at the beginning. We are still hunters and gatherers. Our ancestors couldn't outrun a lion, but we did have wits. We knew how to kill, yes, but we also knew how to run and climb—and how to use the environment to recover our wits."

Today, we find ourselves continually on the alert, chased by an unending stampede of two-thousand-pound automobiles and four-thousand-pound SUVs. Even inside our homes the assault continues, with unsettling, threatening images charging through the television cable into our living rooms and bedrooms. At the same time, the urban and suburban landscape is rapidly being stripped of its peace-inducing elements.

A widening circle of researchers believes that the loss of natural habitat, or the disconnection from nature even when it is available, has enormous implications for human health and child development. They say the quality of exposure to nature affects our health at an almost cellular level.

Brooks taught her students about the ecology of vacant lots through the lens of "biophilia," the hypothesis of Harvard University scientist and Pulitzer Prize–winning author Edward O. Wilson. Wilson defines biophilia as "the urge to affiliate with other forms of life." He and his colleagues argue that humans have an innate affinity for the natural world, probably a biologically based need integral to our development as individuals. The biophilia theory, though not universally embraced by biologists, is supported by a decade of research that reveals how strongly and positively people respond to open, grassy landscapes, scattered stands of trees, meadows, water, winding trails, and elevated views.

At the cutting edge of this frontier, added to the older foundation of ecological psychology, is the relatively new interdisciplinary field of ecopsychology. The term gained currency in 1992, through the writing of historian and social critic Theodore Roszak. In his book *Voice of the Earth*, Roszak argued that modern psychology has split the inner life from the outer life, and that we have repressed our "ecological unconscious" that provides "our connection to our evolution on earth." In recent years, the meaning of the term "ecopsychology" has evolved to include nature therapy, which asks not only what we do to the earth, but what the earth does for us—for our health. Roszak considers that a logical extension of his original thesis.

As he points out, the American Psychiatric Association lists more than three hundred mental diseases in its Diagnostic and Statistical Manual, a large number of them associated with sexual dysfunction. "Psychotherapists have exhaustively analyzed every form of dysfunctional family and social relations, but 'dysfunctional environmental relations' does not exist even as a concept," he says. The Diagnostic and Statistical Manual "defines 'separation anxiety disorder' as 'excessive anxiety concerning separation from home and from those to whom the individual is attached.' But no separation is more pervasive in this Age of Anxiety than our disconnection from the natural world." It's time, he says, "for an environmentally based definition of mental health."

Ecopsychology and all of its budding branches, reinforcing Wilson's biophilia hypothesis, have fueled a new surge of research into the impact of nature on human physical and emotional health. Professor Chawla, the international expert on urban children and nature, is skeptical about some of the claims made in the name of biophilia, but she also argues that one does not have to adopt unreservedly the entire thesis to believe that Edward O. Wilson and the ecopsychology movement are on to something. She calls for a common-sense approach, one that recognizes "the positive effects of involvement with nature on health, concentration, creative play, and a developing bond with the natural world that can form a foundation for environmental stewardship."

The idea that natural landscapes, or at least gardens, can be therapeutic and restorative is, in fact, an ancient one that has filtered down through the ages. Over two thousand years ago, Chinese Taoists created gardens and greenhouses they believed to be beneficial for health. By 1699, the book *English Gardener* advised the reader to spend "spare time in the garden, either digging, setting out, or weeding; there is no better way to preserve your health."

In America, mental-health pioneer Dr. Benjamin Rush (a signer of the American Declaration of Independence), declared, "digging in the soil has a curative effect on the mentally ill." Beginning in the 1870s, the Quakers' Friends Hospital in Pennsylvania used acres of natural landscape and a greenhouse as part of its treatment of mental illness. During World War II, psychiatry pioneer Carl Menninger led a horticulture therapy movement in the Veterans Administration Hospital System. In the 1950s, a wider movement emerged, one that recognized the therapeutic benefits of gardening for people with chronic illnesses. In 1955, Michigan State University awarded the first graduate degree in horticultural/occupational therapy. And in 1971, Kansas State University established the first horticultural therapy degree curriculum.

Today, pet therapy has joined horticultural therapy as an accepted health-care approach, particularly for the elderly and children. For example, research has shown that subjects experienced significant decreases in blood pressure simply by watching fish in an aquarium. Other reports link pet ownership to a lowering of high blood pressure and improved survival after heart attacks. The mortality rate of heart-disease patients with pets was found to be one-third that of patients without pets. Aaron Katcher, a psychiatrist on the faculty of the University of Pennsylvania's Schools of Medicine, Dentistry, and Veterinary Medicine, has spent over a decade investigating how social relationships between human beings and other animals influence human health and behavior. Katcher and Gregory Wilkins, an expert on animal-facilitated therapy in residential treatment centers, tell of an autistic child who spent several sessions with passive dogs before encountering Buster, a hyperactive adolescent dog brought from a local animal shelter. At first the autistic child ignored the dogs—but at a later session, "without any other change in regimen, the patient eagerly ran into the therapy room and within minutes said his first new words in six months: 'Buster Sit!'" The child learned to play ball with Buster and give him food rewards— and also learned to seek out Buster for comfort.

The evidence of the therapeutic value of gardens and pets is convincing. What do we know, though, about the next step—the influence of unstructured natural landscapes and experiences in nature on human development and health? Poets and shamen have recognized that link for millennia, but science began to explore it relatively recently.

Most of the new evidence connecting nature to well-being and restoration focuses on adults. In the *American Journal of Preventive Medicine*, Howard Frumkin, chairman of the department of environmental and occupational health at Emory University's School of Public Health, considers this a mostly overlooked field in modern medicine, even though many studies credit exposure to plants or nature with speeding up recovery time from injury. Frumkin points to a ten-year study of gallbladder surgery patients, comparing those who recovered in rooms facing a grove of trees to those in rooms with a view of a brick wall; the patients with the view of trees went home sooner. Perhaps not unexpectedly, research revealed Michigan prison inmates whose cells faced a prison courtyard had 24 percent more illnesses than those whose cells had a view of farmland. In a similar vein, Roger Ulrich, a Texas A&M researcher, has shown that people who watch images of natural landscape after a stressful experience calm markedly in only five minutes: their muscle tension, pulse, and skin-conductance readings plummet.

Gordon Orians, professor emeritus of zoology at the University of Washington, says such research suggests that our visual environment profoundly affects our physical and mental well-being, and that modern humans need to understand the importance of what he calls "ghosts," the evolutionary remnants of past experience hard-wired into a species' nervous system.

The childhood link between outdoor activity and physical health is clear. The Centers for Disease Control (CDC) reports that the number of overweight adult Americans increased over 60 percent between 1991 and 2000. According to CDC data, the U.S. population of overweight children between ages two and five increased by almost 36 percent from 1989 to 1999. And two out of ten of America's children are clinically obese—four times the percentage of childhood obesity reported in the late 1960s. In the United States, children ages six to eleven spend about thirty hours a week looking at a TV or computer monitor. This study also found that the amount of TV that children watched directly correlated with measures of their body fat. The television to junk food obesity correlations are not as direct as they might seem. For example, the obesity epidemic has coincided with the greatest increase in organized sports for children in history. What are kids missing that soccer and Little League cannot provide? Generalized, hour-to-hour physical activity is the likely absent ingredient. The physical and emotional exercise that children enjoy when they play in nature is more varied and less time-bound than organized sports.

While it's true that heart disease and other negative effects of children's physical inactivity usually take decades to develop, another result is more readily documented: kids get depressed.

Biophilia and Emotional Health

Nature is often overlooked as a healing balm for the emotional hardships in a child's life. You'll likely never see a slick commercial for nature therapy, as you do for the latest antidepressant pharmaceuticals. But parents, educators, and health workers need to know what a useful antidote to emotional and physical stress nature can be. Especially now.

A 2003 survey, published in the journal *Psychiatric Services*, found the rate at which American children are prescribed antidepressants almost doubled in five years; the steepest increase—66 percent—was among preschool children. "A number of factors acting together or independently may have led to escalated use of antidepressants among children and adolescents," said Tom Delate, director of research at Express Scripts, the pharmacy benefits group that conducted the survey. "These factors include increasing rates of depression in successive age groups, a growing awareness of and screening for depression by pediatricians and assumptions that the effectiveness experienced by adults using antidepressant medications will translate to children and adolescents." The growth in such prescriptions written for children occurred even though antidepressants were never approved for children younger than eighteen—with the exception of Prozac, which was approved as a treatment for children in 2001, after the rise in juvenile prescriptions began. The findings were announced a month after the Food and Drug Administration asked pharmaceutical companies to add explicit product labeling warnings about alleged links between antidepressants and suicidal behavior and thoughts, especially among children. In 2004, data analysis by Medco Health Solutions, the nation's largest prescription benefit manager, found that between 2000 and 2003 there was a 49 percent increase in the use of psychotropic drugs—antipsychotics, benzodiazepines, and antidepressants. For the first time, spending on such drugs, if medications for attention disorders are included, surpassed spending on antibiotics and asthma medications for children.

Although countless children who suffer from mental illness and attention disorders do benefit from medication, the use of nature as an alternative, additional, or preventive therapy is being overlooked. In fact, new evidence suggests that the need for such medications is intensified by children's disconnection from nature. Although exposure to nature may have no impact on the most severe depressions, we do know that nature experiences can relieve some of the everyday pressures that may lead to childhood depression. I've mentioned the Ulrich study and a few others that focused on adults; in *The Human Relationship with Nature*,

Peter Kahn points to the findings of over one hundred studies that confirm that one of the main benefits of spending time in nature is stress reduction.

Cornell University environmental psychologists reported in 2003 that a room with a view of nature can help protect children against stress, and that nature in or around the home appears to be a significant factor in protecting the psychological well-being of children in rural areas. "Our study finds that life's stressful events appear not to cause as much psychological distress in children who live in high-nature conditions compared with children who live in low-nature conditions," according to Nancy Wells, assistant professor of design and environmental analysis in the New York State College of Human Ecology at Cornell. "And the protective impact of nearby nature is strongest for the most vulnerable children—those experiencing the highest levels of stressful life events."

Wells and colleague Gary Evans assessed the degree of nature in and around the homes of rural children in grades three through five. They found that children with more nature near their home received lower ratings than peers with less nature near their home on measures of behavioral conduct disorders, anxiety, and depression. Children with more nature near their homes also rated themselves higher than their corresponding peers on a global measure of self-worth. "Even in a rural setting with a relative abundance of green landscape, more [nature] appears to be better when it comes to bolstering children's resilience against stress or adversity," Wells and Evans reported.

One reason for the emotional benefits of nature may be that green space fosters social interaction and thereby promotes social support. For instance, a Swedish study shows that children and parents who live in places that allow for outdoor access have twice as many friends as those who have restricted outdoor access due to traffic. Of course, no one would argue that nature's solace is *entirely* dependent on the social interaction that nature may encourage. After a classroom discussion I conducted at the University of San Diego about nature and childhood, Lauren Haring, a twenty-year-old student, described the importance of nature to her emotional health:

> Growing up [in Santa Barbara, California], I lived in a house that had a fairly big back yard and a creek across the street. It was when I was by myself that the environment meant the most to me. Nature was the one place where, when everything in my life was going bad, I could go and not have to deal with anyone else.
>
> My dad died of brain cancer when I was nine. It was one of the most difficult times for my family and myself. Going out into nature was one outlet that I had, which truly allowed me to calm down and not think or worry.
>
> I really believe that there is something about nature—that when you are in it, it makes you realize that there are far larger things at work than yourself. This helps to put problems in perspective. And it is the only place where the issues facing me do not need immediate attention or resolution. Being in nature can be a way to escape without fully leaving the world.

Richard Herrmann, a nature photographer, also understands the healing qualities of nature, which helped him through a tragic time. He told me:

> My first memories of being affected by the natural world were from my youth growing up at Pacific Grove, not far from the burned-out cannery of Cannery Row. I remember being four years old, and looking into a tide pool, and being mesmerized by the tiny fishes swimming through the shimmering water, and the anemones and crabs scurrying about. I was transfixed; I could have looked at the same pool for days. To me, the tide pool represented perfection, and calmness. I also remember my father returning from fishing in the bay with sacks of colorful rock cod . . . I found them beautiful. They represented special treasures from the sea.
>
> I was a kid who could not sit still for more than a few minutes, so

school was painful for me. But nature always gave me this incredible calmness and joy. I could literally sit and fish, or crab, for hours without getting bored, even if I wasn't catching anything.

Later, I needed this calmness again when my father was killed in a car accident when I was fourteen. I was lost, and the temptations and distractions were many in the late sixties. Drugs were everywhere. I remember being absolutely in pain and stress most days, but I would find solace by walking by myself to an area of coast oak woodland— just walking, looking at the undercover of poison oak . . . seeing salamanders, colorful mushrooms, and lichens. It all made sense to me. I experienced great calmness there that I could not find anywhere else.

As an adult, giving presentations at local high schools, I noticed that I can get teenagers to focus and calm down by showing images of the natural world. Being close to nature saved my life.

Herrmann's own experience helped him encourage his fourteen-year-old daughter—who is dyslexic—to employ nature to balance her life and reduce her stress. Finding solace raising lambs in a 4-H program has, he says, "really turned her around in school."

Elsewhere, in Wellesley, Massachusetts, the Institute for Child and Adolescent Development's Therapeutic Garden won the President's Award for Excellence from the American Society of Landscape Architects. In a 1999 interview with the online professional journal *The Massachusetts Psychologist*, Sebastiano Santostefano, director of the institute, explained his view that nature has power to shape the psyche, and that it can play a significant role in helping traumatized children. He found that playing outdoors, whether along a river or in an alleyway, "is how a kid works through issues." "We have a small hill, a mound—and for one kid at a certain point in therapy it was a grave; for another, it was the belly of a pregnant woman," he said. "The point is obvious: children interpret and give meaning to a piece of landscape, and the same piece can be interpreted differently. Usually, if you [use] traditional puppets and games, there are limits. A policeman puppet is usually a policeman;

a kid rarely makes it something else. But with landscape, it's much more engaging, and you're giving the child ways of expressing what's within."

The Re-naturing of Childhood Health

With a sense of urgency, some health professionals say that we should act now on the available knowledge. For example, Emory's Howard Frumkin suggests that public-health experts expand their definition of environmental health beyond concern about, say, toxic dumps, to encompass how the environment can heal. He recommends that environmental-health research be done in collaboration with architects, urban planners, park designers, landscape architects, pediatricians, and veterinarians. Others argue that increased awareness of nature's power to improve physical and emotional health should also guide the way classrooms are conceived, houses built, and neighborhoods shaped. And, as the coming chapters explain, the evolving research can help us rediscover the link between human creativity and experiences in nature, and could offer a new branch of therapy for such syndromes as attention-deficit disorder.

Elaine Brooks taught her community college students that each of us—adult or child—must earn nature's gift by *knowing* nature directly, however difficult it may be to glean that knowledge in an urban environment.

How ironic it is, Brooks told me one day, that the reality of life in beautiful California "is that we rarely experience any of these natural settings directly and intimately, but rather live our lives in large, sprawling urban areas." Even when we drive to mountains and deserts, "it is not unusual to make a day trip, stopping only for coffee or a snack along the way. The entire experience occurs within an automobile looking out." Yet, "the look, feel, odor, sounds of a landscape surround every individual from the very beginning of life. The landscape is the place where we exist, where our real daily world is bounded." As a species, we crave the very shapes we now allow to be scraped away.

Brooks's students are grateful for what she taught them. So am I. She would have been the first person to point out that the natural world offers us no warranties. Elaine passed away in 2003. As she lay dying from a brain tumor, drifting in and out of a deepening sleep, her friends pinned snapshots of Fay Avenue Extension to the walls around her bed, and took turns sitting beside her. Perhaps, as she traveled a topology of dreams, she saw the future from the branches of that imaginary tree, high above the savanna of La Jolla.

5. A Life of the Senses: Nature vs. the Know-It-All State of Mind

I go to nature to be soothed and healed,
and to have my senses put in tune once more.
—John Burroughs

Children need nature for the healthy development of their senses, and, therefore, for learning and creativity. This need is revealed in two ways: by an examination of what happens to the senses of the young when they lose connection with nature; and by witnessing the sensory magic that occurs when young people—even those beyond childhood—are exposed to even the smallest direct experience of a natural setting.

The Boyz of the Woods

In just a few weeks, a group of boyz of the 'hood become the boyz of the woods. At the Crestridge Ecological Reserve, 2,600 acres of mountainous California between the cities of El Cajon and Alpine, a dozen members of the Urban Corps, ages eighteen to twenty-five—all but one of them male, all of them Hispanic—follow two middle-aged Anglo women—park docents—through sage and patches of wild berries.

As members of the city-sponsored Urban Corps, they attend a charter school that emphasizes hands-on conservation work. They've spent the past few weeks at the nature preserve clearing trails, pulling out non-native plants, learning the art of tracking from a legendary former Border Patrol officer, and experiencing a sometimes baffling explosion of senses. The young people wear uniforms: light-green shirts, dark-green pants, military-style canvas belts. One of the docents wears a blue sunbonnet, the other a baggy T-shirt and day pack.

"Here we have the home of the dusky-footed wood rat," says Andrea Johnson, a docent who lives on a ridge overlooking this land.

She points at a mound of sticks tucked under poison oak. A wood rat's nest looks something like a beaver's lodge; it contains multiple chambers, including specialized indoor latrines and areas where leaves are stored to get rid of toxins before eating. The nests can be as tall as six feet. Wood rats tend to have houseguests, Johnson explains. "Kissing bugs! Oh my, yes," she says. Kissing bugs, a.k.a. the blood-sucking assassin bug.

"This is one reason you might not want a wood-rat nest near your house. Kissing bugs are attracted to carbon dioxide, which we all exhale. Consequently, the kissing bug likes to bite people around their mouths," Johnson continues, fanning herself in the morning heat. "The bite eats away the flesh; my husband has a *big scar* on his face."

One of the Urban Corpsmen shudders so hard that his pants, fashionably belted far to the south of his hips, try to head farther south.

Leaving the wood-rat's lair, the docents lead the Urban Corps members through clusters of California fuchsia and laurel sumac into cool woods where a spring seeps into a little creek. Carlos, a husky six-footer with earrings and shaved head, leaps nimbly from rock to rock, his eyes filled with wonder. He whispers exclamations in Spanish as he crouches over a two-inch-long tarantula hawk, a wasp with orange wings, dark-blue body, and a sting considered one of the most painful of any North American insect. This wasp is no Rotarian; it will attack and paralyze a tarantula five times its size, drag it underground, plant a single egg, and seal the chamber on its way out. Later, the egg hatches into a grub that eats the spider alive. Nature is beautiful, but not always pretty.

Several of the young men spent their early childhood in rural Central America or on Mexican farms. Carlos, who now works as a brake technician, describes his grandmother's farm in Sinaloa, Mexico. "She had pigs, man. She had land. It was fine." Despite their current urban habitats, these young first- and second-generation immigrants experienced nature more directly when they were small children than have most North Americans. "In Mexico, people know how hard it is to own a piece of land up here, so they value it. They take care of it. People who live on this side of the border don't value land so much. Take it for granted. Too much cream on the taco, or something." But right now the boyz of the woods aren't so serious. They begin to tease a nineteen-year-old with a shy grin and a hickey the size of a tarantula hawk.

"He's been sleepin' with his window open again," someone says. "Blair Witch got him."

"Nah, man," says Carlos, laughing, "*Chupacabras* chewed him," referring to Latin America's half-bat, half-kangaroo, razor-clawed, goat-sucking mythological beast, most recently reported in Argentina. Or maybe it was just the kissing bug.

Over the weeks, Carlos has observed closely and sketches the plants and animals in notebooks. Along with the other students, he has watched a bobcat stalk game, heard the sudden percussion of disturbed rattlesnake dens, and felt a higher music. "When I come here, I can *exhale*," says Carlos. "Here, you *hear* things; in the city, you can't hear anything because you can hear everything. In the city, everything is *obvious*. Here, you get closer and you see more."

Losing Our Senses

Not that long ago, the sound track of a young person's days and nights was composed largely of the notes of nature. Most people were raised on the land, worked the land, and were often buried on the same land. The relationship was direct.

Today, the life of the senses is, literally, electrified. One obvious contributor is electronics: television and computers. But simpler, early technologies played important roles. Air-conditioning, for example: The

U.S. Census Bureau reports that in 1910, only 12 percent of housing had air conditioning. People threw open their sash windows and let in night air and the sound of wind in leaves. By the time the baby boomers came along, approximately half our homes were air-conditioned. By 1970, that figure was 72 percent, and by 2001, 78 percent.

In 1920, most farms were miles from a city of any size. Even by 1935, fewer than 12 percent of America's farms had electricity (compared to 85 percent of urban homes); not until the mid-1940s were even half of all U.S. farm homes electrified. In the 1920s, farmers gathered at feed stores or cotton gins to listen to the radio, or created their own wired networks by connecting several homes to a single radio. In 1949, only 36 percent of farms had telephone service.

Few of us are about to trade our air conditioners for fans. But one price of progress is seldom mentioned: a diminished life of the senses. Like the boyz of the 'hood, as human beings we need direct, natural experiences; we require fully activated senses in order to feel fully alive. Twenty-first century Western culture accepts the view that because of omnipresent technology we are awash in data. But in this information age, vital information is missing. Nature is about smelling, hearing, tasting, seeing below the "transparent mucous-paper in which the world like a bon-bon is wrapped so carefully that we can never get at it," as D. H. Lawrence put it, in a relatively obscure but extraordinary description of his own awakening to nature's sensory gift. Lawrence described his awakening in Taos, New Mexico, as an antidote to the "know-it-all state of mind," that poor substitute for wisdom and wonder:

> Superficially, the world has become small and known. Poor little globe of earth, the tourists trot round you as easily as they trot round the Bois or round Central Park. There is no mystery left, we've been there, we've seen it, we know all about it. We've done the globe and the globe is done.
>
> This is quite true, superficially. On the superficies, horizontally,

we've been everywhere and done everything, we know all about it. Yet the more we know, superficially, the less we penetrate, vertically. It's all very well skimming across the surface of the ocean and saying you know all about the sea. . . .

As a matter of fact, our great-grandfathers, who never went anywhere, in actuality had more experience of the world than we have, who have seen everything. When they listened to a lecture with lantern-slides, they really held their breath before the unknown, as they sat in the village school-room. We, bowling along in a rickshaw in Ceylon, say to ourselves: "It's very much what you'd expect." We really know it all.

We are mistaken. The know-it-all state of mind is just the result of being outside the mucous-paper wrapping of civilization. Underneath is everything we don't know and are afraid of knowing.

Some of us adults recognize the know-it-all state of mind in ourselves, sometimes at unlikely moments.

Todd Merriman, a newspaper editor and father, remembers an illuminating hike with his young son. "We were walking across a field in the mountains," he says. "I looked down and saw mountain lion tracks. They were fresh. We immediately headed back to the car, and then I saw another set of tracks. I knew they had not been there before. The lion had circled us." In that moment of dread and excitement, he became intensely aware of his surroundings. Later, he realized that he could not remember the last time he had used all of his senses so acutely. The near encounter jarred something loose.

How much of the richness of life have he and his son traded for their daily immersion in indirect, technological experience? Today, Merriman often thinks about that question—usually while he is sitting in front of a computer screen.

IT DOESN'T TAKE an encounter with a lion for us to recognize that our sensory world has shrunk. The information age is, in fact, a myth, despite songwriter Paul Simon's phrase, "These are the days of miracle and wonder. . . . Lasers in the jungle," and all that. Our indoor life feels downsized, as if it's lost a dimension or two. Yes, we're enamored with our gadgets—our cell phones connected to our digital cameras connected to our laptops connected to an e-mail-spewing satellite transponder hovering somewhere over Macon, Georgia. Of course, some of us (I include myself here) love the gizmology. But quality of life isn't measured only by what we gain, but also by what we trade for it.

Instead of spending less time at the office, we work on Internet Time. A billboard on the freeway near my home advertises an online banking service. It shows a chipper young woman in front of her computer saying, "I expect to pay bills at 3 A.M." Electronic immersion will continue to deepen. Researchers at the Massachusetts Institute of Technology's Media Laboratory are working to make computers invisible in the home. In New York, architects Gisue and Mojgan Hariri promote their idea of a dream Digital House, with walls of LCD screens.

As electronic technology surrounds us, we long for nature—even if the nature is synthetic. Several years ago, I met Tom Wrubel, founder of the Nature Company, the pioneering mall outlet for all things faux flora and fauna. In the beginning, the store, which became a nationwide chain, was aimed primarily at children. In 1973, Wrubel and his wife, Priscilla, noted a common thread in nature-oriented retailing: the emphasis was on *getting* to nature. "But once you got to the mountains or wherever, what do you do, except shoot or catch things," he said. "So we emphasized books and gadgets to use in nature."

The Wrubels caught and accelerated a wave—what the Nature Company's president, Roger Bergen, called "the shift from activity-orientation in the 1960s and '70s, to knowledge-orientation in the '80s." The Nature Company marketed nature as mood, at first to children primarily. "We go for strong vertical stone elements, giant archways. Gives you the feeling that you're entering Yosemite Canyon. At the entrances, we place stone creeks with running water—but these creeks are modernistic, an architect's dream of creekness," Tom Wrubel explained. His version of nature was both antiseptic and whimsical. Visitors walked through the maze of products: dandelion blossoms preserved within crystalline domes; designer bird-feeders; inflatable snakes and dinosaurs; bags of Nature Company natural cedar tips from the mountains of New Mexico; "pine cones in brass cast from Actual Cones," according to the display sign. In the air: the sounds of wind and water, buzzing shrimp, snapping killer whales—courtesy of "The Nature Company Presents: Nature," available on audiotape and compact disk. "Mood tapes" were also available, including "Tranquility," a forty-seven-minute, musically scored video the catalog described as a "deeply calming, beautiful study in the shapes and colors of clouds, waves, unfolding blossoms and light."

Wrubel sincerely believed that his stores stimulated concern for the environment. Perhaps he was right.

Such design emphasis now permeates malls across the country. For example, Minnesota's Mall of America now has its own UnderWater World. John Beardsley, a curator who teaches at the Harvard Design School, describes this simulated natural attraction in *Earthworks and Beyond: Contemporary Art in the Landscape:* "You're in a gloomy boreal forest in the fall, descending a ramp past bubbling brooks and glass-fronted tanks stocked with freshwater fish native to the northern woodlands. At the bottom of the ramp, you step onto a moving walkway and are transported through a 300-foot-long transparent tunnel carved into a 1.2-million-gallon aquarium. All around you are the creatures of a succession of ecosystems: the Minnesota lakes, the Mississippi River, the Gulf of Mexico, and a coral reef."

There, according to the mall's promotional line, you'll "meet sharks, rays, and other exotic creatures face to face." This "piece of concocted nature," as Beardsley terms it, "is emblematic of a larger phenomenon." Beardsley calls it the growing "commodification of nature: the increasingly pervasive commercial trend that views and uses nature as a sales gimmick or marketing strategy, often through the production of replicas or simulations." This can be presented on a grand scale; more often, the commodification of nature occurs in smaller, subtler ways. As Beardsley points out, this phenomenon is new only in scale and to the degree that it permeates everyday life. "For at least five centuries—since the 15th-century Franciscan monk Fra Bernardino Caimi reproduced the shrines of the Holy Land at Sacro Monte in Varallo, Italy, for the benefit of pilgrims unable to travel to Jerusalem—replicas of sacred places, especially caves and holy mountains, have attracted the devout," he writes. The 1915 Panama-Pacific International Exposition in San Francisco included a small railroad, according to Beardsley, that "featured fabricated elephants, a replica of Yellowstone National Park complete with working geysers, and a mock-up Hopi village." But now, "almost everywhere we look, whether we see it or not, commodity culture is reconstructing nature. Synthetic rocks, video images of forests, Rainforest Cafés."

Mall and retail design is one way to package nature for commercial purposes, but the next stage goes a step further by using nature itself as an advertising medium. Researchers at the State University of New York at Buffalo are experimenting with a genetic technology through which they can choose the colors that appear on butterfly wings. The announcement of this in 2002 led writer Matt Richtel to conjure a brave new advertising medium: "There are countless possibilities for moving ads out of the virtual world and into the real one. Sponsorship-wise, it's time for nature to carry its weight." Advertisers already stamp their messages into the wet sands of public beaches. Cash-strapped municipalities hope corporations agree to affix their company logo on parks in exchange for dollars to keep the public spaces maintained. "The sheer popularity" of simulating nature or using nature as ad space "demands that we acknowledge, even respect, their cultural importance," suggests Richtel. Culturally important, yes. But the logical extension of synthetic nature is the irrelevance of "true" nature—the certainty that it's not even worth looking at.

True, our experience of natural landscape "often occurs within an automobile looking out," as Elaine Brooks said. But now even that visual connection is optional. A friend of mine was shopping for a new luxury car to celebrate her half-century of survival in the material world. She settled on a Mercedes SUV, with a Global Positioning System: just tap in your destination and the vehicle not only provides a map on the dashboard screen, but talks you there. But she knew where to draw the line. "The salesman's jaw dropped when I said I didn't want a backseat television monitor for my daughter," she told me. "He almost refused to let me leave the dealership until he could understand why." Rear-seat and in-dash "multimedia entertainment products," as they are called, are quickly becoming the hottest add-on since rearview mirror fuzzy dice. The target market: parents who will pay a premium for a little backseat peace. Sales are brisk; the prices are falling. Some systems include wireless, infrared-connected headsets. The children can watch *Sesame Street* or play Grand Theft Auto on their PlayStation 2 without bothering the driver.

Why do so many Americans say they want their children to watch less TV, yet continue to expand the opportunities for them to watch it? More important, why do so many people no longer consider the physical world worth watching? The highway's edges may not be postcard perfect. But for a century, children's early understanding of how cities and nature fit together was gained from the backseat: the empty farmhouse at the edge of the subdivision; the variety of architecture, here and there; the woods and fields and water beyond the seamy edges—all that was and is still available to the eye. This was the landscape that we watched as children. It was our drive-by movie.

Perhaps we'll someday tell our grandchildren stories about our version of the nineteenth-century Conestoga wagon.

"You did *what?*" they'll ask.

"Yes," we'll say, "it's true. We actually *looked out the car window.*" In our useful boredom, we used our fingers to draw pictures on fogged glass as we watched telephone poles tick by. We saw birds on the wires and combines in the fields. We were fascinated with roadkill, and we counted cows and horses and coyotes and shaving-cream signs. We stared with a kind of reverence at the horizon, as thunderheads and dancing rain moved with us. We held our little plastic cars against the glass and pretended that they, too, were racing toward some unknown destination. We considered the past and dreamed of the future, and watched it all go by in the blink of an eye.

> Soap
> May do
> For lads with fuzz
> But sir, you ain't
> the kid you wuz
> *Burma-Shave.*

Is roadside America really so boring today? In some stretches, yes, but all the others are instructive in their beauty, even in their ugliness. Hugh A. Mulligan, in an Associated Press story about rail travel, quoted novelist John Cheever's recollection of the "peaceable landscape" once seen by suburban rail commuters: "It seemed to me that fishermen and lone bathers and grade-crossing watchmen and sandlot ballplayers and owners of small sailing craft and old men playing pinochle in firehouses were the people who stitched up the big holes in the world made by people like me." Such images still exist, even in this malled America. There is a real world, beyond the glass, for children who look, for those whose parents encourage them to truly see.

The Rise of Cultural Autism

In the most nature-deprived corners of our world we can see the rise of what might be called cultural autism. The symptoms? Tunneled senses, and feelings of isolation and containment. Experience, including physical risk, is narrowing to about the size of a cathode ray tube, or flat panel if you prefer. Atrophy of the senses was occurring long before we came to be bombarded with the latest generation of computers, high-definition TV, and wireless phones. Urban children, and many suburban children, have long been isolated from the natural world because of a lack of neighborhood parks, or lack of opportunity—lack of time and money for parents who might otherwise take them out of the city. But the new technology accelerates the phenomenon. "What I see in America today is an almost religious zeal for the technological approach to every facet of life," says Daniel Yankelovich, the veteran public opinion analyst. This faith, he says, transcends mere love for new machines. "It's a value system, a way of thinking, and it can become delusional."

The late Edward Reed, an associate professor of psychology at Franklin and Marshall College, was one of the most articulate critics of the myth of the information age. In *The Necessity of Experience* he wrote, "There is something wrong with a society that spends so much money, as well as countless hours of human effort—to make the least dregs of processed information available to everyone everywhere and yet does little or nothing to help us explore the world for ourselves." None of our major institutions or our popular culture pay much notice to what Reed called "primary experience"—that which we can see, feel, taste, hear, or smell for ourselves. According to Reed, we are beginning "to lose the ability to experience our world directly. What we have come to mean by the term experience is impoverished; what we have of experience in daily life is impoverished as well." René Descartes argued that physical reality is so ephemeral that humans can only experience their personal, internal interpretation of sensory input. Descartes' view "has become a major cultural force in our world," wrote Reed, one of a number of psychologists and philosophers who pointed to the postmodern acceleration of indirect experience. They proposed an alternative view—ecological psychology (or ecopsychology)—steeped in the ideas of John Dewey, America's most influential educator. Dewey warned a century ago that worship of secondary experience in childhood came with the risk of depersonalizing human life.

North Carolina State professor Robin Moore, director of the National Learning Initiative, takes Reed and Dewey to heart in his contemporary examination of postmodern childhood play. Primary experience of nature is being replaced, he writes, "by the secondary, vicarious, often distorted, dual sensory (vision and sound only), one-way experience of television and other electronic media." According to Moore:

> Children live through their senses. Sensory experiences link the child's exterior world with their interior, hidden, affective world. Since the natural environment is the principal source of sensory stimulation, freedom to explore and play with the outdoor environment through the senses in their own space and time is essential for healthy development of an interior life. . . . This type of self-activated, autonomous interaction is what we call free play. Individual children test themselves by interacting with their environment, activating their potential and reconstructing human culture. The content of the environment is a critical factor in this process. A rich, open environment will continuously present alternative choices for creative engagement. A rigid, bland environment will limit healthy growth and development of the individual or the group.

Little is known about the impact of new technologies on children's emotional health, but we do know something about the implications for adults. In 1998, a controversial Carnegie Mellon University study found that people who spend even a few hours on the Internet each week suffer higher levels of depression and loneliness than people who use the Net infrequently. Enterprising psychologists and psychiatrists now treat Internet Addiction, or IA as they call it.

Even as we grow more separate from nature, we continue to separate from one another physically. The effects are more than skin deep, says Nancy Dess, senior scientist with the American Psychological

Association. "None of the new communication technologies involve human touch; they all tend to place us one step removed from direct experience. Add this to control-oriented changes in the workplace and schools, where people are often forbidden, or at least discouraged, from any kind of physical contact, and we've got a problem," she says. Without touch, infant primates die; adult primates with touch deficits become more aggressive. Primate studies also show that physical touch is essential to the peace-making process. "Perversely, many of us can go through an average day and not have more than a handshake," she adds. Diminishing touch is only one by-product of the culture of technical control, but Dess believes it contributes to violence in an ever more tightly wired society.

Frank Wilson, professor of neurology at the Stanford University School of Medicine, is an expert on the co-evolution of the hominid hand and brain; in *The Hand,* he contends that one could not have evolved to its current sophistication without the other. He says, "We've been sold a bill of goods—especially parents—about how valuable computer-based experience is. We are creatures identified by what we do with our hands." Much of our learning comes from doing, from making, from feeling with our hands; and though many would like to believe otherwise, the world is not entirely available from a keyboard. As Wilson sees it, we're cutting off our hands to spite our brains. Instructors in medical schools find it increasingly difficult to teach how the heart works as a pump, he says, "because these students have so little real-world experience; they've never siphoned anything, never fixed a car, never worked on a fuel pump, may not even have hooked up a garden hose. For a whole generation of kids, direct experiences in the backyard, in the tool shed, in the fields and woods, has been replaced by indirect learning, through machines. These young people are smart, they grew up with computers, they were supposed to be superior—but now we know that something's missing."

The Infinite Reservoir

Not surprisingly, as the young grow up in a world of narrow yet over-whelming sensory input, many of them develop a wired, know-it-all state of mind. That which cannot be Googled does not count. Yet a fuller, grander, more mysterious world, one worthy of a child's awe, is available to children and the rest of us. Bill McKibben, in *The Age of Missing Information*, argues that "the definition of television's global village is just the contrary—it's a place where there's as little variety as possible, where as much information as possible is wiped away to make 'communications' easier." He describes his personal experience with a nearby mountain: "The mountain says you live in a particular place. Though it's a small area, just a square mile or two, it took me many trips to even start to learn its secrets. Here there are blueberries, and here there are bigger blueberries . . . You pass a hundred different plants along the trail—I know maybe twenty of them. One could spend a life-time learning a small range of mountains, and once upon a time people did."

Any natural place contains an infinite reservoir of information, and therefore the potential for inexhaustible new discoveries. As Robert Michael Pyle says, "Place is what takes me out of myself, out of the limited scope of human activity, but this is not misanthropic. A sense of place is a way of embracing humanity among all of its neighbors. It is an entry into the larger world."

During my visits with middle school, high school, and college students, a discussion of the senses would inevitably come about when we talked about nature. Sometimes I would ask directly, other times the students would raise the subject in the classroom or later, through essays. Their verbal answers were often hesitant, searching. This was apparently not a subject that many, if any, had confronted before. For some young people, nature is so abstract—the ozone layer, a faraway rain forest—that it exists beyond the senses. For others, nature is simple background, a disposable consumer item. One young man in a Potomac, Maryland, classroom described his relationship with nature as shaky, at best. "Like most I exploit what it gives and I do with it what I please," he said. He thought of nature "as a means to an end or a tool. Something made to be used and admired not something to live. Nature to me is like my house or even like my cluttered room. It has things in it which can be played with. I say play away, do what you want with it, it's your house." He made no mention of the senses, saw or understood no complexity. I admired his honesty.

Yet other young people, when prompted, did describe how experiences in nature excited their senses. For example, one boy recalled his sensory experience when camping, "the red and orange flames dancing in the darkness, the smoky fumes rising up, burning my eyes and nostrils. . . ."

The experience of irrepressible Jared Grano, a ninth-grader whose father is a middle-school principal, sends a positive message to parents who worry that they might be alienating their kids from nature by taking them on the sometimes-dreaded family vacation. He complained that, although vacations are supposed to be for getting away from it all, "Unfortunately, I had to take them all with me! My parents, younger brother, and younger sister would all be traveling with me in an oven on wheels for over a week. The Grand Canyon? I was in no hurry to see the canyon. I figured it would be there for me later." When the family arrived, Jared gazed at "the massive temples of the canyon." His first thought was, "It looks like a painting." He was impressed by the beauty and majesty of the surroundings. "But after seeing the canyon from several different vantage points, I was ready to leave. Although the canyon was magnificent, I felt that I was not part of it—and without being part of it, it seemed little more than a giant hole in the ground." But the vacation was young, and the know-it-all state of mind penetrable. After the Grand Canyon, his family drove to smaller Walnut Canyon National Monument, near Flagstaff, Arizona. Jared assumed that Walnut

Canyon would be similar to the Grand Canyon, "interesting to look at, but nothing to hold my attention."

Nine hundred years ago, the Sinagua people built their homes under cliff overhangs. Twenty miles long, four hundred feet deep and a quarter mile wide, the canyon is populated with soaring turkey vultures, and elk and javelina. Life zones overlap, mixing species that usually live apart; cacti grow beside mountain firs. Jared described details of the path they walked, how the bushes were low and straggly and looked as though they had been there for many years, and the shape of the tall green pines across the gap. "As we followed the path down into the canyon, the skies grew suddenly dark. It began raining and the rain quickly turned to sleet," Jared wrote. "We found shelter in one of the ancient Indian caves. Lightning lit up the canyon and the sound of thunder reverberated in the cave. As we stood waiting for the storm to end, my family and I talked about the Indians who once lived here. We discussed how they cooked in the caves, slept in the caves, and found shelter in the caves—just as we were doing." He looked out across the canyon through the haze of rain. "I finally felt that I was a part of nature." The context of his life shifted. He was immersed in living history, witnessing natural events beyond his control, keenly aware of it all. He was *alive.*

Surely such moments are more than pleasant memories. The young don't demand dramatic adventures or vacations in Africa. They need only a taste, a sight, a sound, a touch—or, as in Jared's case, a lightning strike—to reconnect with that receding world of the senses.

The know-it-all state of mind is, in fact, quite vulnerable. In a flash, it burns, and something essential emerges from its ashes.

6. The "Eighth Intelligence"

BEN FRANKLIN LIVED a block from Boston Harbor when he was a boy. In 1715, when Ben was nine, his eldest brother was lost at sea, but Ben was not deterred. "Living near the water, I was much in and about it, learned early to swim well, and to manage boats, and when in a boat or canoe with other boys I was commonly allowed to govern, especially in any case of difficulty," he wrote later.

This love of water and his bent toward mechanics and invention merged and led to one of his earliest experiments.

One windy day, Ben was flying a kite from the bank of the Mill Pond, a holding area for water from high tide. In a warm wind, Ben tied the kite to a stake, threw off his clothes and dove in.

"The water was pleasantly cool, and he was reluctant to leave it, but he wanted to fly his kite some more," biographer H. W. Brands writes. "He pondered his dilemma until it occurred to him that he need not forgo one diversion for the other." Climbing out of the pond, Ben untied the kite and returned to the cool water. "As the buoyancy of the water diminished gravity's hold on his feet, he felt the kite tugging him forward. He surrendered to the wind's power, lying on his back and letting the kite pull him clear across the pond without the least fatigue and with the greatest pleasure imaginable."

He applied a scientist's mind to the lessons of the senses, and used his direct experience with nature to solve a problem. Today, of course, we have moved much scientific experimentation to the electronic ether. But surely the foundation of such experimentation remains the kind of direct experience that Ben enjoyed as he surrendered to the wind's power.

Nature Smart: Paying Attention

Howard Gardner, a professor of education at Harvard University, developed his influential theory of multiple intelligences in 1983. Gardner argued that the traditional notion of intelligence, based on I.Q. testing, was far too limited; he instead proposed seven types of intelligences to account for a broader range of human potential in children and adults. These included: linguistic intelligence ("word smart"); logical-mathematical intelligence ("number/reasoning smart"); spatial intelligence ("picture smart"); bodily-kinesthetic intelligence ("body smart"); musical intelligence ("music smart"); interpersonal intelligence ("people smart"); and intrapersonal intelligence ("self smart").

More recently, he added an eighth intelligence: naturalist intelligence ("nature smart"). Charles Darwin, John Muir, and Rachel Carson are examples of this type. Gardner explained:

> The core of the naturalist intelligence is the human ability to recognize plants, animals, and other parts of the natural environment, like clouds or rocks. All of us can do this; some kids (experts on dinosaurs) and many adults (hunters, botanists, anatomists) excel at this pursuit. While the ability doubtless evolved to deal with natural kinds of elements, I believe that it has been hijacked to deal with the world of man-made objects. We are good at distinguishing among cars, sneakers, and jewelry, for example, because our ancestors needed to be able to recognize carnivorous animals, poisonous snakes, and flavorful mushrooms.

Gardner's monumental work, which has helped shape public and private education, used findings from neurophysiology research to pinpoint parts of the brain that correlate to each identified intelligence; he showed that humans could lose one of the specific types of intelligence through disease or injury. Naturalist intelligence is not as clearly linked to biological evidence.

"Were I granted another lifetime or two, I would like to rethink the nature of intelligence with respect to our new biological knowledge, on the one hand, and our most sophisticated understanding of the terrain of knowledge and societal practice, on the other," he wrote in 2003.

The Montessori movement, along with other education approaches, has made this connection for decades. However, the impact of nature experience on early childhood development is, in terms of neuroscience, understudied. Gardner's designation of the eighth intelligence suggests another rich arena for research, but his theory has immediate application for teachers and parents who might otherwise overlook the importance of natural experience to learning and child development.

Professor Leslie Owen Wilson teaches courses in educational psychology and theories of learning in the School of Education at the University of Wisconsin. Her university offers one of the premier graduate programs in environmental education. She, for one, awaits more definitive biological evidence. Nonetheless, she offers a list of descriptors for children with the eighth intelligence. Such children, she writes:

1. Have keen sensory skills, including sight, sound, smell, taste, and touch.
2. Readily use heightened sensory skills to notice and categorize things from the natural world.
3. Like to be outside, or like outside activities like gardening, nature walks, or field trips geared toward observing nature or natural phenomena.
4. Easily notice patterns from their surroundings—likes, differences, similarities, anomalies.
5. Are interested in and care about animals or plants.
6. Notice things in the environment others often miss.

7. Create, keep, or have collections, scrapbooks, logs, or journals about natural objects—these may include written observations, drawings, pictures and photographs, or specimens.
8. Are very interested, from an early age, in television shows, videos, books, or objects from or about nature, science, or animals.
9. Show heightened awareness of and concern for the environment and/or for endangered species.
10. Easily learn characteristics, names, categorizations, and data about objects or species found in the natural world.

Some teachers, as we will see later, are making good use of their knowledge of the eighth intelligence. However, the problem with such a helpful list of indicators is that some adults may incorrectly use it to interpret naturalistic intelligence as a separate intelligence, one somehow relegated to a stereotype: Nature Boy or Nature Girl, the kids who collect snakes or hover over the classroom aquarium (if the classroom is lucky enough to have one). It's unlikely that Ben Franklin's teachers thought of him as a Nature Boy, but surely his intensified senses and ability to see natural connections were related to his transcendent experiences in nature. Children are able to attune themselves to all kinds of learning if they have appropriate developmental experiences.

Gardner has drawn needed attention to the fact that intelligence should not be narrowly defined as linguistic or logical-mathematical. Further, he emphasizes that children may have several of the eight intelligences, or all, in different degrees. Wilson's first descriptor is "keen sensory skills." Certainly all the intelligences teach children to pay attention, but as we will see in a later chapter, there is probably something peculiar to experiences in nature that work particularly well in attuning attention—and not only because nature is interesting.

Janet Fout, a West Virginia environmental activist, told me that when her daughter was small she encouraged her to note the details, to detect them with all of her senses. Janet's own affinity with the natural world began early. Now in her early fifties, Janet was raised in her grandmother's house in town. Her grandmother had moved there after forty years of harsh living in rural West Virginia. The simple white house was fronted by one of the few remaining dirt roads in Huntington. Day and evening, she and the other kids in her neighborhood spent hours playing hide-and-seek or freeze-tag. A water maple in the front yard offered her a branch low enough to grab, wrap a leg around, and pull herself up, and served as her personal hideout and escape, "a place where I could contemplate my life and future, undisturbed, and feed my wild, wild dreams." Her recollections are rich with sensory learning, with paying attention:

> My Grandma generally had to threaten a switching to get me to come inside, and the sinuous willow tree in our neighbor's yard provided her with all the fine keen switches she needed to coerce me—even when the weather turned "bad." What we call "bad" weather now was seen by me as an opportunity. I never judged the weather then but took advantage of the shifting winds. Summer rains sent me charging inside in search of a swimsuit and back outside to drench myself, fully clothed if my swimsuit wasn't found. Rain on the dirt road at Twelfth Street had a smell all it's own—different as it hit the gray dirt instead of asphalt, bricks, or concrete.
>
> When rainfall was especially heavy, I headed for Monroe Avenue, where backed-up storm drains would provide an instant "swimming pool" with thigh-high water where I waded and splashed. Leaves became sailing ships that dodged the perils of being swept away in the whirlpool of the storm drain. A good hard rain meant mudpies were in the making and my creative juices, like the rain in the gutters, began to flow. If a storm unleashed its full fury with thunder and lightning, I huddled bravely on the red-metal glider on the big front porch with others emitting appropriate cries of awe or terror. Fluke storms associated with unexpected cold fronts, transforming giant raindrops to icy hail, were the best of all—the sultry heat of a summer day magically dissipated. Hail as big as golfballs made great missiles to hurl at imagined foes.

Sometimes on a summer night close to bedtime, I would fill a jar with lightning bugs, bring it inside to my darkened room, and marvel at the iridescent and random illumination these marvelous insects emanated— liberating one in my room and returning the remaining jarful to freedom. Quietly I would lie in bed, watching this flying light-form, now isolated like me, from others of its kind. Soon mesmerized and calmed by the occasional tiny signal light, I drifted off to sleep.

Almost since the birth of her daughter, Julia Fletcher, mother and child spent time together in nature, not only in the mountains, but also in the semi-natural nature of their own yard. This time heightened Julia's powers of observation. Janet recalls, "One of our favorite games was making names for unusual colors we saw in nature. 'That one's candlelight,' Julia would say as we watched the sunset. I used to tease her that she could always go to work naming new colors for the Crayola crayon company!"

Janet and Julia also invented nature games. As they wandered through the woods, they would listen for "the sounds they could not hear." Janet called this game "The Sound of a Creature Not Stirring." A list might include:

sap rising
snowflakes forming and falling
sunrise
moonrise
dew on the grass
a seed germinating
an earthworm moving through the soil
cactus baking in the sun
mitosis
an apple ripening
feathers
wood petrifying
a tooth decaying

a spider weaving its web
a fly being caught in the web
a leaf changing colors
a salmon spawning

And then this list might expand beyond nature, such as the sound that occurs . . .

after the conductor's baton ceases to rise

Although Julia's adult life is just getting under way, Janet believes that early attention to nature's details played a major role in Julia's speech development, writing, and artwork, and that her daughter's keen attention to detail will continue to serve her well. "Unlike many of her peers, Julia is not easily impressed by 'stuff,'" says Janet. "What's real, what's enduring—a view from a mountaintop, a soaring bird of prey, a rainbow after a summer's rain—these things leave a lasting impression on her." Julia is in college and Janet's sphere of motherly influence has waned, of course. Her daughter spends less time outdoors. But Julia has not lost her love of nature, solitude, and simple pleasures. "These values are rooted deeply in those early years," says Janet, the years when she and Julia listened to the sounds of creatures not stirring.

Coming to Our Senses

One of the world's leading experts on butterflies, Robert Michael Pyle, teaches children about the insects by first placing a living butterfly on their noses, so that the butterfly can become the teacher.

"Noses seem to make perfectly good perches or basking spots, and the insect often remains for some time. Almost everyone is delighted by this: the light tickle, the close-up colors, the thread of a tongue probing for droplets of perspiration. But somewhere beyond delight lies enlightenment. I have been astonished at the small epiphanies I see in the eyes of a child in truly close contact with nature, perhaps for the first time. This can happen to grown-ups too, reminding them of something they never knew they had forgotten."

Perhaps the eighth intelligence is the intelligence within nature, the lessons waiting to be delivered if anyone shows up.

This is how Leslie Stephens views the educational necessity of nature. An at-home mother especially attuned to nature, she grew up in San Diego, a self-described "tomboy," roaming Tecolote Canyon with her Weimaraner, Olga, by her side. In those years, Tecolote Canyon was a wild place, at the edge of a housing tract, filled with chaparral and sage. Coyotes and deer found their way there through suburban tracts. Her family spent most summer afternoons at Shell Beach in La Jolla and every August she traveled to her grandparents' home at Ryan Dam, on the Great Falls of the Missouri River in Montana. When she was thirteen, the arm of the canyon where she played as a child was plowed up by bulldozers and homes were built.

When she became a parent, her family moved to the edge of another canyon, called Deer Canyon. It is, she says, "our little wilderness, narrow and deep." She wants her children to learn from this edge of another universe, as she did. The canyon stimulates not only their spirits, but also their intellect. She tells how, when she was a girl, her canyon taught her a broader definition of shelter, and gave her "a deep understanding of how the world works":

> A child who is allowed to run free in a place that is natural will very quickly begin to look around for a special shelter. The interior framework of bushes is inspected and judged for its suitability to act as a fort. Trees, especially mature ones, provide towering castles, and the best climbing branches are claimed as "rooms." In contrast, the exposure a child feels running across a grassy, sunny slope or wide, open field allows her to feel the lack of shelter. It is only through experiencing both opposites that children begin to understand each part more deeply.

Nature also teaches kids about friendship, or can. Sure they can learn that elsewhere, but there's something different about friendship forged outdoors.

When I was my children's age, after school or on weekends anyone who wanted to be with friends just headed down to the old oak that grew along the seasonal creek. It was a great climbing tree and someone had tied a heavy rope from one of the sturdier branches. We would run, jump, and grab onto the rope and swing wildly, clearing the creek bed filled with smooth boulders and rocks. I do not recall anyone getting hurt there and upon reflection I think it may be that even though we tested each other's limits, we knew our own. Pecking order established itself in an unspoken manner. But we were friends and we accepted each other. It was enough just to be together. The wildness of our place bonded us and we felt a connection that went beyond verbal exchanges to a deeper knowing.

Stephens's recollection brings to mind the fascinating, if skimpy, studies that suggest children who spend more time playing outdoors have more friends. Certainly the deepest friendships evolve out of shared experience, particularly in environments in which all the senses are enlivened. On one level, discovering—or rediscovering—nature through the senses is simply a way to learn, to pay attention. And paying attention is easier when you're actually doing something, rather than only considering how it might be done.

John Rick, the middle-school teacher who educated me about the growing number of legal and regulatory restrictions on natural play, grew up in the 1960s. His family's house backed up on vacant land. At that time there were only three local television stations, one of them in Spanish. Computers and Game Boys didn't exist. He spent his free hours exploring the land, as countless children did at that time. Rick says:

I can remember how furious my dad used to get when he never had a shovel in the garage. That was because I had taken it to dig foxholes deep enough to crouch inside and put plywood over the top. We even took the time to disguise the cover with plants and dirt. A lot of the time the roof caved in on us, but we learned. There were other adventures, too: swings from trees, kites on two thousand feet of string.

My dad helped when he could, but most of the time he left us to try things: to experiment, test, fail, or succeed. We learned so much more than we ever would have with someone showing us the right way to do things every time. Our failures gave us a deep, intrinsic understanding of how things worked. We understood the laws of physics long before we took the class.

Schoolhouse in a Tree

Nature can stimulate the eighth intelligence (and probably all the others) in countless ways. But I have a soft spot in my heart for tree houses, which have always imparted certain magic and practical knowledge.

Rick's story reminded me of my early career as neighborhood tree-house architect, at nine or ten years old. I couldn't catch a ground ball well, but I could climb a trunk and nail a board with style. One summer I directed a crew of five or six boys in the appropriation of "spare" lumber from nearby building projects. In the 1950s, we did not consider it stealing—though it certainly was. Mountains of lumber, some of it crusted with concrete, would rise next to basement holes that became small lakes after summer storms. Carpenters looked the other way as we carted off four-by-eight sheets of plywood and two-by-fours. Our pockets bulged with nails that we collected from the ground.

We picked the largest oak in the state, we figured: a tree that must have been two hundred years old. We erected a four-story tree house with a sealed bottom floor that we entered through a trap door on the floor of the second story. Each ascending level became more elaborate and larger as the branches of the tree opened out. The top floor was a crow's nest that could only be reached by leaving the third story and crouch-walking out ten feet on a thick branch, transferring to a higher branch that dipped down close to the first one, and then traversing that branch to the crow's nest—forty feet above the ground. The tree house was serviced by ropes and pulleys and two baskets. This tree house became our galleon, our spaceship, our Fort Apache, and from it we could see out over the cornfields and north to the great, dark woods. To think of that tree house today, within the context of our litigious society, makes me shudder.

I returned years later and the old tree was doing just fine. The only sign of civilization within its branches were two or three gray two-by-fours. If you drive across the Midwest today, or for that matter across any of wooded America, you can see similar artifacts, the skeletons of tree houses past. But you won't see many new tree houses. More often than not, adults build the ones that do exist, sometimes for themselves.

Adults have appropriated tree-house building, just as they have Halloween. (Perhaps the better word is reappropriated: the Medicis built a marble tree house during the Renaissance, and a town near Paris was famous in the mid-nineteenth century for its tree-house restaurants.) Elaborate books for adults advise tree-house builders to rest boards on major branches and close to the trunk; to brace boards to resist wind and twisting; to use natural-fiber manila rope, rather than nylon rope. They advise that the floor be tilted slightly to allow water runoff; that the ladder not be nailed to the trunk, but tied to the tree and self-supported. And so on.

As tree-house architect, I could have used such information, but did fine without it. We built our tree house well enough for our needs. None of my fellow builders was injured, at least not seriously. Ours was a learning tree. Through it we learned to trust ourselves and our abilities.

Recently, I talked about the art and education of tree-house building with a friend, architect Alberto Lau, who is also the construction scheduler for several new schools in my city. Alberto grew up in Guatemala. "Only in this affluent society would kids be able to get construction materials free," he said, shaking his head. But later, he sent me a list of what my young associates and I may well have learned while building that tree house:

- You learned the most common sizes of lumber, 4' × 8' sheets of plywood, and 2" × 4" studs; also, about the sizes of nails.
- You probably figured out that diagonal bracing stiffened the structure, whether the bracing was applied at a corner or to hold up the platform or floor of the tree house.
- You learned about hinges, if you used those to attach the trap door.
- You probably learned the difference between screws and nails.
- You learned about ladders, if that is how you got from one story to the next.
- You learned about pulleys.
- You learned that framing must strengthen openings such as windows or the trap doors.
- You probably learned to slope the roof in imitation of real homes, or because you were beginning to understand that a slope would shed rain.
- You probably learned to place the framing narrow side up; you were beginning to learn about "strength of materials," a subject taught in engineering schools.
- You learned how to cut with a handsaw.
- You learned about measurement, and three-dimensional geometry.
- You learned how the size of your body relates to the world: your arms and legs to the diameter of the tree trunk; your height to the tree height; your legs to the spacing of the ladder rungs; your reach to the spacing of the tree branches; your girth to the size of the trap door; the height from which you could safely jump, etc.

"One more thing," he added. "You probably learned from your failures more than from success. Perhaps a rope broke from too much weight; a board or 2 × 4 pulled off because you used nails that were too small. You also learned, by practicing, one of the essential principles of engineering: you can solve any large or complex problem by breaking it down into smaller, simpler problems. Perhaps you broke the tree-house-building problem down like this: which tree to choose; how to climb the tree; where on the tree to build the house; what materials were needed; where to get the materials; what tools are needed; where to get the tools; how much time is needed; how many people are needed to do the job; how to get the materials up the tree; how to cut the materials; how to build the floor; how to build the walls; how to build windows; how to build the roof."

Conventional memory holds that, in past decades, tree-house building and other nature-based engineering escapades were conducted mainly by boys; those girls who did participate were considered tomboys—when you think about it, a strange, ambivalent term. But the fact is, we don't know that girls were so demure. In the absence of good longitudinal studies of how kids have experienced nature, we can't assume that girls—in some significant number—weren't building tree houses or underground forts or conducting any number of similarly muddy experiments in physics. Janet Fout, for example, didn't build tree houses, but she wove elaborate weed houses within the hollowed confines of brush and bushes.

When I mentioned my own recollections to Elizabeth Schmitt, a clinical social worker, that tree-house building was something boys did, she bristled and offered a different memory:

> My parents married the day after my dad, a navy pilot from WWII, graduated from Columbia on June 2, 1948. As New Yorkers, they were thrown into the life of rural Pennsylvania where my dad, a mining engineer, was employed by Bethlehem Steel Company. In a small company town we called "Toy Town" because the company houses all looked the same, I roamed and played with all the kids. We played baseball together, and built huts and tree houses. Boys and girls did this together. I was as active as any boys there and *not* a tomboy.

One positive trend is that outdoor opportunities are expanding for women, and therefore for girls. By 2000, the Sporting Goods Manufacturers Association reported that females comprised 44 percent of tent campers and 50 percent of day campers. If kid-built tree houses were as common today as when Elizabeth Schmitt or Janet Fout were girls, I wonder what the gender balance of the construction crews would be.

As it turns out, Alberto's daughter, Erin, a University of Southern California student, grew up building tree houses in a Scripps Ranch canyon. Later, the local community association made a practice of tearing down tree houses and forts there. Even so, in her tree house and canyon, Erin grew a dream:

> The quiet wisdom of nature does not try to mislead you like the landscape of the city does, with billboards and ads everywhere. It doesn't make you feel like you have to conform to any image. It's just there, and it accepts everyone.
>
> Living where I did allowed me to be outside building forts from age five to fourteen. And to jump to a large conclusion, it influenced the way in which I saw the built world. I am a landscape architecture major because of the pressing need in this world for the reintroduction of the natural landscape into the unwelcoming built environment. Why can't mini-ecosystems be introduced into the middle of the city? Can we design parks so that they are as chaotic as nature, yet safe for an evening walk?

Idealistic? Let's hope so, considering the alternative. Which brings us back to Ben Franklin. As H. W. Brands tells the story, Ben and his friends liked to hunt small fish in Mill Pond. But their shuffling through the water stirred up mud, clouding the water, which didn't help the fishing. Their solution: to build a jetty extending into the marsh. Ben, with his eye on stones piled at a nearby building site, told his gang to wait until the masons had gone. "The boys waited, the men departed, and the construction commenced," writes Brands. "After several hours and much struggling, the jetty was completed, to the boys' satisfaction and pride. The foreman of the building crew, arriving next morning, was less admiring. A cursory investigation revealed the whereabouts of the missing stones, from which the foreman deduced the identity of those responsible for their removal. The boys were remanded to their parents' custody and chastisement. . . . " Though young Ben "pleaded the civic usefulness of the construction," his father pointed out that the first civic virtue was honesty.

Whether the boy learned more about civic honesty or practical rebellion is unclear. But for Ben, as for Erin, nature was a place to use all the senses—and to learn by doing.

7. The Genius of Childhood: How Nature Nurtures Creativity

I played around our yard some and talked to the fence posts, sung songs and made the weeds sing . . .

— Woody Guthrie

Art critic Bernard Berenson, echoing the words of the psychologist Erik Erikson, father of human developmental theory, theorized that creativity begins "with the natural genius of childhood and the 'spirit of place.'" He once described how, as he looked back on his seventy years, and recalled his moments of greatest happiness, they were usually times when he lost himself "all but completely in some instant of perfect harmony":

> In childhood and boyhood this ecstasy overtook me when I was happy out of doors . . . A silver haze shimmered and trembled over the lime trees. The air was laden with their fragrance. The temperature was like a caress. I remember . . . that I climbed up a stump and felt suddenly immersed in Itness. I did not call it by that name. I had no need for words. It and I were one. Surely most children are like that. I have retained that faculty through the years.

Robin Moore would agree with Berenson. As a champion for outdoor play, Moore has written that natural settings are essential for healthy child development because they stimulate all the senses and integrate informal play with formal learning. According to Moore, multisensory experiences in nature help to build "the cognitive constructs necessary for sustained intellectual development," and stimulate imagination by supplying the child with the free space and materials for what he calls children's "architecture and artifacts." "Natural spaces and materials stimulate children's limitless imaginations and serve as the medium of inventiveness and creativity observable in almost any group of children playing in a natural setting," says Moore.

Early theoretical work in this field was done by Cambridge architect Simon Nicholson, the son of two of Britain's most prominent twentieth-century artists, Ben Nicholson and Barbara Hepworth. In a 1990 obituary for Nicholson, the *Guardian* of London described Nicholson's contention that everybody is innately creative but that modern society suppresses the creative instinct, while promoting artists as a gifted elite, "who, as it happens, have all the fun." Nicholson's "loose-parts" theory has been adopted by many landscape architects and child's-play experts. Nicholson summed up his theory this way: "In any environment, both the degree of inventiveness and creativity, and the possibility of discovery, are directly proportional to the number and kind of variables in it." A "loose-parts" toy, as Nicholson defined it, is open-ended; children may use it in many ways and combine it with other loose parts through imagination and creativity. A typical list of loose parts for a natural play area might include water, trees, bushes, flowers, and long grasses, a pond and the creatures within it, along with other living things, sand (best if it can be mixed with water), places to sit in, on, under; structures that offer privacy and views. Go beyond that play area, to woods, fields, and streams, and the parts become looser and even more potent to the imagination.

One might argue that a computer, with its near-infinite coding possibilities, is history's deepest box of loose parts. But binary code, made of two parts—× and 0—has its limits. Nature, which excites all the senses, remains the richest source of loose parts.

The loose-parts theory is supported by studies of play that compare green, natural play areas with blacktop playgrounds. Swedish studies found that children on asphalt playgrounds had play that was much more interrupted; they played in short segments. But in more natural playgrounds, children invent whole sagas that they carried from day to day to day—making and collecting meaning.

The growing number of such studies, comparing patterns of creative play in green versus built spaces, "are consistent with the notion that green space supports healthy child development," according to a review of the literature by Andrea Faber Taylor and Frances Kuo at the Human–Environment Research Laboratory at the University of Illinois.

In Sweden, Australia, Canada, and the United States, studies of children in schoolyards with both green areas and manufactured play areas found that children engaged in more creative forms of play in the green areas. One of these studies found that a more natural schoolyard encouraged more fantasy and make-believe play in particular, which provided ways for boys and girls to play together in egalitarian ways; another reported that children showed a greater sense of wonder. The researchers defined creative play widely: playing with action figures and dolls; role-playing on imaginary battlefields and planets, and in mythical landscapes with fairies and queens; elaborate jump-rope routines; constructing buildings or objects from loose materials; and exploring the environment.

Researchers have also observed that when children played in an environment dominated by play structures rather than natural elements, they established their social hierarchy through physical competence; after an open grassy area was planted with shrubs, the quality of play in what the study termed "vegetative rooms" was very different. Children used more fantasy play, and their social standing became based less on physical abilities and more on language skills, creativity, and inventiveness.

In their review of these studies, Taylor and Kuo cautioned that in some of them children were self-selecting the spaces in which they played. Children, when given a choice, may choose green spaces when they intend to engage in creative play. Taylor's and Kuo's own studies demonstrated that children have greater ability to concentrate in more natural settings. In their study, children also selected where they wanted to play. These studies, therefore, do not prove a direct link between nature-play and creativity. Nonetheless, the possibility that creative children prefer natural areas for their play raises its own crucial question: What happens when creative children can no longer choose a green space in which to be creative?

Nature and Famous Creators

Curious about the influence of nature in the early development of the famously creative, I asked my teenage son, Matthew, to spend some summer library time searching through biographies for examples. He took on this job with enthusiasm. I offered to pay him for his time, but he declined money, as is his way. Realizing how much work he was in for, I persisted. Would any other kind of compensation do?

"How about StarCraft, Dad," he said.

"A video game?"

"Computer game."

I acquiesced. He headed for the library and hauled back the first stack of biographies. Excited, he brought me the first passage he found, from a biography of the great science-fiction author—the man who also originated the principles of the geostationary communication satellite—Arthur C. Clarke. Clarke grew up in Minehead, England, a coastal town on the Bristol Channel, with boyhood "vistas of the Atlantic Ocean that created the illusion of infinite space," as biographer Neil McAleer tells it. On that shore, McAleer wrote, the young Clarke "built battlements of sand and explored the tidewater pools."

> During the winter months [Clarke] often cycled home in the dark, with the stars and moon illuminating his route in clear weather. Such starry evenings influenced Clarke's budding cosmic consciousness. The

silent night sky above him stirred his imagination and brought forth images of the future. Men would walk on the moon someday, he knew, and later they would leave their boot prints on the red sands of Mars. Even the gulf between our sun and other stars would be bridged eventually, and their planets explored by the descendants of our species.

In his later years, Clarke admitted that the only place where he was ever completely relaxed was by the edge of the sea, or weightless within it.

I added Matthew's collection to other examples I had found. Joan of Arc first heard her calling, at age thirteen, "toward the hour of noon, in summer, in my father's garden." Jane Goodall, at two years of age, slept with earthworms under her pillow. (Don't try this at home.) John Muir described "reveling in the wonderful wildness" around his boyhood home in Wisconsin. Samuel Langhorne Clemens held down an adult job as a printer at fourteen, but when his working day ended at three in the afternoon, he headed to the river to swim or fish or navigate a "borrowed" boat. One can imagine that it was there, as he dreamed of becoming a pirate or a trapper or scout, that he became "Mark Twain." The poet T. S. Eliot, who grew up alongside the Mississippi River, wrote, "I feel that there is something in having passed one's childhood beside the big river which is incommunicable to those who have not." And the imagination of biophilia's patron, E. O. Wilson (whose boyhood nickname was "Snake"), was ignited while exploring the "woods and swamps in a languorous mood . . . [forming] the habit of quietude and concentration."

In *Edison: Inventing the Century*, biographer Neil Baldwin tells how "Little Al," as Edison was nicknamed, wandered away one day while visiting his sister's farm. Her husband found him sitting in a box of straw. The little boy explained, "I saw baby chickens come out of eggs the old hen was sitting on so I thought I could make little gooses come out of the goose eggs if I sat on them. If the hens and geese can do it, why can't I?" Later, seeing the egg stain on Al's pants, and that he was upset, his sister comforted him, reportedly saying, "It's all right, Al . . . If no one ever tried anything, even what some folks say is impossible, no one would ever learn anything. So you just keep on trying and maybe some day you'll try something that will work.'"

Or consider Eleanor Roosevelt, one of the more creative public figures in American history. In *Eleanor and Franklin*, Joseph P. Lash tells how, "as she passed from childhood to adolescence, the beauty of nature spoke to her awakening senses." He goes on:

> The changes of the seasons, the play of light on the river, the color and coolness of the woods began to have the profound meaning to her that they would retain throughout her life. When she was a young girl, she wrote a half century later, "there was nothing that gave me greater joy than to get one of my young aunts to agree that she would get up before dawn, that we would walk down through the woods to the river, row ourselves the five miles to the village in Tivoli to get the mail, and row back before the family was at the breakfast table."

She disappeared into the woods and fields for hours, where she would read her books and write stories filled with awe and rooted in the metaphors of nature. In "Gilded Butterflies," a particularly fanciful short story Lash recounts in his book, Eleanor unconsciously describes her own future. In her story, she is lying on her back in the long grass one hot summer day, when she is startled by the voices of butterflies. "Curiosity sharpening my ears I began to hear what they were saying." One butterfly blurts out, "Pooh! I'm not going to sit on a daisy always. I have higher aspirations in life. I am going to know a great deal and to see everything. I won't stay here to waste my life. I mean to know something before I've finished." For Eleanor, literature, nature, and dreams were forever linked. We can only imagine how this little girl would have developed without her time in nature, but surely her fragile power needed protection as it grew, and time and space to hear an inner voice.

For Beatrix Potter, the connection between the mystery of nature and imagination is even more direct. Potter, one of the most famous children's authors, exhibited ruthless collecting abilities. As her biographer Margaret Lane tells it, Beatrix and her brother "were not squeamish, and there was a toughness about some of their experiments which would have surprised their parents."

The two siblings "smuggled home innumerable beetles, toadstools, dead birds, hedgehogs, frogs, caterpillars, minnows and sloughed snakeskins. If the dead specimen were not past skinning, they skinned it; if it were, they busily boiled it and kept the bones. They even on one occasion, having obtained a dead fox from heaven knows where, skinned and boiled it successfully in secret and articulated the skeleton." Everything they brought home, they drew or painted, and sewed the pieces of drawing paper together to make their books of nature. The depictions were realistic for the most part, "but here and there on the grubby pages fantasy breaks through. Mufflers appear round the necks of newts, rabbits walk upright, skate on ice, carry umbrellas, walk out in bonnets . . ."

Nature offers a well from which many, famous or not, draw a creative sense of pattern and connection. As Moore points out, nature experiences "help children understand the realities of natural systems through primary experience. They demonstrate natural principles such as networks, cycles, and evolutionary processes. They teach that nature is a uniquely regenerative process." An appreciation of these patterns is essential in fostering creativity, which of course is not the sole domain of the arts, but of science and even politics.

Richard Ybarra, a political operative from California and son-in-law of the late labor leader Cesar Chavez, describes Chavez's seemingly inexhaustible power of spirit and energy and how his early childhood prepared him for a deep understanding of natural—including human—systems:

> He always had a connection to nature that went back to his days growing up on a farm on the Gila River. He always had the river connection. Even his magical life-twists carried him full circle back to the

very river region where his life began. His dad raised him to understand the land, soils, water and how things work. His mom raised him to know about herbs and all that nature produced. It is obvious in so many ways that his genius was very much derived from life's simplest and most basic processes and systems. He could always see with great clarity, no matter the complexities or challenges.

Of course, not everyone with childhood experience in nature is affected in this particular way, and not every child who is touched becomes a Chavez, Roosevelt, Potter, or Clarke—or, thankfully, Joan of Arc. Creativity draws from other immersions as well. When Matthew and I explored the biographies of more recent creators, mentions of nature as inspiration began to fade. Creative people who came of age in the 1970s—rock stars among them—seldom described inspirational childhood experiences in nature. So, it seems, creativity occurs without natural influences, but it may have a different tempo.

Nature, Creativity, and Ecstatic Places

Economist Thorstein Veblen once offered an alternative way to define serious research. Its outcome, he said, "can only be to make two questions grow where one question grew before." By this definition, Edith Cobb was a good researcher. She offered a deep box of loose parts, and influenced a generation of childhood researchers.

In 1977, after years of dedicated (if not strictly scientific) research, Cobb published her influential book, *The Ecology of Imagination in Childhood*. Though she had a degree from the New York School of Social Work, Cobb was not a sociologist; her expertise came mainly from her many hours of observing and documenting children at play, and her years of reflection on what she had learned about children's relationships with nature. She based much of her analysis on a collection of some three hundred volumes of autobiographical recollections of childhood by creative thinkers from diverse cultures and eras. She concluded that inventiveness and imagination of nearly all of the creative people she studied was rooted in their early experiences in nature.

Drawing also on her observations of children's behavior, Cobb posited that the child's "capacity to go out and beyond the self derives from the plasticity of response to environment in childhood." She wrote, "In the creative perceptions of poet and child we are close to the biology of thought itself—close, in fact, to the ecology of imagination, . . ." Creative thinkers, she believed, return in memory to renew the power and impulse to create at its very source, a source which they describe as the experience of emerging not only into the light of consciousness, but into a living sense of kinship with the outer world. These experiences, Cobb believed, take place primarily in the middle years of childhood. "Memories of awakening to the existence of some potential, aroused by early experiences of self and world, are scattered through the literature of scientific and aesthetic invention. Autobiographies repeatedly refer to the cause of this awakening as an acute sensory response to the natural world."

Many years after Edith Cobb wrote her pioneering and controversial work, environmental psychologist Louise Chawla—who had been inspired to specialize in this area by *The Ecology of Imagination in Childhood*—closely examined Cobb's research. Although she found it flawed in technique, she was intrigued by the questions it raised. She concluded Cobb's theory must be amended to allow for different degrees of experience. It is possible, she writes, that the developing consciousness of all children involves what Cobb described as a dynamic sense of relationship with their place. "Only in some children, however, is this experience so intense that it burns itself into memory to animate adult life." For example, businesspeople and politicians report less emphasis on nature experiences in early childhood than do artists. This does not mean that early childhood experiences in nature do not shape future politicians or captains of industry; they may just be less likely to report them. Certainly the biographies of Edison and Benjamin Franklin suggest that the very foundations of modern industry and design grew first in the waters and woods and farmlands of childhood.

Chawla has not rejected Cobb's theory, but argues instead that the relationship between creativity and environment is more complex than Cobb imagined. For example, transcendent childhood experiences in nature were "never reported when a child did not enjoy freedom within an alluring natural or urban environment." Transcendence did not require spectacular scenery, "but could be evoked by environments as small as a patch of weeds at the edge of a sleeping porch, or during freedom as brief as an escape [into nature] during a school outing."

Chawla's own research further suggests a deep but still vaguely understood link between creativity and early experiences in nature. "The good thing, from what we are finding, is that nature isn't only important to future geniuses," she says. So-called regular people also report these transcendent moments in nature. "Many threads come together to form the final creative fabric, and experience in nature is one of them."

In her more recent work, Chawla explores "ecstatic places." She uses the word "ecstatic" in its original meaning. The contemporary synonym is delight or rapture, but the word's ancient Greek roots—*ek statis*—as some sources have it, mean "outstanding" or "standing outside ourselves." These ecstatic moments of delight or fear, or both, "radioactive jewels buried within us, emitting energy across the years of our lives," as Chawla eloquently puts it, are most often experienced in nature during formative years.

Author Phyllis Theroux wrote a moving description of an ecstatic moment she had on a sleeping porch, as she watched a clump of weeds lit by morning sun, the cockleburs "like bumblebees quivering on harp wires . . . golden, translucent, amazing sheaves of wheat. The light drove down the shafts of the stalks, making a cool fire of the dew that collected at the roots. My eyes would contemplate the cockleweeds without searching for the adjectives that even now elude me. I would simply hang off the mattress, staring at the sight, getting my bearings, not knowing why." Theroux continued:

> Could it be, and this is the question of a speculative, unmarveling adult, that every human being is given a few signs like this to tide us over when we are grown? Do we all have a bit or piece of something that we instinctively cast back on when the heart wants to break upon itself and causes us to say, "Oh yes, but there was this," or "Oh yes, but there was that," and so we go on?

Reviewing the conditions in which ecstatic memories are made, Chawla was "struck by the fragility of their setting." Ecstatic memories require space, freedom, discovery, and "an extravagant display for all five senses." When these requirements are met, even in cities, nature nurtures us. And behind these requirements hover "that difficult-to-define yet effusive quality of loveliness. . . . This combination of conditions cannot be taken for granted." Ecstatic places offer our children, and us, even more than Cobb suggested. As Chawla explains, ecstatic memories give us "meaningful images; an internalized core of calm; a sense of integration with nature; and for some, a creative disposition. Most of these benefits are general human advantages, whether or not we make our way in the world as creative thinkers."

Playgrounds for Poets

Most children today are hard-pressed to develop a sense of wonder, to induce what Berenson called the "spirit of place" while playing video games or trapped inside a house because of the fear of crime. Asked to name their favorite special places, children often describe their room or an attic—somewhere quiet. A common characteristic of special places is quietness, peacefulness, Chawla emphasizes. So finding wonder outside of nature is surely possible. But electronics or the built environment do not offer the array of physical loose parts, nor the physical space to wander.

Many years ago, I interviewed Jerry Hirshberg, founding director and president of Nissan Design International, the Japanese auto company's design center in America. This was one of several such centers established by Japan's car manufacturers up and down the California coast. When I asked Hirshberg why these centers existed, he explained that the Japanese know their strengths and ours: their specialty was tight, efficient manufacturing; ours was design. The Japanese, said Hirshberg, recognized that American creativity comes largely from our freedom, our space—our physical space and our mental space. He offered no academic studies to support his theory; nonetheless, his statement rang true, and it has stayed with me. Growing up, many of us were blessed with natural space and the imagination that filled it.

America's genius has been nurtured by nature—by space, both physical and mental. What happens to the nation's intrinsic creativity, and therefore the health of our economy, when future generations are so restricted that they no longer have room to stretch? One might argue that the Internet has replaced the woods, in terms of inventive space, but no electronic environment stimulates all the senses. So far, Microsoft sells no match for nature's code.

Nature is imperfectly perfect, filled with loose parts and possibilities, with mud and dust, nettles and sky, transcendent hands-on moments and skinned knees. What happens when all the parts of childhood are soldered down, when the young no longer have the time or space to play in their family's garden, cycle home in the dark with the stars and moon illuminating their route, walk down through the woods to the river, lie on their backs on hot July days in the long grass, or watch cockleburs, lit by morning sun, like bumblebees quivering on harp wires? What then?

Creativity is so difficult to define and measure, so subjective by definition. Surely this limits our ability to apply scientific inquiry. Therefore, part of this discussion must take place where control groups never venture, in the realms of the poet, artist, or philosopher. Nature may inspire different kinds of creativity and different art than the built environment. Contemporary urban poets have moved away from Wordsworth and the Romantics, whose metaphors were shaped by sublime natural forces, whose rhythms were so often set by the cycles of nature. The newer language of art emanates from the human-built environment, from the street, from computers. This urban or electronic expression of creativity speaks to and for modern ears and eyes, and it has its own rhythms and metaphors.

Parents who wish to raise their children in a climate conducive to modern—or postmodern—creativity do well to expose them to that world, but not at the exclusion of the natural world.

Nature—the sublime, the harsh, and the beautiful—offers something that the street or gated community or computer game cannot. Nature presents the young with something so much greater than they are; it offers an environment where they can easily contemplate infinity and eternity. A child can, on a rare clear night, see the stars and perceive the infinite from a rooftop in Brooklyn. Immersion in the natural environment cuts to the chase, exposes the young directly and immediately to the very elements from which humans evolved: earth, water, air, and other living kin, large and small. Without that experience, as Chawla says, "we forget our place; we forget that larger fabric on which our lives depend."

8. Nature-Deficit Disorder and the Restorative Environment

WITH IDEALISM AND TREPIDATION, a graduating college student anticipates becoming a teacher; but she is puzzled and upset by the school environment she experienced during her training. "With all of the testing in schools there is no time for physical education, let alone exploring the outdoors," she says. "In one of my kindergarten classes, the kids get to run to a fence and then run back. That's their P.E. They have to stay on the blacktop, or they can use one of the two swings available." She doesn't understand why P.E. is so limited, or why the playground can't be more conducive to natural play. Many educators share her sentiment.

At least her school has recess. As the federal and state governments and local school boards began to push for higher test scores in the early part of the decade, about a dozen states halved or even canceled recess. They consider such breaks a waste of potential academic time, or too much of a liability, or there is concern over violence on the playground. As of this writing, only seven states even require elementary schools to hire certified physical education instructors. This has occurred in a country where 40 percent of five- to eight-year-olds suffer cardiac risk factors such as obesity.

Now, for some good news. Studies suggest that nature may be useful as a therapy for Attention Deficit Hyperactivity Disorder (ADHD), used with or, when appropriate, even replacing medications or behavioral therapies. Some researchers now recommend that parents and educators make available more nature experiences—especially green places—to children with ADHD, and thereby support their attentional functioning and minimize their symptoms. Indeed, this research inspires use of the broader term, *nature-deficit disorder,* as a way to help us better understand what many children experience, whether or not they have been diagnosed with ADHD. Again, I am not using the term nature-deficit disorder in a scientific or clinical sense. Certainly no academic researchers use the term, yet; nor do they attribute ADHD entirely to a nature deficit. But based on accumulating scientific evidence, I believe the concept—or hypothesis—of nature-deficit disorder is appropriate and useful as a layperson's description of one factor that may aggravate attentional difficulties for many children.

First, consider the diagnosis and current treatments of choice.

Nearly 8 million children in the U.S. suffer from mental disorders, and ADHD is one of the more prevalent ones. The disorder often develops before age seven, and is usually diagnosed between the ages of eight and ten. (Some people use the acronym ADD, for attention deficit disorder, to mean ADHD without the hyperactive component. But ADHD is the more accepted medical diagnosis.) Children with the syndrome are restless, and have trouble paying attention, listening, following directions, and focusing on tasks. They may also be aggressive, even antisocial, and may suffer from academic failure. Or, in the language of the American Psychiatric Association: "The essential feature of ADHD is a persistent pattern of inattention and/or hyperactivity, impulsivity . . . more frequently displayed and more severe than is typically observed in individuals at a comparable level of development." Some of the uninformed public tends to believe that poor parenting and other social factors produce the immature behavior associated with ADHD, but ADHD is now considered by many researchers to be an organic disorder associated with differences in the brain morphology of children.

Critics charge that often-prescribed stimulant medications such as methylphenidate (Ritalin) and amphetamines (Dexedrine), though necessary in many cases, are overprescribed, perhaps as much as 10 to 40 percent of the time. Methylphenidate is a central nervous system stimulant and shares many of the pharmacological effects of amphetamine, methamphetamine, and cocaine. Contrasting sharply with medical practices elsewhere in the world, use of such stimulants increased 600 percent between 1990 and 1995, and continues to rise in numbers, especially for younger children. Between 2000 and 2003, spending on ADHD for preschoolers increased 369 percent. Both boys and girls are diagnosed with ADHD, but approximately 90 percent of the young people placed on medication—often at the suggestion of school officials—are boys.

One child psychiatrist explains: "My prejudice is that girls with ADHD whose symptoms are similar to boys with typical symptoms of ADHD are not common." Notice that he said "prejudice." Much about ADHD remains a medical and political mystery.

The massive increase in ADHD diagnoses and treatment may, in fact, be a matter of recognition: ADHD has been there all the time, called by other names or missed entirely, causing suffering for children and their families. Another explanation boils down to availability: three decades ago the currently used medications were not widely known or as intensely marketed by pharmaceutical companies, and not yet fully trusted by physicians—and we're lucky to have them now. Nonetheless, the use of such medications and the causes of ADHD are still in dispute. As of this writing, the latest culprit is television. The first study to link television-watching to this disorder was published in April 2004. Children's Hospital and Regional Medical Center in Seattle maintains that each hour of TV watched per day by preschoolers increases by 10 percent the likelihood that they will develop concentration problems and other symptoms of attention-deficit disorders by age seven.

This information is disturbing. But television is only part of the larger environmental/cultural change in our lifetime: namely, that rapid move from a rural to a highly urbanized culture. In an agricultural society, or during a time of exploration and settlement, or hunting and gathering—which is to say, most of mankind's history—energetic boys were particularly prized for their strength, speed, and agility. As mentioned earlier, as recently as the 1950s, most families still had some kind of agricultural connection. Many of these children, girls as well as boys, would have been directing their energy and physicality in constructive ways: doing farm chores, baling hay, splashing in the swimming hole, climbing trees, racing to the sandlot for a game of baseball. Their unregimented play would have been steeped in nature.

The "Restorative Environment"

Even without corroborating evidence, many parents notice significant changes in their hyperactive child's behavior when they hike in mountains or enjoy other nature-oriented outings.

"My son is still on Ritalin, but he's so much calmer in the outdoors that we're seriously considering moving to the mountains," one mother says.

Could it simply be that he needs more physical activity?

"No, he gets that, in sports," says the mother. "There's just something calming to him about being outside in nature."

Many physicians and psychologists agree. "Our brains are set up for an agrarian, nature-oriented existence that came into focus five thousand years ago," says Michael Gurian, a family therapist and best-selling author of *The Good Son* and *The Wonder of Boys*. "Neurologically, human beings haven't caught up with today's overstimulating environment. The brain is strong and flexible, so 70 to 80 percent of kids adapt fairly well. But the rest don't. Getting kids out in nature can make a difference. We know this anecdotally, though we can't prove it yet."

New studies may offer that proof.

This research builds on the well-established attention-restoration theory, developed by a husband-and-wife research team, Stephen and Rachel Kaplan. Environmental psychologists at the University of Michigan, the Kaplans were inspired by philosopher and psychologist William James. In 1890, James described two kinds of attention: directed attention and fascination (i.e., involuntary attention). In the early 1970s, the Kaplans began a nine-year study for the U.S. Forest Service. They followed participants in an Outward Bound–like wilderness program, which took people into the wilds for up to two weeks. During these treks or afterward, subjects reported experiencing a sense of peace and an ability to think more clearly; they also reported that just being in nature was more restorative than the physically challenging activities, such as rock climbing, for which such programs are mainly known.

The positive effect of what the Kaplans came to call "the restorative environment" was vastly greater than the Kaplans expected it to be. According to the Kaplans' research, too much directed attention leads to what they call "directed-attention fatigue," marked by impulsive behavior, agitation, irritation, and inability to concentrate. Directed-attention fatigue occurs because neural inhibitory mechanisms become fatigued by blocking competing stimuli. As Stephen Kaplan explained in the journal *Monitor on Psychology*, "If you can find an environment where the attention is automatic, you allow directed attention to rest. And that means an environment that's strong on fascination." The fascination factor associated with nature is restorative, and it helps relieve people from directed-attention fatigue. Indeed, according to the Kaplans, nature can be the most effective source of such restorative relief.

In a paper presented to the American Psychological Society in 1993, the Kaplans surveyed more than twelve hundred corporate and state office workers. Those with a window view of trees, bushes, or large lawns experienced significantly less frustration and more work enthusiasm than those employees without such views. Like similar studies on stress reduction, this study demonstrated that a person does not have to live in the wilderness to reap nature's psychological benefits—including the ability to work better and think more clearly.

Subsequent research has supported the Kaplans' attention-restoration theory. For example, Terry A. Hartig, an associate professor of applied psychology at the Institute for Housing and Urban Research at Uppsala University in Gävle, Sweden, along with other researchers, compared three groups of backpacking enthusiasts; a group who went on a wilderness backpacking trip showed improved proofreading performance, while those who went on an urban vacation or took no vacation showed no improvement. In 2001, Hartig demonstrated that nature can help people recover from "normal psychological wear and tear"—but nature also improves the capacity to pay attention. Hartig emphasizes that he does not test the extremes—say, the Sierras versus East Los Angeles. Rather, his studies have focused on what he describes as "typical local conditions." As described in *Monitor on Psychology*, Hartig asked participants to complete a forty-minute sequence of tasks designed to exhaust their directed-attention capacity. After the attention-fatiguing tasks, Hartig then randomly assigned participants to spend forty minutes "walking in a local nature preserve, walking in an urban area, or sitting quietly while reading magazines and listening to music," the journal reported. "After this period, those who had walked in the nature preserve performed better than the other participants on a standard proofreading task. They also reported more positive emotions and less anger."

Nature's Ritalin

Attention-restoration theory applies to everyone, regardless of age. But what about children, especially those with ADHD?

"By bolstering children's attention resources, green spaces may enable children to think more clearly and cope more effectively with life stress," writes Nancy Wells, assistant professor at the New York State

College of Human Ecology. In 2000, Wells conducted a study that found that being close to nature, in general, helps boost a child's attention span. When children's cognitive functioning was compared before and after they moved from poor- to better-quality housing adjacent to natural, green spaces, "profound differences emerged in their attention capacities even when the effects of the improved housing were taken into account," according to Wells.

Swedish researchers compared children within two daycare settings: at one, the quiet play area was surrounded by tall buildings, with low plants and a brick path; at the other, the play area, based on an "outdoors in all weather" theme, was set in an orchard surrounded by pasture and woods and was adjacent to an overgrown garden with tall trees and rocks. The study revealed that children in the "green" day care, who played outside every day, regardless of weather, had better motor coordination and more ability to concentrate.

Some of the most important work in this area has been done at the Human-Environment Research Laboratory at the University of Illinois. Andrea Faber Taylor, Frances Kuo, and William C. Sullivan have found that green outdoor spaces foster creative play, improve children's access to positive adult interaction—and relieve the symptoms of attention-deficit disorders. The greener the setting, the more the relief. By comparison, activities indoors, such as watching TV, or outdoors in paved, non-green areas, increase these children's symptoms.

In a survey of the families of ADHD children ages seven to twelve, parents or guardians were asked to identify after-school or weekend activities that left their child functioning especially well or particularly poorly. Activities were coded as "green" or "not green." Green activities, for example, included camping and fishing. Not-green activities included watching television, playing video games, doing homework. Some activities, such as rollerblading, were labeled ambiguous. The controls in this study were more complex than space allows me to describe, but suffice it to say, the research team was careful to account for variables. They found that greenery in a child's everyday environment, even views of green through a window, specifically reduces attention-deficit symptoms. While outdoor activities in general help, settings with trees and grass are the most beneficial. As they reported in the journal *Environment and Behavior,* "compared to the aftereffects of play in paved outdoor or indoor areas, activities in natural, green settings were far more likely to leave ADD children better able to focus, concentrate. Activities that left ADD children in worse shape were far more likely to occur indoors or outdoors in spaces devoid of greenery."

They also found that the positive influence of near-home nature on concentration may be more pronounced for girls (ages six to nine) than for boys. On average, the greener a girl's view from home, the better she concentrates, the less she acts impulsively, and the longer she can delay gratification. This helps her do better in school, handle peer pressure, and avoid dangerous, unhealthy, or problem behaviors. She is more likely to behave in ways that foster success in life, according to the researchers. Perhaps, if girls are less biologically prone to ADHD, as some mental health professionals believe, they may exhibit milder symptoms and may also have a more robust, healthy response to the treatment—whether pharmaceutical or green.

Based on the study, the University of Illinois issued this informal advice regarding girls to parents, caregivers, and others. The information also applies to boys:

- Encourage girls to study or play in rooms with a view of nature.
- Encourage children to play outdoors in green spaces, and advocate recess in green schoolyards. This may be especially helpful for renewing children's concentration.
- Plant and care for trees and vegetation at your residence, or encourage the owner to do so.
- Value and care for the trees in your community. Caring for trees means caring for people.

In addition to its work in the housing projects of inner-city Chicago, the Human-Environment Research Laboratory has also examined nature's impact on children with ADHD in middle-class settings. There, as in the public housing development, parents reported that their children exhibited fewer symptoms of ADHD after spending time in green surroundings. "You could say that the kids who had greener settings were just richer," says Kuo. "But that doesn't explain the fact that even rich kids do better after being in green settings . . ." In the report:

> Participants were asked if they had had any experiences, either positive or negative, related to any aftereffects of green settings on their child's attention. One parent said she had recently begun taking her son to the local park for 30 minutes each morning before school because the weather was nice, and they "had some time to kill." She then said, "Come to think of it, I have noticed his attitude toward going to school has been better, and his schoolwork has been better this past week. I think it's because spending time at the park is pleasurable, peaceful, quiet, calming."

Another parent reported that his son could hit golf balls or fish for hours, and that during these times the boy was "very relaxed" and his attention-deficit symptoms minimal. "When I read the results of your study, they hit me in the face," he told the researchers. "I thought, yes, I've seen this!"

So had some of the parents I interviewed. Noticing that their children's ADHD symptoms were calmed by natural settings, they applied common sense; they were already encouraging their kids to spend more time outdoors, and they felt affirmed when I told them about the Illinois studies.

Taylor's and Kuo's more recent research findings are equally provocative. According to an unpublished study (which Taylor emphasizes is "a work in progress"), attention performance for unmedicated children clinically diagnosed with ADHD was better after a simple twenty-minute walk in a park, with a natural setting, than it was after a walk through well-kept downtown and residential areas.

Expanding such knowledge, and applying it in practical ways, will be the next challenge. Although today's common medications for ADHD offer temporary gains, including sustained attention and academic productivity, these medications may do little for a child's long-term success, either socially or academically. The medications can also have unpleasant side effects, among them sleep disruption, depression, and growth suppression of approximately half an inch per year on average, as reported in a large randomized trial funded by the National Institute of Mental Health. A second class of treatment—behavioral therapies—teaches children how to self-monitor attention and impulsive behavior, but the success of these therapies has been mixed.

More time in nature—combined with less television and more stimulating play and educational settings—may go a long way toward reducing attention deficits in children, and, just as important, increasing their joy in life. Researchers at the Human-Environment Research Laboratory believe that their findings—if replicated and broadened by additional research—point to nature therapy as a potential third course of treatment, applied either in concert with medication and/or behavioral therapy, or on its own. Behavioral therapy and nature therapy, if used collaboratively, might teach the young how to visualize positive experiences in nature when they need a calming tool. One psychiatrist who works with ADHD children relates how he sometimes slides into mild depressions. "I grew up fly-fishing in Michigan, and that was how I found peace as a child," he says. "So, when I begin to feel depressed, I use self-hypnosis to go there again, to call up those memories." He calls them "meadow memories." Though he is a firm believer in the proper use of the currently available medications for ADHD, he is encouraged by the possibility that nature therapy might offer him another professional tool. And, as Kuo points out, prescribing "green time" for the treatment of ADHD has other advantages: it's widely accessible, free of side effects, nonstigmatizing, and inexpensive.

If it's true that nature therapy reduces the symptoms of ADHD, then the converse may also be true: ADHD may be a set of symptoms aggravated by lack of exposure to nature. By this line of thinking, many children may benefit from medications, but the real disorder is less in the child than it is in the imposed, artificial environment. Viewed from this angle, the society that has disengaged the child from nature is most certainly disordered, if well-meaning. To take nature and natural play away from children may be tantamount to withholding oxygen.

An expanded application of attention-restoration theory would be useful in the design of homes, classrooms, and curricula. New York's Central Park, the first professionally designed urban park in America, was originally seen as a necessary aid to both civic consciousness and public health. It was construed as a place where all New Yorkers, regardless of class, age, or health, would benefit from fresh air. If nature-deficit disorder, as a hypothetical condition, affects all children (and adults) whether or not they have some biological propensity for attention deficit, then nature therapy at the societal and individual levels will do the greatest good for the greatest number of people.

Research on the impact of nature experiences on attention disorders and on wider aspects of child health and development is in its infancy, and easily challenged. Scientists doing some of the best of this research are the first to point that out. "For many of us, intuition emphatically asserts that nature is good for children," write Taylor and Kuo, in an overview of the research to date. "Beyond these intuitions, there are also well-reasoned theoretical arguments as to why humans in general—and therefore children—might have an inborn need for contact with nature." Yes, more research is needed, but we do not have to wait for it. As Taylor and Kuo argue, "given the pattern of statistically reliable findings all pointing the same direction and persisting across different subpopulations of children, different settings, and in spite of design weaknesses, at some point it becomes more parsimonious to accept the fact that nature does promote healthy child development." If, as a growing body of evidence recommends, "contact with nature is as important to children as good nutrition and adequate sleep, then current trends in children's access to nature need to be addressed."

Even the most extensive research is unlikely to capture the full benefits of direct, natural experience. One aspect sure to elude measurement—a phenomenon that will be discussed later in these pages—is the contribution of nature to the spiritual life of the child, and therefore to the adult. This we know: As the sign over Albert Einstein's office at Princeton University read, "Not everything that counts can be counted, and not everything that can be counted counts." We don't have to wait for more, needed, research to act on common sense, or to give the gift of nature—even when it might seem to be too late.

Touching the Sky with a Stick

On a Sunday afternoon, a half-dozen teenagers gathered in defense attorney Daniel Ybarra's office not far from where I live. These teenagers—several diagnosed with ADHD—were on probation. They looked like your usual troubled teenage suspects: a gang member wearing a white net skullcap and black jersey; a girl with orange hair, her fingernails chewed to the quick; another boy with a black skullcap with a bandana tied around his head. He was wearing a sealskin Tlingit medicine pouch around his neck.

"You gonna carry your bus tokens in that, now?" one of the teens teased.

They had just returned from two chaperoned weeks living with tribal people in Ketchikan, Alaska, and in the southwestern Alaskan village of Kake, population 750. Kake is on an island served by a ferry that comes once every five days. The young people had been ordered to Alaska by a superior court judge who has an interest in alternative approaches to punishment.

For years, Ybarra had dreamed of pulling at-risk kids out of their urban environment and exposing them to nature. With the blessing of the judge, he acted. He convinced Alaska Airlines to provide inexpensive airline tickets, raised contributions from law school classmates, a professional football player, and the United Domestic Workers union.

Some of the teenagers Ybarra took under his wing had never been to the mountains or beyond earshot of a combustion engine. The farthest one girl had been from her inner city home was a trip to a suburb. Suddenly they were transported to a place of glaciers and *takus*—storms that come out of nowhere, with winds that can blow a forest flat. They found themselves among grizzlies on the beaches, sea elephants that loomed up from the channel, and bald eagles that sat ten to a branch, as common as sparrows.

Tlingit villages face the sea, as they have for thousands of years, and life still revolves around the ocean's harvest. Although the Tlingits have their own problems with substance abuse, they retain pieces of what so many young people have lost. The boy with the black skullcap said: "I never seen a place so dark at night. I seen seals, bears, whales, salmon jumpin'—and I caught crabs and oysters, and as soon as we caught 'em, we ate 'em. I felt like I was in a past life." A girl dressed in neo-hippie garb added: "I never saw a bear before. I'm scared of bears, but when I saw them, I had no stress. I was calm, free. You know what was great? Picking berries. It was addictive. Like cigarettes." She laughed. "Just the picking, just being out in the bushes."

One of the young men said he almost refused to get on the airplane to come home. But he returned determined to become an attorney specializing in environmental law.

They learned about *sha-a-ya-dee-da-na*, a Tlingit word that loosely translates as "self-respect," by being in nature, and by associating with people who had never been separated from it.

"I met a little boy and spent a lot of time with him," said one of the young women in the room. She had long, dark hair and eyes as bright as the midnight sun. "One day I was outside—this was right before we went into a sweat lodge—and he asked me, 'Can you touch the sky with a stick?' I answered, 'No, I'm too short.' He looked at me with disgust and said, 'You're weak! How do you know you can't touch the sky with a stick if you don't even try?'" Recalling the riddle, the young woman's eyes widened. "This was the first time I've ever been spoken to like that by a four-year-old."

When she came home, her mother was not at the airport to pick her up. She returned to an empty house.

"Last night, I looked out at the trees and I thought of Kake," she said.

Anyone who has spent much time around addicts or gang members understands how disarming—and manipulative—they can be. Yet on this afternoon, I saw no evidence of the con artist in their eyes. At least for a while—a day, a week, a year, or perhaps even a lifetime—they were changed.

PART III

THE BEST OF INTENTIONS:
WHY JOHNNIE AND JEANNIE DON'T PLAY OUTSIDE ANYMORE

Our children no longer learn how to read

the great Book of Nature

from their own direct experience or how to interact creatively

with the seasonal transformations of the planet.

They seldom learn where their water comes from or where it goes.

We no longer coordinate our human celebration with

the great liturgy of the heavens.

—WENDELL BERRY

9. Time and Fear

NOW THAT WE KNOW more about the wide-ranging value of direct experience in nature, it's time to look more deeply into the hurdles that must be crossed to increase that exposure. Some of these obstacles are cultural or institutional—growing litigation, education trends that marginalize direct experience in nature; some are structural—the way cities are shaped. Other barriers are more personal or familial—time pressures and fear, for example. A shared characteristic of these institutional and personal barriers is that those of us who have erected them have usually done so with the best of intentions.

When my son Jason was nine, I picked him up from school one afternoon and we stopped at a neighborhood park to play catch. The expanse of grass was filling up with children's soccer teams. Jason and I moved from the center to the edge of the park and found a patch of green with no soccer players. We began to toss a ball back and forth. A mother of one of Jason's classmates approached. I knew this athletic woman; she was extremely committed to her children's academic and athletic achievements. She drove herself even harder.

"Whatcha doing?" she asked, with a smile. "Waiting for a team?"

"Nope. Just playing catch," I answered, tossing the ball to Jason.

"Ah . . . killing time," she said.

When did playing catch in a park become a form of killing time? This mother had the best of intentions, of course. Most of us do. Yet, as the pace of American life, especially for children, has quickened—as we have striven to improve schools, increase productivity, accumulate more wealth, and provide a more technological education—the consequences of our intentions are not always what we intend.

Our lives may be more productive, but less inventive. In an effort to value and structure time, some of us unintentionally may be killing dreamtime. In our worry about our children's safety we may take actions that, in some ways, decrease our children's safety. Institutions that have traditionally introduced the young to the outdoors are now adopting policies that, in some cases, actually separate children from nature. Even some environmental organizations are hastening that separation—unconsciously, with the best of intentions—and risking the future of environmentalism and the health of the earth itself.

Okay, back to the park.

My purpose in telling this anecdote is not to diminish the importance of soccer. Certainly, organized sports get kids outside, and these activities offer attributes all their own. Still, we need to find a better balance between organized activities, the pace of our children's lives, and their experiences in nature. That mission will be difficult, but attainable.

Eighty percent of Americans live in metropolitan areas, and many of these areas are severely lacking in park space. Support for existing parks atrophied in recent decades. For example, only 30 percent of Los Angeles residents live within walking distance of a park, according to the Trust for Public Land.

More to the point, parks increasingly favor what Robin Moore, president of the International Association for the Child's Right to Play, calls the "commercialization of play." Moore charts a broad "international trend toward investing public funds in sports areas rather than in multichoice space for free play." He adds, "For-profit indoor play centers are developing around the world. Until now, they have offered a narrow range of gross motor activity." Meanwhile, vacant lots are vanishing, and the nature of suburban development is changing. Suburban fields that might have been left open in earlier decades are being erased, replaced by denser, planned developments with manicured green areas maintained through strict covenants. "Most countries do not even have a general guideline for play space allocation," Moore reports.

From 1981 to 1997, the amount of time children spent in organized sports increased by 27 percent. In 1974, the U.S. Youth Soccer Association had approximately 100,000 members; today, the association has nearly 3 million. Demand for playing fields is up. Expenditures on parks are falling. When parks are offered, the designers focus on reducing liability. Encouraging a variety of play styles is less of a priority. A flat patch of grass or artificial turf (now being considered for several parks by the city of Seattle) may be perfect for organized sports, but not for unstructured or natural play. When a park is graded to create a playing field, children gain soccer capacity, but they lose places for self-directed play. Indeed, research suggests that children, when left to their own devices, are drawn to the rough edges of such parks, the ravines and rocky inclines, the natural vegetation. A park may be neatly trimmed and landscaped, but the natural corners and edges where children once played can be lost in translation.

Ironically, as mentioned earlier, the childhood obesity epidemic (with a complex set of causes) has coincided with a dramatic increase in children's organized sports. This does not mean, of course, that organized sports contribute to obesity, but that an over-scheduled, over-organized childhood may. Such a childhood, without nature, is missing vital ingredients.

IT TAKES TIME—loose, unstructured dreamtime—to experience nature in a meaningful way. Unless parents are vigilant, such time becomes a scarce resource, not because they intend it to shrink, but because time is consumed by multiple, invisible forces; because our culture currently places so little value on natural play. During my travels across the country to research *Childhood's Future*, I asked a class of fifth- and sixth-graders at Jerabek Elementary in San Diego to describe their schedules. The comment of one girl was typical:

> I don't really have much time to play at all because I have piano les-
> sons. My mom makes me practice for about an hour every day, and
> then I have my homework, and that's about an hour's worth, and then
> I got soccer practice, and that's from five-thirty to seven, and then
> there's no time left over to play. On weekends we usually have soccer
> games, and I have to practice piano and then I have to do yard work,
> and then I have the chores, and then I'm free to play—which is only
> about two hours, three hours something like that.

I was intrigued with the way children defined play: often, their defi-nition did not include soccer or piano lessons. Those activities were more like work.

How do young people feel when they do have extra, unscheduled time?

"I sort of feel free, like I can do anything in the world that I want to. It's a good feeling," one boy told me. "I know I don't have homework, and I know I don't have soccer practice or anything like that, and it's just a really good feeling that you can get out and go hike or bike ride."

In a classroom at Kenwood Elementary School in Miami, I asked if anybody worried about getting into good colleges or getting good jobs in the future. More than half of the children raised their hands. These were fourth-graders. A serious little girl, eyebrows scrunched up behind her glasses, explained, "Well, you should not stare out the window or dream. You should get your mind on your work because you can never get a college education if you don't." A central concern is how parents model their own use of time—their attitude about where time fits into their busy lives. In a classroom in Potomac, Maryland, ninth-grader Courtney Ivins clearly expressed this effect. As people grow older, nature's magnificence "gets easier to overlook," she surmises. "Snow not only brings a chance to miss school, but it also provides a means for adventure. . . . snowmen, igloos, and snowball fights." But for many adults, she observes, "snow is just another one of life's many hassles. The roads are slippery, traffic is increased, and sidewalks are ready to be shoveled."

So where has all the time gone, or shifted to? Time researchers sometimes ignore obvious variables. But in recent years, several studies have offered a fairly clear snapshot of time use. For example, time-analysis studies done at the University of Michigan's Institute for Social Research showed that from 1981 to 1997, the amount of time children up to age twelve spent studying increased by 20 percent. As with the growth of organized sports, the increase in homework and study time is not necessarily a bad trend—except that, so often, mounting pressure eclipses unstructured time and natural play.

As for adults, a Stanford University study reveals that as Internet use grows, Americans spend less time with friends and family, reading newspapers, or watching television. (Outdoors activities are not mentioned in the study.) They spend more time working for their employers at home, without cutting back their hours in the office. Also, according to the Stanford survey, time spent on the Internet grows with the number of years a person is connected. In 2004, the University of California, Berkeley, found that Americans spend 170 minutes a day watching TV and movies, nine times as many minutes as they spend on physical activities. We're in our cars 101 minutes a day, five times the amount of time we spend exercising. As sprawl pushes the urban envelope, we spend more time on the road; the proportion of workers who commuted for 30 minutes or more a day jumped from 20 percent in 1990 to 34 percent in 2000. We devote, on average, only 19 minutes a day, or 5 percent of our time, to physical leisure-time activities.

Do these findings mean we are lazy? No, we are just busy, according to Gladys Block, professor of epidemiology and public-health nutrition at the University of California, Berkeley, and the study's coauthor. We take fewer vacation days and work harder than the Japanese or Europeans. In 2001, Americans logged 1,821 work hours, compared with 1,467 for German workers. (People in the middle-America states are the least physically active, according to the study. The survey also indicates that African-Americans report less physical or leisure-time activities than other ethnic groups. This could reflect the fact that more African-Americans live in low-income neighborhoods, and so are less likely to have parks and safe places to walk.) Weekends are no longer for recreation, but for the undone chores that pile up during the week. And in a landmark Canadian survey, researchers found that both parents cut back on sleep to handle all their responsibilities. No time to sleep. No time for snow.

Or so it seems.

Nature Time Is Not Leisure Time

The reasons for our time poverty are more complex than workaholism or greed. Other factors include technological change and employers who intentionally squeeze the last drop of employees' energy. These forces are difficult to resist, especially when a family's economic security seems chronically at risk. Bottom line: We want to do what's best for our children. If working more helps us do that, so be it. If enrolling Suzie in Suzuki violin lessons develops her musical capabilities and self-discipline, so be it.

This understandable impulse is one reason why the emerging evidence of nature's necessity to children's healthy development is so important. We can now look at it this way: *Time in nature is not leisure time; it's an essential investment in our children's health* (and also, by the way, in our own). American parents have become too accustomed to the media mantra that dismisses us as selfish strivers who care more about our Lexuses than our children. But, if anything, most parents have an acutely tuned sense of responsibility—to the point where they consider relaxation and leisure, for themselves or their children, a self-indulgent luxury. By taking nature experience out of the leisure column and placing it in the health column, we are more likely to take our children on that hike—more likely to, well, have fun. Such a change in outlook is crucial. The stakes are high, and the consequences more evident when children reach their teen years. Tonia Berman, a high school biology teacher in my city, describes the usual roster of teen problems. She sees kids who don't get enough to eat at home, who brave neighborhood violence after school, and increasingly, she witnesses another kind of suffering: what she calls the Superchild syndrome. "We've heard all about the Supermom," she says, "the woman who tries to do everything perfectly, who pursues a high-pressure career, agonizes over the family's dinner menu, drills her kids with flash cards, rushes to charity events . . . and so on." Indeed, parenting magazines are full of cautionary tales about how Supermoms (and Superdads, too) can crash and burn. "But what about the kids who are running on the same treadmill, sometimes even faster?"

When Berman asked her students to write essays about their time pressure, one teenager itemized her schedule, as well as her response to it. Here, she said, is a partial list: "I play tennis during tennis season, lead a community service club as president, take a community college course in how to work with people with disabilities, volunteer in the community, work as a child care helper at my place of worship, take six extremely advanced classes (for extra credit when I enter college), am a really good friend, and counsel my peers because I would not turn a friend or other person down."

Over winter and spring breaks, this student continues her volunteer work, and studies to get a head start on the next semester. She prides herself on personal honesty, but cries inside when she sees other students, who cheat, do better on tests. "I am a very worryful person (is that a word?)," she wrote. "I am the type of person that thinks about things a great deal." After a particularly stressful few weeks, she fell into a slump that scared her. What if she couldn't get back to her schedule?

What then? "I considered suicide. I didn't really care about myself and would rather hurt myself than my parents or friends. I suffered so they would not have to know what I was going through—my weaknesses, my failures, the hatred I felt at the world." This isn't just a reflection of eternal teen angst, but a singular example of why there is a growing rate of adolescent suicides and attempted-suicides. Could she turn to her parents for help? She felt she could not. "They pass right by who I am, looking only for what they want to see." She says that she might not be here today if not for people like Mrs. Berman, her biology teacher, who reached out to her in time.

Instilling self-discipline is an essential value in parenting, but so is the nurturing of creativity and wonder. With greater knowledge about the measurable value of exposing children to nature, parents may have an easier time finding that balance. Certainly many parents are concerned about overprogramming their children, and hunger for a different approach. Tina Kafka, the mother of college students, wonders if her children will remember much of what she has scheduled into their lives:

> When I think of my own childhood, I particularly remember those special times when I was climbing my tree, or playing pirates in the wash behind my house, or sliding down the wash sides on a piece of cardboard. But I realize now, after talking with my mother—who said she scheduled a lot of my childhood, arranging for friends to come over, all that—that the free time in the wash may not have actually occupied that many hours of my childhood. But those hours are the moments I remember absolutely vividly. Even with my own children, I am often amazed how some activity that I have carefully planned pales in their long-term memories compared to another activity that was completely spontaneous and hardly memorable to me. As adults, we can plan a million things to take up our kids' time in a meaningful way, but what really clicks into their inner being is beyond our control. Sometimes I wonder why we think we need so much control.

10. The Bogeyman Syndrome Redux

Man's heart, away from nature, becomes hard; [the Lakota] knew that lack of respect for growing, living things soon led to lack of respect for humans too.

—LUTHER STANDING BEAR (C. 1868–1939)

FEAR IS THE MOST potent force that prevents parents from allowing their children the freedom they themselves enjoyed when they were young. Fear is the emotion that separates a developing child from the full, *essential* benefits of nature. Fear of traffic, of crime, of stranger-danger—and of nature itself.

The boundaries of children's lives are growing ever tighter. A 1991 study of three generations of nine-year-olds found that, between 1970 and 1990, the radius around the home where children were allowed to roam on their own had shrunk to a ninth of what it had been in 1970. In the winter 2003 issue of *American Demographics* magazine, TNS Intersearch reported that 56 percent of today's parents say that by the time they were ten years old they were allowed to walk or bike to school. Today, only 36 percent of those same parents say their own kids should be allowed similar freedoms. A separate study by Taylor Research and Consulting found that 41 percent of children ages eight to eleven worry about being safe in their neighborhoods.

When landscape and play expert Robin Moore studied the San Francisco Bay region in 1980, he combined his findings with a review of international research and came to "one inescapable conclusion": Increasing residential and arterial traffic "was the one universal factor above all others that restricted the development of children's spatial range, thereby limiting children's knowledge of the community environment—including its natural characteristics and components."

My unscientific hunch, however, is that since 1980, fear of strangers —and beyond that a generalized, unfocused fear—has come to outrank the fear of traffic. For all of these reasons, many children never get to know their neighborhoods or parks or the surviving natural areas at their fringes.

Long before the terror of 9/11 magnified our generalized fear, I spent a day with the Fitzsimmons family in Swarthmore, Pennsylvania. They lived in a Victorian house; the porch swing in front creaked slightly in the wind. Swarthmore is an idyllic town filled with old trees and young children and wide sidewalks, where, as Beth Fitzsimmons told me later, there is one rule: Nobody can hurt trees or children. This is, in short, the last place where one would expect parents to express fear. Yet, Beth said:

> When I was a little kid, there were woods at the foot of my street, and I would get up at six o'clock in the morning and go down there for two or three hours and pick blueberries by myself, and nobody ever had to worry about it. . . . Guns and drugs are the reasons that we say no to things that our kids would probably like to do. There are a lot of lunatics out there. It's so different. Even if [my daughter] Elizabeth goes down to Crum Creek behind the college, I want her to take the dog and make sure she's with at least one friend.

I was surprised to find the fear as intense in Kansas as it was in Pennsylvania. One father said:

> I have a rule. I want to know where my kid is twenty-four hours a day, seven days a week. I want to know where that kid is. Which house. Which square foot. Which telephone number. That's just my way of dealing with it. Both of my kids have heard my preaching that the world is full of crazy people. And it is. There're nuts running loose.

People that need to go through years of therapy and need to be incarcerated. They're out there driving around in cars and they've got guns on their seats. They're out there. And you have to deal with that situation. I'd be hesitant to let my kids go over to the park alone. Everyone tells you to never leave your kids alone.

Also in Kansas, a pleasant middle-aged teacher spoke with sorrow about how daily life is colored by fear.

I was standing in line the other day at the airport and a little kid was going around to look behind the counter, and his mother said to him, 'Do you want somebody to snatch you? Don't walk away from me like that.' And here I'm standing behind them in line, and I'm saying to myself, well, I really didn't *look* like a child snatcher. But we teach our kids so young to be aware of everything. They lose their time to be innocent. My seventh-graders have had to deal with situations that we didn't know about until we were adults. Teaching kids intelligent caution around strangers is certainly important; how to say 'no' to potential child abusers is essential. But we need to create a balanced view of danger. The damage that has been caused when you have families teaching their kids never to talk to another adult in a society where you desperately need more communication—what does that do to the kid?

In the oddest ways, many Americans' view of the woods has reverted to ancient irrationality, conjuring dread behind the branches.

Scared Stupid

In the early 1990s, Joel Best, then a professor and chairman of the sociology department at California State, Fresno, had conducted a study of stranger-danger—Halloween terrorism, in particular; all those reports of candy laced with drugs or pins, razor blades or poison. He reviewed seventy-six specific stories and rumors reported from 1958 to 1984 in the *New York Times*, the *Chicago Tribune*, the *Los Angeles Times* and the *Fresno Bee*. "We couldn't find a single case of any child killed or seriously injured by candy contamination," he said. "The Halloween sadist is an urban myth." In 2001, Best—now a professor at the University of Delaware—updated his findings in his book *Damn Lies and Statistics.* "Every year since 1950, the number of American children gunned down has doubled." So goes a widely quoted statement, which originated in a Children's Defense Fund report in the mid-1990s. Best calls it the most inaccurate social statistic ever circulated. "If the number doubled each year, there must have been two children gunned down in 1951, four in 1952, eight in 1953, and so on," he writes. In 1983, the number of American children gunned down would have been 8.6 billion (about twice the Earth's population at the time). By this doubling process, the number of American kids shot in 1987 alone would have been greater than the estimated total of the world's population—from the time of the first humans. "Monster hype," Best calls this.

At the time, I dubbed the phenomenon the "Bogeyman syndrome."

At the height of the first missing-children panic, a decade ago, some missing-children organizations were claiming that four thousand children a year were being killed by strangers in the course of abduction. Wrong, said David Finklehor, co-director of the Family Research Laboratory at the University of New Hampshire, who conducted the National Incidents Study of Missing Children with the Justice Department in 1990, considered the most comprehensive and accurate report on this subject. Most of the abductors weren't strangers, but family members or someone the family knew. Second, the actual annual figure of stranger abductions was two hundred to three hundred and it still is.

Today, Finklehor calls the stranger-snatcher epidemic "an optical illusion" caused by the generalized social anxiety, new coordination between law enforcement and the missing-children groups, and media excitability. Make that media market-driven excitability. In a five-year study of local newscasts aired in Los Angeles in the 1990s, Frank Gilliam, a professor of political science at UCLA and associate director of the Center for the Study of American Politics and Public Policy, found that local TV news is creating a powerful "crime script" in the public's mind—a distorted shorthand that we carry around in our heads. "The nightly news, much more visceral and powerful than print media, actually promotes racism and violence," he says. "Viewers now automatically link race with crime."

Isn't TV simply telling us unpleasant, though accurate, news? "No," says Gilliam. "Violent crime coverage, connected to race, has disproportionately come to dominate local news." In Los Angeles, coverage of violence overwhelmingly outstrips the incidents of violent crime—by a factor of as much as 30 to 1 in the case of murder. Some TV newsrooms work hard to provide balance and context to crime coverage. But Gilliam insists that "body-bag" news coverage, by conditioning us to "crude stereotypes of members of racial minority groups," is shaping public policy and spreading inaccurate fear.

Such fear may actually make our children less safe. In 1995, a "shyness inventory" revealed that 48 percent of people surveyed described themselves as shy, up from 40 percent in the mid-1970s. "People see social interactions as more dangerous than they are," says Lynn Henderson, a clinical psychologist and visiting scholar at Stanford. She worries that, as more parents keep their children inside the house or under rigid control, youngsters will be deprived of chances to become self-confident and discerning, to interact with neighbors, or to learn how to build real community—which is one defense against sociopaths.

Excessive fear can transform a person and modify behavior permanently; it can change the very structure of the brain. The same can happen to a whole culture. What will it be like for children to grow up in socially and environmentally controlled environments—condominiums and planned developments and covenant-controlled housing developments surrounded with walls, gates, and surveillance systems, where covenants prevent families from planting gardens? One wonders how the children growing up in this culture of control will define freedom when they are adults.

Parents may now buy a cheerfully colored, three-ounce bracelet called the global positioning system (GPS) personal locator, and lock it on their child's wrist. If the water-resistant bracelet is cut or forcefully removed, its continuous signal activates an alarm and notifies the manufacturer's emergency operators. At least at first glance, resistance to global personal tracking seems not only futile but also selfish—because we love our children and want to protect them. But guaranteed safety, or the illusion of it, can only be bought at a dangerous price. Imagine future generations of children who have been raised to accept the inevitability of being electronically tracked every day, every second, in every room of their lives, in the un-brave new world. Such technology may work in the short run, but it may also create a false sense of security and serve as a poor substitute for the proven antidotes to crime: an active community, more human eyes on the streets, and self-confident children.

When Nature Becomes the Bogeyman

Stranger danger isn't the only reason families draw the boundaries of children's life tighter. Children and adults are even beginning to see nature as our natural enemy—a bogeyman, a stand-in for other, less identifiable reasons for fear.

Has our relationship with the outdoors reversed, or more accurately, regressed? Earlier generations of Americans were not sanguine about their chances of survival in the great outdoors. As development encroaches on the territories of bears and mountain lions, wild animals do sometimes attack humans—and remind us why many of our forebears perceived nature as a threat.

Our greatest parks, once viewed as refuges from urban ills, are becoming suspect—at least in the media. A few years ago, a motel handyman confessed to the FBI that he killed three Yosemite sightseers just outside the national park, and later decapitated a naturalist in the park. Other recent stories may have jarred Americans' confidence in the outdoors. In Washington's Olympic National Park in 1998, there were eighty-two car break-ins, forty-seven cases of vandalism, sixty-four incidents involving drug and alcohol abuse, one sexual assault, and one aggravated assault with a weapon. The park's rangers now carry semi-automatic weapons. Also in 1998, in the Great Smoky Mountains, a deranged landscaper who enjoyed singing gospel music shot and killed National Park Service ranger Joe Kolodski. Elsewhere, two park rangers were shot, one fatally, in Oregon's Oswald West State Park.

Movies tap into this fear. The 1930s Wolfman seems mild compared with the terror exploited in the lengthening string of summer-camp slasher films or *The Blair Witch Project*, a horror movie set in the forest.

Jerry Schad, a naturalist of repute and the author of a series of *Afoot and Afield* guides to the Southern California backcountry, works tirelessly to help young people bond with the natural world. He reports:

> Every semester I invite the students in my Survey of Physical Science course at Mesa College on a trip to Mt. Laguna Observatory. The students are required to write a short report on what they learned or what impressed them the most. As the years go by, fewer and fewer students have any notion of what is out there one hour east of San Diego. Relatively few now have ever seen the Milky Way until (perhaps) the date of the trip. Most are very impressed with what they see and learn, but for a significant number the trip is downright frightening. Several have mentioned the trees in the forest at dusk in the same sentence as *Blair Witch Project*.

In the 1970s, concern about outdoor air pollution, energy conservation, and fear of strangers converged with advances in technology; new houses, workplaces, public buildings, and schools became virtual biospheres, sealed from the outside with windows that don't open. Seeking a safe alternative to outdoor play, some parents drive their children to fast-food restaurants and let them loose in admission-free indoor tunnel-mazes and accompanying "ball pits."

Real dangers do exist in nature, but the threat is greatly exaggerated by the media. Reality is different. Take the park scare, for example.

Joe Kolodski was only the third U.S. Park Service ranger killed in the line of duty in the agency's 82-year history. As the *Seattle Times* reports, the crime rate in the Olympic National Forest "wasn't exactly a crime wave," considering that the park counted 4.6 million visits. No city that size could claim so little crime. Some 286 million people trekked through America's national parks last year, and few of them suffered much more than mosquito bites.

In fact, the crime rate is falling in most wilderness parks. From 1990 to 1998, reported robberies in the national parks dropped from 184 to 25, murders from 24 to 10, and rapes from 92 to 29. Yosemite is, in fact, one of the safest of the nation's parks. The killing of the young naturalist in Yosemite, though tragic, was the first murder reported there in a decade.

Worried about lions, tigers, and bears? The number of attacks is miniscule. Or West Nile virus? Mosquitoes, who love a good nightlight, can transfer that bug indoors, too. And the brown recluse spider—often more deadly than any rattlesnake—prefers staying indoors. Brown recluse spiders take refuge in clothing that has been placed on the floor; they bite when trapped and pressed between the patient's skin and clothing. We may fear the outdoors, but kids may generally face more dangers in their own home. The Environmental Protection Agency now warns us that *indoor* air pollution is the nation's number one environmental threat to health—and it's from two to ten times worse than outdoor air pollution. A child indoors is more susceptible to spores of toxic molds growing under that plush carpet; or bacteria or allergens carried by household vermin; or carbon monoxide, radon, and lead dust. The allergen level of newer, sealed buildings can be as much as two hundred times greater than that of older structures. *Pediatric Nursing* journal reports that those indoor ball-pit playgrounds at the fast-food restaurants can spread serious infectious diseases: "Although these commercial food establishments must adhere to the Food and Drug Administration's model of sanitation and food protection," none of their guidelines followed the "Centers for Disease Control recommendations for cleaning and disinfecting the areas in which these children play."

Some experts link indoor play (not to mention fast food) to the epidemic of childhood obesity. Ironically, a generation of parents fixated on being buff is raising a generation of physical weaklings. Two-thirds of American children can't pass a basic physical: 40 percent of boys and 70 percent of girls ages six to seventeen can't manage more than one pull-up; and 40 percent show early signs of heart and circulation problems, according to a new report by the President's Council on Physical Fitness and Sports.

So where is the greatest danger? Outdoors, in the woods and fields? Or on the couch in front of the TV? A blanket wrapped too tightly has its own consequences. One is that we may end up teaching our children, in the same breath, that life is too risky but also not real—that there is a medical (or if that fails, a legal) remedy for every mistake. In 2001, the *British Medical Journal* announced that it would no longer allow the word "accident" to appear in its pages, based on the notion that when most bad things happen to good people, such injuries could have been foreseen and avoided, if proper measures had been taken. Such absolutist thinking is not only delusional, but dangerous.

11. Don't Know Much About Natural History: Education as a Barrier to Nature

To a person uninstructed in natural history, his country or sea-side stroll is a walk through a gallery filled with wonderful works of art, nine-tenths of which have their faces turned to the wall.

—THOMAS HUXLEY

DAVID SOBEL TELLS this story: A century ago, a boy ran along a beach with his gun, handmade from a piece of lead pipe. From time to time, he would stop, aim, and shoot at a gull. Today, such activity would be cause for time spent in juvenile hall, but for young John Muir, it was just another way to connect with nature. (Muir, it should be noted, was a bad shot, and apparently never killed a seagull.) Muir went on to become one of the initiators of modern environmentalism.

"Whenever I read Muir's description of shooting at seagulls to my students, they're shocked. They can't believe it," says Sobel, co-director of the Center for Place-based Education at Antioch New England Graduate School. He uses this example to illustrate just how much the interaction between children and nature has changed. Practitioners in the new fields of conservation psychology (focused on how people become environmentalists) and ecopsychology (the study of how ecology interacts with the human psyche) note that, as Americans become increasingly urbanized, their attitudes toward animals change in paradoxical ways.

To urbanized people, the source of food and the reality of nature are becoming more abstract. At the same time, urban folks are more likely to feel protective toward animals—or to fear them. The good news is that children today are less likely to kill animals for fun; the bad news is that children are so disconnected from nature that they either idealize it or associate it with fear—two sides of the same coin, since we tend to fear or romanticize what we don't know. Sobel, one of the most important thinkers in the realm of education and nature, views "ecophobia" as one of the sources of the problem.

Explaining Ecophobia

Ecophobia is fear of ecological deterioration, by Sobel's definition. In its older, more poetic meaning, the word ecophobia is the fear of home. Both definitions are accurate.

"Just as ethnobotanists are descending on tropical forests in search of new plants for medical uses, environmental educators, parents, and teachers are descending on second- and third-graders to teach them about the rainforests," Sobel writes in his volume, *Beyond Ecophobia: Reclaiming the Heart in Nature Education.* "From Brattleboro, Vermont, to Berkeley, California, schoolchildren . . . watch videos about the plight of indigenous forest people displaced by logging and exploration for oil. They learn that between the end of morning recess and the beginning of lunch, more than ten thousand acres of rainforest will be cut down, making way for fast-food, 'hamburgerable' cattle."

In theory, these children "will learn that by recycling their *Weekly Readers* and milk cartons, they can help save the planet," and they'll grow up to be responsible stewards of the earth, "voting for environmental candidates, and buying energy-efficient cars." Or maybe not. The opposite may be occurring, says Sobel. "If we fill our classrooms with examples of environmental abuse, we may be engendering a subtle form of dissociation. In our zest for making them aware of and responsible for the world's problems, we cut our children off from their roots." Lacking direct experience with nature, children begin to associate it with fear and apocalypse, not joy and wonder. He offers this analogy of disassociation: In response to physical and sexual abuse, children learn to cut themselves off from pain. Emotionally, they turn off. "My fear is that our environmentally correct curriculum similarly ends up distancing children from, rather than connecting them with, the natural world. The natural world is being abused and they just don't want to have to deal with it."

To some environmentalists and educators, this is contrarian thinking—even blasphemy. To others, the ecophobia thesis rings true. Children learn about the rain forest, but usually not about their own region's forests, or, as Sobel puts it, "even just the meadow outside the classroom door." He points out that "It is hard enough for children to understand the life cycles of chipmunks and milkweed, organisms they can study close at hand. This is the foundation upon which an eventual understanding of ocelots and orchids can be built."

By one measure, rain-forest curriculum is developmentally appropriate in middle or high school, but not in the primary grades. Some educators won't go that far, but they do agree with Sobel's basic premise that environmental education is out of balance. This issue is at the crux of the curriculum wars, particularly in the area of science. One teacher told me, "The science frameworks bandied about by state and local education boards have swung back and forth between the hands-on experiential approach and factoid learning from textbooks."

If educators are to help heal the broken bond between the young and the natural world, they and the rest of us must confront the unintended educational consequences of an overly abstract science education: ecophobia and the death of natural history studies. Equally important, the wave of test-based education reform that became dominant in the late 1990s leaves little room for hands-on experience in nature. Although some pioneering educators are sailing against the wind, participating in an international effort to stimulate the growth of nature education in and outside classrooms (which will be described in later chapters), many educational institutions and current educational trends are, in fact, part of the problem.

Silicon Faith

John Rick, who was quoted earlier in these pages about his community's restrictions on natural play, is a dedicated educator who left engineering to teach eighth-grade math. Rick is dismayed that nature has disappeared from the classroom, except for discussions of environmental catastrophe.

I asked Rick to describe an imaginary classroom saturated with the natural sciences and hands-on nature learning. "I keep coming back to a class devoid of nature," he answered. "Unfortunately, a class devoid of nature looks just like any classroom you would walk into today. We have industrialized the classroom to the extent that there is no room for nature in the curriculum." Curriculum standards adopted in the name of school reform restrict many districts to the basics of reading, writing, and mathematics. These are vital subjects, of course, but in Rick's opinion—and I share it—education reform has moved too far from what used to be called a well-rounded education. Rick elaborated:

> The society we are molding these kids toward is one that values consumer viability. The works of John Muir, Rachel Carson, or Aldo Leopold are seldom if ever taught to children in the public schools. Even in the sciences, where nature could play such an important role, the students study nature in a dry, mechanized way. How does the bat sonar work, how does a tree grow, how do soil amenities help crops grow? Kids see nature as a lab experiment.
>
> The alternative? I imagine a classroom that turns outward, both figuratively and literally. The grounds would become a classroom, buildings would look outward, and gardens would cover the campus. The works of naturalists would be the vehicle by which we would teach reading and writing. Math and science would be taught as a way to understand the intricacies of nature, the potential to meet human needs, and how all things are interlaced. A well-rounded education would mean learning the basics, to become part of a society that cherished nature while at the same time contributing to the well-being of mankind. Progress does not have to be patented to be worthwhile.

Progress can also be measured by our interactions with nature and its preservation. Can we teach children to look at a flower and see all the things it represents: beauty, the health of an ecosystem, and the potential for healing?

Public education is enamored, even mesmerized, by what might be called silicon faith: a myopic focus on high technology as salvation. In 2001, the Alliance for Childhood, a nonprofit organization in College Park, Maryland, released "Fool's Gold: A Critical Look at Computers in Childhood," a report supported by more than eighty-five experts in neurology, psychiatry, and education, including Diane Ravitch, former U.S. assistant secretary of education; Marilyn Benoit, president-elect of the American Academy of Child and Adolescent Psychiatry; and primate researcher Jane Goodall. "Fool's Gold" charged that thirty years of research on educational technology had produced just one clear link between computers and children's learning. (On some standardized tests, "drill-and-practice programs appear to improve scores modestly—though not as much or as cheaply as one-on-one tutoring.") The co-signers of the "Fool's Gold" report went so far as to call for a moratorium on computer use in early childhood education, until the U.S. surgeon general can ascertain whether computers are hazardous to the health of young children. The public response was surprising. After "Fool's Gold" was released, MSNBC conducted an online poll of subscribers, asking if they supported such a moratorium. Of three thousand people who answered, 51 percent agreed. And these were Internet users.

The problem with computers isn't computers—they're just tools; the problem is that overdependence on them displaces other sources of education, from the arts to nature. As we pour money and attention into educational electronics, we allow less fashionable but more effective tools to atrophy. Here's one example: We know for a fact that the arts stimulate learning. A 1995 analysis by the College Board showed that students who studied the arts for more than four years scored forty-four points higher on the math portion and fifty-nine points higher on the verbal section of the SAT. Nonetheless, over the past decade, one-third of the nation's public-school music programs were dropped. During the same period, annual spending on school technology tripled, to $6.2 billion. Between early 1999 and September 2001, educational technology attracted nearly $1 billion in venture capital, according to Merrill Lynch and Company. One software company now targets babies as young as one day old. Meanwhile, many public school districts continue to shortchange the arts, and even more districts fail to offer anything approaching true hands-on experience with nature outside the classroom.

In some school districts, the arts are making a tentative comeback. The same cannot be said of hands-on nature education—yet. In recent years, farsighted educators and environmental organizations have made important inroads into the classroom and the public consciousness of the young, especially at the primary and secondary levels. Experiential, environment-based, or place-based education offers a promising alternative. Proponents of the arts revival in schools have successfully argued that the arts stimulate learning in math and science. Based on early research, a similar argument could now be made that nature education stimulates cognitive learning and reduces attention deficits.

Nonetheless, the school district in my own county—the sixth-largest district in America—illustrates the lack of synchronicity. San Diego County, larger in size and population than some states, is an ecological and sociological microcosm of America. It is, in fact, a place with more endangered and threatened species than any other county in the continental United States. The United Nations declared it one of the Earth's twenty-five "hot spots" of biodiversity. Yet, as of this writing, not one of the forty-three school districts within this county offers a single elective course in local flora and fauna. A few volunteers, including docents from the local Natural History Museum, do what they can. Across the nation, such neglect is the norm.

The Death of Natural History

Though current waves of school reform are less than nature-friendly, individual teachers—with help from parents, natural history museum docents, and other volunteers—can do much to improve the situation without organized, official sanction. To be truly effective, however, we must go beyond the dedication of individual teachers and volunteers, to question the assumptions and context of the nature–student gap. We should do everything we can to encourage the incipient movement of what is sometimes called "experiential education." We should also challenge some of the driving forces behind our current approach to nature, including a loss of respect for nature and the death of natural history in higher education.

A few years ago, I sat in the cluttered office of Robert Stebbins, professor emeritus at the Museum of Vertebrate Zoology at the University of California, Berkeley. He grew up ranging through California's Santa Monica Mountains, where he learned to cup his hands around his mouth and "call in the owls." For him, nature was still magical. For more than twenty years, Stebbins's reference work, *A Field Guide to Western Reptiles and Amphibians*, which he wrote and illustrated, has remained the undisputed bible of herpetology, and inspired countless youngsters to chase snakes. To Stebbins, our relationship with nature has been undermined by a shift in values.

For a decade, he and his students drove to the California desert to record animal tracks in areas frequented by all-terrain vehicles, or ATVs; Stebbins discovered that 90 percent of invertebrate animal life—insects, spiders, and other arthropods—had been destroyed in the ATV-scarred desert areas. While I spoke with him, he dropped scores of slides into an old viewer. "Look," he said. "Ten years of before-and-after photos." Grooves and slashes, tracks that will remain for centuries. Desert crust ripped up by rubber treads, great clouds of dirt rising high into the atmosphere; a gunshot desert tortoise, with a single tire track cracking its back; aerial photographs taken near Blythe, California, of ancient and mysterious Indian intaglios, carved images so large that they can only be perceived from the air. Across the flanks and back and head of a deer-like intaglio were claw marks left by ATVs. "If only these people knew what they were doing," said Stebbins.

What upset him most was not the destruction that had already occurred, but the devastation yet to come and the waning sense of awe—or simple respect—toward nature that he sensed in each successive generation. "One time, I was out watching the ATVs. I saw these two little boys trudging up a dune. I went running after them. I wanted to ask them why they weren't riding machines—maybe they were looking for something else out there. They said their trail bikes were broken. I asked them if they knew what was out there in the desert, if they'd seen any lizards. 'Yeah,' one of them said, 'But lizards just run away.' These kids were bored, uninterested. If only they knew."

Even among children who participate in nature activities, a conservation ethic is not assured. In a classroom in Alpine, California, I visited elementary-school pupils who reported spending far more time outside than I had heard reported in most settings across the country. Some of the students in this science class had watched bobcats play on the ridges; one boy had watched a mountain lion thread its way across his parents' acreage. Many of these young people were growing up in this far exurb in the mountains because their parents wanted them to be exposed to more nature. One boy said, "My mom didn't like the city because there was hardly any nature, so mom and dad decided to move here to Alpine. We live in an apartment. My grandma lives even farther out and she has huge property—most of it is grass, but part of it is just trees. I like to go there, because she has a baby mountain lion that comes down into her yard. When I was there on Sunday, we were going out to feed the goats and we saw a bobcat trying to catch birds. It's really cool."

I was glad to find a group of kids who seemed to enjoy nature as much as I had, but as they spoke, it became clear that, for nearly half of them, their favorite interaction with nature was vehicular, on small four-wheel ATVs, or "quads." "My dad and me ride in the desert and most of the time we don't follow the tracks. My dad races off-road cars. He says it's cool to go out there even if you're on a track because you can still see animals—and also it's fun to race." Another boy: "Every August we go to Utah, and my mom's friend up there has three quads; we ride for the fun of it but mostly to see animals like deer and skunk at night, and if you leave fish guts and go out at night you'll see, like, five black bears come out. It's cool." A third boy: "We go to the desert every weekend and they have races, there's one hill that nobody rides on because it's rocky, so we changed it so you go up, then jump off these cliffs; and up there we'll see snake holes and snakes. On hot days we go out and hunt for lizards." And a girl, displaying no sense of irony, added: "My dad had a four-wheel-drive truck and we go out in the desert, not out in nature or anything."

After the bell rang and the students left, Jane Smith, a teacher at the school for five years, and a social worker before that, raised her hands in exasperation. "It always amazes me. Most of these students don't make the connection that there's a conflict between ATVs and the land. Even after this project we did a week on energy conservation, and they didn't get it. Just didn't see it—and they still don't. Every weekend, Alpine empties out. Families head for the desert and the dunes. And that's the way it is."

Some of these young people, and their parents, are more likely to know the brand names of ATVs than the lizards, snakes, hawks, and cacti of the desert. As my friend, biologist Elaine Brooks, has said, "humans seldom value what they cannot name." Or experience. What if, instead of sailing to the Galápagos Islands and getting his hands dirty and his feet wet, Charles Darwin had spent his days cooped up in some office cubicle staring at a computer screen? What if a tree fell in the forest and no one knew its biological name? Did it exist?

"Reality is the final authority; reality is what's going on out there, not what's in your mind or on your computer screen," says Paul Dayton, who has been seething for years about the largely undocumented sea change in how science—specifically higher education—perceives and depicts nature. That change will shape—or distort—the perception of nature, and reality, for generations to come. Dayton is a professor of oceanography at Scripps Institution of Oceanography in La Jolla. He enjoys a worldwide reputation as a marine ecologist and is known for his seminal ecological studies, which he began in the 1960s, of the benthic (sea bottom) communities in the Antarctic. Two years ago, the Ecological Society of America honored Dayton and colleagues with the prestigious Cooper Ecology Award—marking a first for research of an oceanic system—for addressing "fundamental questions about sustainability of communities in the face of disturbance along environmental gradients." In 2004, the American Society of Naturalists presented him with the E. O. Wilson Naturalist Award.

Now, he sits in his office on a rainy spring day staring at the Pacific Ocean, dark and cold beyond the Scripps Pier. He has a terrarium in the room, where he keeps a giant centipede named Carlos, to whom Dayton feeds mice. Dayton approaches nature with a sense of awe and respect, but he doesn't romanticize it. When he was growing up in snow-clogged logging camps, the family didn't eat if his father didn't hunt. A compact, athletic man with graying hair, an infectious smile, and skin burnished by cold wind and hot sun, Dayton must sometimes feel as if he has slept through a long, hard Arctic night, and awakened in a foreign future in which nothing is named and nature is sold in stores or deconstructed into pure math. He tells me that most of his elite graduate students in marine ecology exhibit "no evidence of training in any type of natural history." Few upper-division ecology majors or undergraduates in marine ecology "know even major phyla such as arthropods or annelids."

Sitting a few feet away from him (and farther from Carlos), Bonnie Becker, a National Park Service marine biologist at Cabrillo National Monument, says Dayton's view is accurate. Recently, she realized that—despite her prior training—she could identify few of the more than one thousand marine invertebrate species that live off Point Loma. So she set up an informal tutoring group, mostly students teaching other students. "Word has gotten out," she says. "You know, have a beer and teach me everything you know about limpets." The people who name the animals, or even know the names, are fast becoming extinct. In San Diego and Orange counties, no more than a half-dozen people can come close to naming a significant number of marine invertebrates, and these are mainly museum workers and docents, and a few local government workers who monitor wastewater treatment and sewage outfalls. These people have few opportunities to pass on their knowledge to a new generation. "In a few years there will be nobody left to identify several major groups of marine organisms," Dayton says. "I wish I were exaggerating."

What we can't name can hurt us. "A guy in Catalina sent me photos of a snail he found," Dayton says. "The snail is moving north. It's not supposed to be where the guy found it. Something is going on with this snail or with its environment." Global warming? Maybe. "But if you don't know it's an invasive species, then you detect no change." It's easy enough to blame the public schools for a pervading ignorance, but Dayton places much of the responsibility on the dominance of molecular biology in higher education. Not that he has anything against molecular biology, and not that he doesn't encounter professors who buck the trend. But, he says, the explicit goal of the new philosophy of modern university science education is to get the "ologies"—invertebrate zoology, ichthyology, mammalogy, ornithology, and herpetology—"back in the nineteenth century where they belong." Shortly after I spoke with Paul Dayton at his Scripps office, he presented a paper, now in high demand as a reprint, at the American Society of Naturalists Symposium. In it he underscores the greater threat:

> The last century has seen enormous environmental degradation: many populations are in drastic decline, and their ecosystems have

been vastly altered. . . . These environmental crises coincide with the virtual banishment of natural sciences in academe, which eliminate the opportunity for both young scientists and the general public to learn the fundamentals that help us predict population levels and the responses by complex systems to environmental variation. . . . The groups working on molecular biology and theoretical ecology have been highly successful within their own circles and have branched into many specialties. These specialists have produced many break-throughs important to those respective fields. However . . . this re-ductionist approach has contributed rather little toward actual solutions for the increasingly severe global realities of declining pop-ulations, extinctions, or habitat loss . . . We must reinstate natural sci-ence courses in all our academic institutions to insure that students experience nature first-hand and are instructed in the fundamentals of the natural sciences.

What specifically, I asked Dayton, can be done to improve the situ-ation? His answer was not hopeful. "Not only is there a huge elitist prejudice against natural history and for microbiology, [but] simple eco-nomics almost rule out a change, because good natural history classes must be small." Nonetheless, he hopes that greater public knowledge about the generational nature deficit will encourage politicians to "start demanding that universities teach the fundamentals of biology and ex-plicitly define these fundamentals to include real natural history."

Unfortunately, finding anybody with enough natural history knowl-edge to teach such classes will be difficult. Dayton suggests that higher education "offer the courses and hire young professors eager to do the right thing" and organize the older naturalists, fading in number, to mentor the young students "never offered the opportunity to learn any natural history." At least one organization, the Western Society of Nat-uralists, has stepped to the plate with support for the training of young naturalists. If education and other forces, intentionally or unintention-ally, continue to push the young away from direct experience in nature, the cost to science itself will be high. Most scientists today began their careers as children, chasing bugs and snakes, collecting spiders, and feeling awe in the presence of nature. Since such untidy activities are fast disappearing, how, then, will our future scientists learn about nature?

"I fear that they will not," says Dayton, staring out at that lost horizon. "Nobody even knows that this wisdom about our world has been driven from our students."

RASHEED SALAHUDDIN, a high school principal who heads my local school district's one-week outdoor-education program, sees the corrosive effect of nature-fear. "Too many kids are associating nature with fear and catastrophe, and not having direct contact with the outdoors," he says. Salahuddin brings sixth-graders to the mountains and shows them the wonder. "Some of these kids are from Eastern Europe, Africa, and the Middle East. They view the outdoors, the woods, as a dangerous place. They associate it with war, with hiding—or they view it in a solely utilitarian way, as a place to gather firewood."

Inner-city kids of all ethnic backgrounds show similar responses, he says. Some have never been to the mountains or the beach—or the zoo, even though it's within sight of their homes. Some of them spend their entire childhood inside an apartment, living in fear. They associate nature with the neighborhood park, which is controlled by gangs. "What does this say about our future?" asks Salahuddin. "Nature has been taken over by thugs who care absolutely nothing about it. We need to take nature back."

12. Where Will Future Stewards of Nature Come From?

> *[What is the] extinction of a condor to a child*
> *who has never seen a wren?*
> —NATURALIST ROBERT MICHAEL PYLE

RECENTLY, I ASKED A committed and effective environmentalist—a person active in the creation of Southern California's ocean-to-mountains San Dieguito River Park—this question: When the park is completed, and the vast stretches of land and water are preserved, how will kids play in it?

"Well, they'll go hiking with their parents . . ." He paused.

Would a kid be able to wander freely on this land, and, say, build a tree house? My friend became pensive.

"No, I don't think so—I mean, there are plenty of more constructive ways to experience nature." When asked how he first interacted with the outdoors, the environmentalist answered, sheepishly, "I built forts and tree houses."

He understands the paradox here, but does not know quite what to do about it. Many of the traditional activities in nature are destructive. To some people, building a tree house or a fort in the woods is not much different than running quads across the dunes. The difference is one of degree: one way of experiencing joy in nature excites the senses, the other way drowns the senses in noise and fumes, and leaves tracks that will last thousands of years.

Working through such distinctions is not easy, but as the care of nature increasingly becomes an intellectual concept severed from the joyful experience of the outdoors, you have to wonder: Where will future environmentalists come from?

If environmental groups, along with Scouting and other traditional outdoors-oriented organizations, wish to pass on the heritage of their movement, and the ongoing care of the earth, they cannot ignore children's need to explore, to get their hands dirty and their feet wet. And they must help reduce the fear that increasingly separates children from nature.

Until recently, most environmental organizations offered only token attention to children. Perhaps their lack of zeal stems from an unconscious ambivalence about children, who symbolize or represent overpopulation. So goes the unspoken mantra: We have met the enemy and it is our progeny. As Theodore Roszak, author of *The Voice of the Earth*, has said: "Environmentalists, by and large, are very deeply invested in tactics that have worked to their satisfaction over the last thirty years, namely scaring and shaming people. . . . I am questioning whether you can go on doing that indefinitely . . . [pushing] that same fear-guilt button over and over again. As psychologists will tell you, when a client comes in with an addiction, they are already ashamed. You don't shame them further."

That environmentalists need the goodwill of children would seem self-evident—but more often than not, children are viewed as props or extraneous to the serious adult work of saving the world. One often overlooked value of children is that they constitute the future political constituency, and their attention or vote—which is ultimately based more on a foundation of personal experience than rational decision-making—is not guaranteed.

Take, as just one example, our national parks.

Welcome to Matrix National Park

To a new generation, the idea of camping at Yosemite is a quaint notion and brings to mind those ancient reruns of Lucy, Desi, Fred, and

Ethel banging around in their Airstream trailer. Some of the largest parks are reporting a peculiar drop-off in attendance over the past few years—a trend that predates the 9/11 terrorist attacks in New York and Washington, D.C. Such a decrease would seem to be good news for overcrowded parks choking on exhaust fumes. But there's a hidden, long-term danger.

First, the numbers. Overall visits to the national park system have remained roughly level over the past decade, but a closer look at the statistics shows that attendance at Eastern urban parks and historical sites has grown, while attendance at the West's major parks has fallen. "Statisticians predict further declines in the next two years," according to *Oregonian* reporter Michael Milstein, in an incisive article about the trend. Indeed, some of the numbers are dramatic. Yosemite National Park attendance has fallen 16 percent since 1996. The number of visitors topped out at the Grand Canyon in 1991, Yellowstone in 1992, and Oregon's Crater Lake National Park in 1995. Mount Rainier National Park attendance dropped from 1.6 million visitors in 1991 to 1.3 million in 2002. Since the late 1980s, the number of Carlsbad Caverns National Park visitors plummeted by nearly half since the late 1980s.

The most important reason for the decline, I believe, is the break between the young and nature—the transition from real-world experience to virtual nature. But a Northern Arizona University study of the nation's parks names two central barriers: shortage of family time and a widely held perception that parks are for viewing scenery, period. Other reasons include shorter vacations; the shrinking American road trip (from 3.5 to 2.5 days); the growth of immigrant groups, particularly in California, with no prior experience with wilderness parks; increased entrance fees, as of this writing as high as twenty dollars per car; and a perception that national parks are for the affluent (a Portland survey of California park visitors showed that more than two-thirds of visitors have incomes of at least fifty thousand dollars a year). What park officials call "windshield tours" are replacing camping. In 2001, the number of visitors who camped in national parks dropped by nearly a third, to its lowest point in a quarter century. The drop-off in camping is especially evident among people younger than thirty, possibly because no one took them camping when they were kids. Consequently, they're not taking their own kids camping. One California survey, cited by Milstein, found that more than eight of ten campers became interested in the outdoors when they were children—but more than half of the camping parties surveyed had no children with them.

But *are* parks for kids anymore? For the *Matrix* generation, much of the natural mystery and risk of the outdoors has been surgically removed. As park officials work to make parks safer and more accessible, the outdoors often ends up feeling more like Disneyland than wilderness. Some kids end up disappointed that the parks aren't *more* Disneyesque. When middle school students sent me their reflections on nature, one boy reported visiting Utah's Rainbow Bridge National Monument, the world's largest natural bridge, which was carved out of the cliffs above modern-day Lake Powell over thousands of years. "The bridge was somewhat disappointing. It was not as perfect as in the brochure," the boy wrote. His parents enhanced the family vacation by renting Jet Skis.

Here's the hidden danger. If park and forest attendance stagnates as the visitor age rises, what happens to the future political constituency for parks and national forests? Not much, if visitor drop were the only change at hand. But that phenomenon appears to be occurring at the exact moment when development and energy interests are rapidly ratcheting up their pressure on the natural environment.

The political wind is currently in their favor. For example, the U.S. Forest Service, currently conducting an update of its fifteen-year plan for Southern California's Cleveland National Forest, is considering several radical proposals for the northern third of the forest. These include the damming of a canyon to create a 100-acre reservoir; two high voltage transmission lines, 28.5 miles and 31 miles long; and a new highway that would open a transportation corridor between Riverside County and Orange County through the national forest.

Theodore Roosevelt created Cleveland National Forest in 1908; since then, the forest has shrunk from 2 million acres to 427,000 fragmented acres. If the proportion of people with hands-on emotional attachment to such endangered places also shrinks, how much forest and parkland will remain in, say, 2108, when our vastly expanded population will likely be desperate for a little breathing room?

The Endangered Environmentalist

The broader issue involves the future of the stewardship ethic, in particular the shrinking genetic pool of environmentalists, conservationists, and other stewards.

In 1978, Thomas Tanner, professor of environmental studies at Iowa State University, conducted a study of environmentalists' formative influences. He probed what it was in their lives that had steered them to environmental activism. He polled staff members and chapter officers of major environmental organizations. "Far and away the most frequently cited influence was childhood experience of natural, rural, or other relatively pristine habitats," according to Tanner. For most of these people, the natural habitats were accessible for unstructured play and discovery nearly every day when they were kids. "Several studies since mine have supported my findings," he said. Studies of environmental activists in locales as diverse as Kentucky and Norway indicate that childhood experiences are significant precursors for adult activism on behalf of the environment. "But for some reason, you don't hear many environmentalists expressing much concern about the intimacy factor between kids and nature."

In other surveys of environmental leaders, according to environmental psychologist Louise Chawla, most "attributed their commitment to a combination of two sources: many hours spent outdoors in a keenly remembered wild or semi-wild place in childhood or adolescence, and an adult who taught respect for nature." The childhoods of environmentalists and naturalists are replete with stories of their childhood inspiration, leading directly to their later activism. E. O. Wilson, the father of biophilia, addressed this in his memoir, *Naturalist*: "Most children have a bug period, and I never outgrew mine. Hands-on experience at the critical time, not systematic knowledge, is what counts in the making of a naturalist. Better to be an untutored savage for a while, not to know the names or anatomical detail. Better to spend long stretches of time just searching and dreaming."

Edmund Morris's description of the boyhood years of the presidential patron of conservation, Theodore Roosevelt, suggests a similar genesis:

> the bookish "Teedie" became aware of the "enthralling pleasures" of building wigwams in the woods, gathering hickory nuts and apples, hunting frogs, haying and harvesting, and scampering barefoot down long, leafy lanes. . . . Even in these early years, his knowledge of natural history was abnormal. No doubt much of it was acquired during his winters [reading] . . . but it was supplemented, every summer, by long hours of observation of the flora and fauna around him.
>
> . . . Teedie's interest in all "curiosities and living things" became something of a trial to his elders. Meeting Mrs. Hamilton Fish on a streetcar, he absentmindedly lifted his hat, whereupon several frogs leaped out of it, to the dismay of fellow passengers. . . . A protest by a chambermaid forced Teedie to move the Roosevelt Museum of Natural History out of his bedroom and into the back hall upstairs. "How can I do the laundry," complained the washerwoman, "with a snapping turtle tied to the legs of the sink?"

We may owe Yosemite to that turtle. Like Roosevelt, writer Wallace Stegner filled his childhood with collected critters, often with no thought to the welfare of the species; such were the times. In his essay, "Finding the Place: A Migrant Childhood," he described the prairie town in Saskatchewan that was his home in his early years. His pets or temporary boarders included burrowing owls, magpies, and a black-footed ferret. He spent many of his young days "trapping, shooting, snaring, poisoning, or drowning out the gophers that gathered in our wheat field. . . . Nobody could have been more brainlessly and immorally destructive. And yet there was love there, too."

In some ways, environmental organizations face the same force of attrition that newspapers now encounter with the aging of their readerships. On average, American newspaper subscribers are in their early and mid-fifties, and climbing, as subscription rates fall. The Sierra Club members' average age is now pushing fifty, and climbing. In a country whose young are more culturally and ethnically diverse than ever (and nature is valued in radically different ways and degrees among some of these cultures), environmentalists look increasingly old and white. All the more reason for environmental and conservation groups to triple their efforts to reach the young—a topic to be addressed in a later chapter. The immediate challenge, however, is for such organizations to ask themselves if their policies, and cultural attitudes, are subtly adding to the separation.

Other organizations, ones that have traditionally linked children to nature, must ask the same question.

Scouting the Future

Madhu Narayan was three months old when her parents, recent immigrants from India, took her camping for the first time. A few years later, they drove across the West, camping as they went. Narayan figures her parents didn't have a lot of money, and camping was an inexpensive way to see their nation of choice. "We moved through days of beautiful weather, and then the rains came," she says. During a lightning storm, the wind blew away the family's tent, and they slept in the car listening to the banshees of wind and rain howl and crash through the woods. Even now, at thirty, Narayan shivers as she tells this story.

She was shaped by such elemental experiences and the mystery that rode with them. Today, as the outdoor education manager for a sprawl-ing Girl Scouts region—covering the California counties of Imperial and San Diego—she wants to offer natural experiences to girls. But there's a problem. The traditional perception of Scouting—for girls or boys—is that nature is the star of the show, the organizing principle, the *raison d'être*; but the raison is shrinking.

At Scout headquarters at San Diego's Camp Balboa, an urban camp-ground created in 1916, Narayan and Karyl T. O'Brien, associate ex-ecutive director of the regional Girl Scouts Council, spread out a stack of literature to describe the rich programs they provide to more than thirty thousand girls. Impressive, but over the past three years, mem-bership in the region has remained flat, even as the population has grown precipitously. This region's council markets itself aggressively. It offers such programs as an overnighter with the city's natural history museum, a daylong junior naturalist program, and popular summer-camp expe-riences. But the overwhelming majority of Girl Scout programs are un-concerned with nature. Included (along with selling cookies) are such offerings as Teaching Tolerance, Tobacco Prevention, Golf Clinic, Self-Improvement, Science Festival, EZ Defense, and Financial Literacy. Soon, Camp CEO will bring businesswomen to a natural setting to mentor girls in job interviewing, product development, and marketing.

The divide between past and future is seen best at the Girl Scout camps in mountains east of the city: one is billed as traditional, with open-air cabins and tents hidden in the trees; the newer camp looks like a little suburbia with street lights. "I flipped when I learned that girls weren't allowed to climb trees at our camps," says O'Brien. Liability is an increasing concern. "When I was a kid, you fell down, you got up, so what; you learned to deal with consequences. I broke this arm twice," says Narayan. "Today, if a parent sends a kid to you without a scratch, they better come back that way. That's the expectation. And as some-one responsible for people, I have to respect that."

Scouting organizations must also respect, or endure, outrageous in-creases in the cost of liability insurance. This is not only an American phenomenon; in 2002, Australia's Scouting organizations Girl Guides and Scouts Australia reported increases of as much as 500 percent in a single year, leading the executive director of Scouts Australia to warn that Scouting could be "unviable" if insurance premiums continued to rise.

Considering the mounting social and legal pressures, Scouting organizations deserve praise for maintaining any link to nature. Narayan pointed out that most of the two thousand girls who attend summer camps are touched by nature, even if indirectly. "But we now feel compelled to put tech labs in camps or computers in a nature center, because that's what people are used to," says O'Brien. Scouting is responding to the same pressures experienced by public schools: as family time and free time have diminished, Americans expect these institutions to do more of society's heavy lifting—more of its social, moral, and political juggling. Ask any Boy Scout how difficult that act can be.

Justly or not, the public image of the Boy Scouts of America has shifted from that of clean-cut boys tying knots and pitching tents to one of adult leaders who ban gays and expel atheists. Like the Girl Scouts, the Boy Scouts struggle to be up-to-date—and marketable. At the new National Scouting Museum in Irving, Texas, displays use virtual-reality technology to allow visitors to climb a mountain, kayak down a river, and conduct simulated rescues on mountain bikes. People for the Ethical Treatment of Animals (PETA) activists launched a campaign to convince the Boy Scouts to drop their fishing merit badge. In 2001, the *Dallas Morning News* reported that some Boy Scout councils across the country were selling off wilderness camps to pay their bills.

For the Boy Scouts and the Girl Scouts, it's not easy being green.

Today's parents push such organizations toward ever safer, more technological activities. Scouting struggles to remain relevant, to be a one-stop shop, to offer something for just about everyone. That may be a good marketing policy. Or not. (An astute book editor once told me: "A book written for everyone is a book for no one.") As the scope of Scouting has widened, the focus on nature has narrowed. But a slim minority of parents and Scout leaders is beginning to argue for a back-to-nature movement. "They're usually the older adults," says O'Brien, "the ones who can remember a different time." Could this set of adults offer a targeted marketing opportunity to future capital campaigns? Rather than accept nature's slide, or suggest that non-nature programs be dropped to make way for the outdoors, why not ask these adults to build a whole new nature wing to Scouting? Interesting possibility, said O'Brien. In fact, it makes sense not only as a marketing tool—define your niche and claim it—but also as a mission.

Scout leaders emphasize that Scouting is an educational program that teaches young people about building character, faith traditions, mentoring, serving others, healthy living, and lifelong learning. Boy Scouts founder Lord Baden-Powell surely sensed that exposure to nature nurtures children's character and health. The best way to advance those educational goals (and, in a marketing sense, revive Scouting) is a return to the core orientation to nature—an approach that many parents and Scout leaders support.

Narayan is one of them. "In my first counseling job, with another organization, I took children with AIDS to the mountains who had never been out of their urban neighborhoods," she says. "One night, a nine-year-old woke me up. She had to go to the bathroom. We stepped outside the tent and she looked up. She gasped and grabbed my leg. She had never seen the stars before. "That night, I saw the power of nature on a child. She was a changed person. From that moment on, she saw everything, the camouflaged lizard that everyone else skipped by. She used her senses. She was *awake*."

An Attachment Theory

The protection of nature depends on more than the organizational strength of stewardship organizations; it also depends on the quality of the relationship between the young and nature—on how, or if, the young attach to nature.

I often wonder: What am I attached to here in Southern California, other than good friends, good work, and the weather? Certainly what attaches me is not the man-made environment, or most of it, a landscape sliced and diced beyond recognition. I do love the parks and older neighborhoods of my city, particularly on those mornings when the fog softens their edges. And I love the beaches. The Pacific Ocean, resisting change, remains the last wilderness for surfing Southern Californians. It is dependable, always there, but at the same time offering mystery and danger—and some of its creatures are larger than human size or ken. I do not surf, but I understand the attachment surfers feel toward the ocean, and once this attachment is made, it is never lost.

When I drive east into the mountains, through Mesa Grande and Santa Ysabel and Julian, I know that these places have entered my heart. They have a mystery distinct from anywhere on Earth. But then always, always, a voice in me says: don't get too attached. Because of urban/suburban sprawl, I have the sense that the fields and streams and mountains that I love here could be gone the next time I drive to the country, and so I cannot entirely commit to them. I wonder about children who cither are never attached to nature, or learn to mistrust that attachment early. Do they exhibit similar characteristics or responses?

Surely children need a quality attachment to land not only for their own health, but in order to feel compelled to protect nature as adults—not only as common-sense conservationists, but as citizens and as voters.

For twenty-five years, psychologist Martha Farrell Erickson and her colleagues have used what they call "attachment theory," an ecological model of child development, as the framework for their ongoing longitudinal study of parent-child interaction. They apply those ideas to preventive intervention with parents in high-risk circumstances. The family's health, related to the health of the surrounding community, has become a growing concern to Erickson.

"The way we usually talk about parent-child attachment is that we rarely see the absence of attachment, even when parents are unreliable, unresponsive, or erratically available. Rather, we see differences in the *quality* of attachment. For example, a child with a parent who is chronically unresponsive (let's say a depressed parent, for example) will protect himself from the pain of rejection by detaching, acting disinterested in the parent—developing what we call an anxious-avoidant attachment."

I suggested to her that some of the same responses or symptoms associated with attachment deficit occur with a poor sense of attachment to land. In my own experience, the rate of development in my part of the country is so fast that attachment to place is difficult; to many of us who came here decades ago (in my case from Kansas), Southern California captures the body, but not the heart. In the world of child development, attachment theory posits that the creation of a deep bond between child and parent is a complex psychological, biological, and spiritual process, and that without this attachment a child is lost, vulnerable to all manner of later pathologies. I believe that a similar process can bind adults to a place and give them a sense of belonging and meaning. Without a deep attachment to place, an adult can also feel lost.

"It's an intriguing idea to approach a child's relationship with nature from the perspective of attachment theory," Erickson said. She continued:

> Children's experience with the natural world seems to be overlooked to a large extent in research on child development, but it would be interesting to examine children's early experiences with nature and follow how those experiences influence the child's long-term comfort with and respect for the natural world—comfort and respect being concepts that are central to the study of parent–child attachment. Given the power of nature to calm and soothe us in our hurried lives, it also would be interesting to study how a family's connection to nature influences the general quality of family relationships. Speaking from personal experience, my own family's relationships have been nourished over the years through shared experiences in nature—from

sharing our toddler's wonder upon turning over a rock and discovering a magnificent bug the size of a mouse, to paddling our old canoe down a nearby creek during the children's school years, to hiking the mountains.

ATTACHMENT TO LAND is not only good for the child, but good for the land as well. As naturalist Robert Finch asserts: "There is a point . . . in our relationship with a place, when, in spite of ourselves, we realize we do not care so much anymore, when we begin to be convinced, against our very wills, that our neighborhood, our town, or the land as a whole is already lost." At this point, he argues, the local landscape is no longer perceived as "a living, breathing, beautiful counterpart to human existence, but something that has suffered irreversible brain death. It may still be kept technically alive—with sewage treatment plants, 'compensatory' wetlands, shellfish reseeding programs, lime treatments for acidified ponds, herbicides for . . . ponds, beach nourishment programs, fenced-off bird sanctuaries, and designated 'green areas'—but it no longer moves, or if it does, it is not with a will of its own."

If a geographic place rapidly changes in a way that demeans its natural integrity, then children's early attachment to land is at risk. If children do not attach to the land, they will not reap the psychological and spiritual benefits they can glean from nature, nor will they feel a long-term commitment to the environment, to the place. This lack of attachment will exacerbate the very conditions that created the sense of disengagement in the first place—fueling a tragic spiral, in which our children and the natural world are increasingly detached.

I am not suggesting the situation is hopeless. Far from it. Conservation and environmental groups and, in some cases, the traditional Scouting organizations are beginning to awaken to the threat to nature posed by nature-deficit disorder. A few of these organizations, as we will see, are helping to lead the way toward a nature-child reunion. They recognize that while knowledge about nature is vital, passion is the long-distance fuel for the struggle to save what is left of our natural heritage and—through an emerging green urbanism—to reconstitute lost land and water. Passion does not arrive on videotape or on a CD; passion is personal. Passion is lifted from the earth itself by the muddy hands of the young; it travels along grass-stained sleeves to the heart. If we are going to save environmentalism and the environment, we must also save an endangered indicator species: the child in nature.

PART IV

THE NATURE-CHILD REUNION

I am well again, I came to life

in the cool winds and crystal waters of the mountains. . . .

—JOHN MUIR

Each new year is a surprise to us.

We find that we had virtually forgotten the note of each bird,

and when we hear it again, it is remembered like a dream,

reminding us of a previous state of existence . . .

The voice of nature is always encouraging.

—HENRY DAVID THOREAU

13. Bringing Nature Home

It is not half so important to know as to feel when introducing a young child to the natural world.

—RACHEL CARSON

ALONE, PARENTS CANNOT heal the broken bond. But each guardian, parent, or other family member can lead the way at home, and within the institutions to which they belong. Educators, city planners, youth nature-program leaders, environmentalists—all of these people will determine the direction of the third frontier, and guide it either toward the end of natural experience, or toward its rebirth in new forms. Parents can encourage institutions to change, but cannot wait for them.

Parents already feel besieged by the difficulty of balancing work and family life. Understandably, they may resist the idea of adding any to-dos to their long list of chores. So here is another way of viewing the challenge: Nature as antidote. Stress reduction, greater physical health, a deeper sense of spirit, more creativity, a sense of play, even a safer life—these are the rewards that await a family when it invites more nature into children's lives.

The Gift of Enthusiasm

A few years ago, Jerry Schad invited me and my sons, then five and eleven, to accompany him and his four-year-old son on a hike along Cottonwood Creek in the mountains east of San Diego. We parked along Sunrise Highway and slipped down a rough path toward a valley far below. The path was a tunnel through chaparral, scrub oak, and manzanita, widened and deepened by countless hikers who have found Cottonwood Creek Falls—named by Schad—primarily because they have read his *Afoot and Afield* guidebooks.

But before I take you on this hike, let me say something about the pressures that parents endure. Simply put, many of us must overcome the belief that something isn't worth doing with our kids unless we do it right. If getting our kids out into nature is a search for perfection, or is one more chore, then the belief in perfection and the chore defeats the joy. It's a good thing to learn more about nature in order to share this knowledge with children; it's even better if the adult and child learn about nature together. And it's a lot more fun.

As we wound our way down the trail, Jason, my older son, held his brother Matthew's hand on the rougher spots while Schad's son, Tom, rushed ahead. Schad told how he grew up in the Santa Clara Valley, now better known as Silicon Valley. He never went camping as a kid. When he was twelve, however, he began sleeping in the backyard during the summers and became fascinated with the night sky, which ultimately led to his career teaching astronomy. As an adult, he favors sleeping on a simple pad beneath the stars in the wilderness.

He spoke with awe about the mysteries of the lost corners of the county, and especially of the night sky. For example, the strange shadows that Venus can cast along the desert floor. Being at a particularly scatological age, the younger boys, Tom and Matthew, were more interested in coyote poop than Venusian shadows. They poked at it and offered an assortment of names for it. Matthew wanted to know why we didn't see any large animals.

"Because they have super powers," I explained.

He stopped in his tracks.

"They can hear and smell us from far away," I added. He was impressed by this, but only briefly. So many rocks to collect; so little time.

The two young boys, competing to be leader of the hike, rushed onward. Small children are not like adults: Schad and I, who had just met,
were overly polite; Matthew and Tom were immediately familiar, trading intimacies and insults as if they had known each other for twenty
years.

"I want to go bushwhacking here!" Tom announced. He disappeared
for a moment into the bushes. "Look out for snakes," he called. "One
could pop his head up any time." Over the years, Tom's father has
sighted two hundred Bighorn sheep, one mountain lion, and a lot of
rattlers. April, Jerry advises, is the month one should be most careful
about snakes. He avoids going off trails or bushwhacking—carving
your own trail through the brush—during that month. Snakes wake
hungry from hibernation then, and are likely to be aggressive.

"Usually, I take Tom on hikes closer to home, but I like bringing him
out here, too," said Schad. "He's able to test himself, to explore and take
some risks. It's important for him to learn good judgment about hiking."

His advice to parents: take your children on easier, shorter hikes,
close to urban areas, because small children tend to get bored long before they grow weary.

Matthew was the first one to hear the falls.

We came to the end of the path at a grove of oaks where Cottonwood
Creek rushes down through the gap. We walked along the creek to the
first of several falls and deep pools that are fed by snowmelt and runoff
from the recent rains. As the boys clambered up the boulders and ran
along the ledges, Schad and I called to them to slow down to look. "See
the darkness?" Schad said to Tom, pointing to stripes of slime that
trailed down a rock face into a deep pool. "Don't step on those; they're
very slick and you'll slip into the water."

The boys skittered like lizards up the rocks. Watching them, Schad
admitted to a vicarious thrill: "When I take Tom with me, I see all of
this freshly, through his eyes." We sat for a while on a boulder overlooking a deep pool; the small boys used the boulder as a slide. At the

precipice, Schad and Jason and I used our bodies to block their descent. After a while, we tired of this and herded Matthew and Tom back up the path, our pockets heavy with rocks Matthew had picked up along the way and insisted we carry.

Tom, once again, took the lead.

His father is proud of his son's energy and surefootedness: "Tom can make it all the way to the top of Cowles Mountain without stopping. We hiked up there the other day and then we came home and Tom was so energized by the hike that he ran around the house nonstop for an hour." Schad smiled. "I wonder what I have created."

WHAT IMPRESSED ME most about Jerry Schad was not his formidable knowledge but his infectious enthusiasm. If such joy is dormant, we must reawaken it. This is not an easy task for parents who previously missed the chance to connect with the outdoors. But that opportunity is still available, and I believe most parents will do this—when they fully understand that nature is not just nice-to-have but a must for healthy childhood development. "If a child is to keep alive his inborn sense of wonder," wrote Rachel Carson, he or she "needs the companionship of at least one adult who can share it, rediscovering with him the joy, excitement, and mystery of the world we live in."

The main thing is to find or rediscover our own sense of joy, excitement, and mystery. André Malraux, the French minister of culture after World War II, once wrote (quoting a priest), "There's no such thing as a grown up person." Certainly it's never too late to rediscover the awe of a child. The most effective way to connect our children to nature is to connect ourselves to nature. If mothers, fathers, grandparents, or guardians already spend time outdoors, they can spend more; they can become birders, anglers, hikers, or gardeners. If children sense genuine adult enthusiasm, they'll want to emulate that interest—even if, when they're teenagers, they pretend to lose it.

Reading about nature with a child is another way, as an adult, to revive a sense of natural wonder. Reading is, of course, a form of indirect experience, but unlike television, reading does not swallow the senses or dictate thought. Reading stimulates the ecology of the imagination. Can you remember the wonder you felt when first reading *The Jungle Book* or *Tom Sawyer* or *Huckleberry Finn*? Kipling's world within a world; Twain's slow river, the feel of freedom and sand on the secret island, and in the depths of the cave? As Louise Chawla points out, environmental educators and activists repeatedly mention nature books as important childhood influences.

Like many children of the 1950s, author Kathryn Kramer grew up on *The Lord of the Rings*. She spent entire summers "on an uncomfortable wicker couch in the living room of our summer place, my legs straight out like those of a stick figure drawn by someone who hasn't the skill to make knees," rereading the trilogy. "Maybe I'd glance up occasionally at the squares of sky through the windows; that seems to be all I wanted of outdoors and glorious summer weather. I had all the weather I needed in Tolkien's books." She was swept away, especially, by J. R. R. Tolkien's description of nature, and cites this wonderful passage:

> They were on an island in a sea of trees, and the horizon was veiled. On the southeastern side the ground fell very steeply, as if the slopes of the hill were continued far down under the trees, like island shores that really are the sides of a mountain rising out of deep waters. . . . In the midst of it there wound lazily a dark river of brown water, bordered with ancient willows, arched over with willows, blocked with fallen willows, and flecked with thousands of faded willow leaves. The air was thick with them, fluttering yellow from the branches; for there was a warm and gentle breeze blowing softly in the valley, and the reeds were rustling, and the willow boughs were creaking.

Page after page of Tolkien's books go on like this, using "more words in English to describe place than most of us use in a lifetime," Kramer says. Today, she reads the trilogy to her seven-year-old son, giving him the gift of this story and, through it, her enthusiasm for the natural world.

A Brief History of Boredom

Especially during summer, parents hear the moaning complaint: "I'm *borrrred.*" Boredom is fear's dull cousin. Passive, full of excuses, it can keep children from nature—or drive them to it.

In summers past (at least through the fog of memory), children were more likely to be pulled or forced out of their boredom. In the late, hot afternoon, the Mickey Mouse Club might have been enough to pull you in from outside, but most of the day's TV offered nothing except soaps and quiz games and an occasional cowboy movie—which made you want to leap up and head outside.

"Well, times have changed," says Tina Kafka, the teacher I quoted earlier. She is a mother of three. "Don't wax too nostalgic," she says. "Even if kids have all the unstructured time in the world, they're not outside playing. They're inside with their video games." She recognizes how carefully planned activities pale in comparison to more spontaneous experiences in her children's long-term memories. She wants to nurture magic in her children's lives. But she's also a realist. "Today, kids just don't go out and play and ride their bikes that much. They're more interested in electronics," Kafka explains. "I'm uncomfortable with them lolling around watching TV, but to be honest, I also get tired of feeling that I have to keep them entertained."

"The word bored isn't in my vocabulary," some of us remember our grandmothers saying. In fact, the word wasn't in anybody's vocabulary until the nineteenth century, according to Patricia Meyer Spacks, a professor of English at the University of Virginia and author of *Boredom: The Literary History of a State of Mind.* In medieval times, according to Spacks, if someone displayed the symptoms we now identify as boredom, that person was thought to be committing something called *acedia,* a "dangerous form of spiritual alienation"—a devaluing of the world and its creator. Who had time for such self-indulgence, what with plague, pestilence, and the labor of survival? Acedia—or, accidie—was considered a sin. Then came the invention of labor-saving machinery, the valuing of the individual, and the "pursuit of happiness." Forget the sin of acedia; now we could afford the emotional state of boredom. And just in time, too. Professor Spacks considers boredom a good thing, at least most of the time. "If life was never boring in pre-modern times," she writes, "neither was it interesting, thrilling or exciting, in the modern sense of these words."

At its best, boredom forces creativity. Today, kids pack the malls, pour into the video archives, and line up for the scariest, goriest summer movies they can find. Yet, they still complain, "I'm *borrrred*." Like a sugared drink on a hot day, such entertainment leaves kids thirsting for more—for faster, bigger, more violent stimuli. This insidious, new kind of boredom is one reason for the rising number of psychiatric problems among children and adolescents, according to an article in *Newsweek* by Ronald Dahl, a professor of pediatrics at the Pittsburgh Medical Center. Dahl suggests this syndrome leads to more doctors prescribing Ritalin and other "stimulants to deal with inattentiveness at school or antidepressants to help with the loss of interest and joy in their lives."

We need to draw an important distinction between a constructively bored mind and a negatively numbed mind. Constructively bored kids eventually turn to a book, or build a fort, or pull out the paints (or the computer art program) and create, or come home sweaty from a game of neighborhood basketball. There are a few things that parents and other caregivers can do to nurture constructive boredom, which can often increase children's openness to nature.

- First: A bored child often needs to spend more time with a parent or other positive adult. Indeed, complaints of boredom may be cries for a parent's attention. Parents or other adults need to be there for their kids, to limit the time they play video games or watch TV, to take them to the library or on long walks in nature, to take them fishing—to help them detach from electronics long enough for their imaginations to kick in.

- Second: Turn off the TV. Any parent who has punished a child by taking away TV privileges and then watched that child play— slowly at first, then imaginatively, freely—will recognize the connection between time, boredom, and creativity. "There's something about television—maybe that it provides so much in the way of audio and visual stimulations that children don't have to generate very much on their own," says Aletha Shuston, co-director of the Center for Research on the Influence of Television on Children at the University of Kansas.

- Third (and this advice pertains to summer programs as well as to time at home): Find a balance between adult direction and child boredom. Too much boredom can lead to trouble; too much supervision can kill constructive boredom—and the creativity that comes with it. "I structure some unstructured time for [my students], times when they can just draw or paint or read and dream, or especially to go outside, with no deadlines or commutes to lessons," says Kafka. "I realize that sounds paradoxical—structuring unstructured time, but you've got to do it."

Sympathetic employers can help. Kafka has the summers off since she works as a teacher. Other parents work at home, either with home businesses or in the traditional stay-at-home role. Today, most parents don't have that kind of flexibility, but they need more (flexible summer workplace hours, for instance) if they're going to guide their kids to use boredom wisely.

Parents can also help push for additional funding for community-based summer recreation programs. Summer camps are godsends to many working parents, especially single parents. A good summer program can literally mean survival for some children who live in rough neighborhoods. Some programs make room for dreamtime. "Adventure playgrounds" provide kids with a supervised (by an adult, at a distance) vacant lot filled with old tires, boards, tools—and places to build and dig. Supervised nature programs help children explore without excessive direction. And teen centers allow teenagers, rather than adults, to create the recreation. Such programs deserve extra support.

Most of all, children need adults who understand the relationship between boredom and creativity, adults willing to spend time in nature with kids, adults willing to set the stage so that kids can create their own play and enter nature through their own imaginations.

Backyard Nature and a Walk in the Woods

Ordinarily, the first physical entry point into nature is the backyard; next come adjacent natural areas, if we're lucky enough to live near them. Yet, many parents who live next to woods, fields, canyons, and creeks say their children never play in those areas—either because of the parents' or child's fear of strangers, or because the kids are just not interested.

Billy Campbell, a South Carolina physician and conservationist, understands that a child's interest in the frontiers around his own home is not usually accidental. He believes the biggest problems faced by children are not the absence of experiences in dramatically picturesque wilderness, but the lack of day-to-day contact with the elements. In addition to the usual barriers, Campbell believes that lack of interest in the outdoors may have something to do with the media's presentation of nature, which can be wonderfully educational, but also overwhelmingly dramatic and extreme. "So kids feel they're not getting enough action. If they don't see a grizzly bear rip apart a caribou calf, then it is boring."

Campbell grew up in the woods—playing army, catching minnows, collecting bird eggs, snakeskins, and bugs. He believes these experiences had a drama all their own and profoundly shaped who he became as an adult. Today, his family's yard joins several hundred acres of woods in a rural area, but he has not assumed that his daughter, Raven, now thirteen, would find the mystery of those woods on her own. He and his wife have consciously introduced her to that more intimate drama:

We took Raven on long hikes before she could walk. We walked to the creek or pond five days a week. We invented games where she would run ahead—we would do sign language of where to go next. She still walks through the one-hundred-year-old woods several times a week to visit her cousins (about 250 yards away). We picked up treasures and brought them home. By the time she was ten, she thought nothing about a six- to ten-mile hike with two thousand feet of climbing (as long as we had food and water—I was in deep doo-doo on one hike when I left the food at home). The point is that for Raven, it is just a part of her world. She never remembers it being some once-a-year thing. She appreciates natural beauty. It was a long time before she realized that she was a little different from her friends and family. Her cousins would whine and complain on much shorter hikes when they came with us. Woods are becoming something scary again—where human predators can snatch kids away. I know we all can't live on farms in rural areas, but we have to find ways to make nature a part of our lives.

One parent's hike is another's forced march, and the same is true for children. Parents must walk a fine line between presenting and pushing their kids to the outdoors. A trip to REI to get just the right camping equipment for a two-week vacation in Yosemite is not a prerequisite or, for that matter, any substitute for more languid natural pastimes that can be had in the backyard.

The dugout in the weeds or leaves beneath a backyard willow, the rivulet of a seasonal creek, even the ditch between a front yard and the road—all of these places are entire universes to a young child. Expeditions to the mountains or national parks often pale, in a child's eyes, in comparison with the mysteries of the ravine at the end of the cul de sac. By letting our children lead us to their own special places we can rediscover the joy and wonder of nature. By exploring those places we enter our children's world and we give these patches of nature a powerful blessing for our children. By expressing interest or even awe at the march of ants across these elfin forests, we send our children a message that will last for decades to come, perhaps even extend generation to generation. By returning to these simple yet enchanted places we see, with our child, how the seasons move and the world turns and how critter kingdoms rise and fall.

"Your job isn't to hit them with another Fine Educational Opportunity, but to turn them on to what a neat world we live in," writes Deborah Churchman in the journal *American Forests,* published by the nation's oldest nonprofit citizens' conservation organization. She recommends re-creating all the dopey, fun things you did as a kid: "Take them down to the creek to skip rocks—and then show them what was hiding under those rocks. Take a walk after the rain and count worms (they're coming up to get air, since their air holes are clogged with water). Turn on the porch light and watch the insects gather (they're nuts about ultraviolet light—for some reason scientists haven't yet figured out). Go to a field (with shoes on) and watch the bees diving into the flowers." Find a ravine, woods, a windbreak row of trees, a swamp, a pond, a vacant and overgrown lot—and go there, regularly. Churchman repeats an old Indian saying: "It's better to know one mountain than to climb many."

In *Lessons from an Urban Wildland,* Robert Michael Pyle describes his childhood haunt, a century-old irrigation channel near his home. The ditch, he writes, was his "sanctuary, playground, and sulking walk," his "imaginary wilderness, escape hatch, and birthplace as a naturalist."

Many of us can remember the small galaxies we adopted as children, the slope behind the neighborhood, the strand of trees at the end of the cul-de-sac. My first special place, like Pyle's, was a ditch, a ravine—dark with mystery, lined with grapevine swings, elms, and tangled bramble. I sat with my dog for hours at the edge of the ravine, poking the dirt, listening to unseen creatures move far below, studying ants as they marched into the abyss. To a four-year-old, such a ravine is as deep and wide and peculiar as the Grand Canyon will be to that same boy, decades later.

These are the "places of initiation, where the borders between ourselves and other creatures break down, where the earth gets under our nails and a sense of place gets under our skin," Pyle writes. These are the "secondhand lands, the hand-me-down habitats where you have to look hard to find something to love." Richard Mabey, a British writer and naturalist, calls such environments, undeveloped and unprotected, the "unofficial countryside." Such habitats are often rich with life and opportunities to learn; in a single decade, Pyle recorded some seventy kinds of butterflies along his ditch.

What if your child has yet to discover such a special place? Then form a joint expedition into the small unknowns—not a forced march, but a mutual adventure. "The kid who yawns when you say 'Let's go outside' may be intrigued enough" to follow you on a trip to gather twigs for making tea, counsels Deborah Churchman.

Encourage your child to get to know a ten-square-yard area at the edge of a field, pond, or pesticide-free garden. Look for the edges between habitats: where the trees stop and a field begins; where rocks and earth meet water. Life is always at the edges. Together, sit at the edge of a pond in August—don't move; wait; wait some more and watch the frogs reappear one at a time. Use all of your senses. Wander through an overgrown garden, a woods, a field, in October. Together, keep a journal; encourage your child to describe, in words and pictures, that tattered bumblebee staggering across autumn leaves, or the two gray squirrels rushing to gather moss and twigs for their winter nests. Ask each other: What was happening in this same spot in June? Did that bumblebee, a bumblebee-lifetime ago, bend flowers as it gathered pollen? If she wishes to, your child can draw outlines of leaves or clouds—or frogs. Later, at home, she can color the drawings and press a flower between the pages, and add details about the weather. Or, she can write a tale from the point of view of the bee: what was it thinking as it looked at you looking at him? What would its summer diary say?

Take a "moth walk," Churchman suggests. "In a blender, mix up a goopy brew of squishy fruit, stale beer or wine (or fruit juice that's been hanging around too long), and sweetener (honey, sugar, or molasses) . . . Then take a paintbrush and a child or two, and go outside at sunset. Slap some of this goo on at least a half-dozen surfaces—trees are best, but any unpainted and untreated wood will do. Come back when it's really dark, and look at what you lured. You'll usually find a few moths, along with several dozen ants, earwigs, and other insects." With help from Internet sites dedicated to birding, track bird migrations. In the winter, look for hibernating insects, galls, or the burrows of animals in or near trees. In the spring, with your child, catch tadpoles, transfer them to an aquarium, and watch them transform into frogs—then return the frogs to the wild. Visit them in August. And hunt for nests abandoned by birds in the fall, and search for the big nests that squirrels make in the fall—because they usually bear their young in the winter.

Gardening is another traditional way to introduce children to nature. Judy Sedbrook, a Master Gardener at Colorado State University Cooperative Extension, advises parents to encourage youthful enthusiasm by planting seeds that mature quickly and are large enough for a child to handle easily: "Vegetables are a good choice for young children. They germinate quickly and can be eaten when mature . . . children may even be encouraged to eat vegetables that they have grown and would otherwise avoid. If you have enough room in the garden, gourds are a good choice. After harvesting, they can be decorated and used as birdhouses." A unique gardening project is the sunflower house. In an eight-by-eight-foot square, parents and kids can plant sunflower seeds or seedlings in a shallow moat, alternating varieties that grow about eight feet high with ones that grow to four feet. You can also plant a few corn plants among the sunflowers; corn discourages Carpophilus beetles, and the sunflowers protect the corn from army worms. Inside, plant a carpet of white clover. As a child plays within the containing protection of the sunflower house, bees, butterflies, and other insects will congregate at the blooms above. Plant seeds of indigenous pollinating plants that provide nectar, as well as roosting and nesting sites, and also help increase the number of pollinating birds and insects. This activity can strengthen interrupted pollination corridors and help reestablish the migration paths of butterflies and hummingbirds; and your child can become a participant in the winged migration, not just an observer.

Capturing Time

Time is the key. It's far easier to recommend that parents take more time for nature than it is for the families to capture that diminished resource. Still, this is not an insurmountable obstacle. For example, a single mother, Teri Konars, tells how she overcame the obstacles of time and lack of nature knowledge:

> Some of my son Adam's earliest memories are of camping. This was when we were living in student housing, and Adam was about five or six. I found an organization called Parents Without Partners, and we began to go on camping trips with them. The first trip was Adam's favorite: the desert. He has big memories of seeing a coyote, and learning to make a needle and thread from a yucca leaf, and [seeing] the stars. Today, he's in his twenties, and he says that experience changed him in profound ways. I had a great time too, but my car died when it was time to come home. It had been daring or foolish to take my old beater on such a trip, but knowing we'd be with other people made it okay. As a single mom, going with a group was the only way to do any camping, because of the fear of the unknown *out there* and the economics of gas, camping equipment, food and all the rest of the expenses, which were not easy on our budget.

Of the stories from other families I have collected over the years, one has special resonance — because of its simplicity. "My family fell into the high-achievement trap," one woman, a PTA officer in Shawnee Mission, Kansas, told me.

> Our son was overstressed. We were overstressed. This realization came to us on one of those nights when all of our voices had raised an octave and all of our eyes were opened just a little wider than normal and we all were just . . . it was just too much. We peaked out. Suddenly we realized we were giving our son the message that he had to achieve in order to be lovable. My husband and I were doing it, too: he was working long hours to be lovable and I was doing all these extracurricular activities to be lovable in the community, and it was just crazy. We were getting less lovable.

So the members of the family made a list of everything they loved to do, and everything they hated to do, and then compared lists. The son surprised them: He didn't really like soccer, which was news to his parents. What he really loved was working in the backyard garden. That surprised his parents, too. Together, they discovered that they all loved being outside, camping, and walking, with no particular destination in mind. The parents cut their overtime work and some of their outside social engagements, and together began going on long walks through the trees, listening to the wind. They won back some time, and reestablished a connection within their family and with nature.

Of course, closing the nature divide is not as simple as making a list. Nor does the solution rest entirely with parents. Parents can work small miracles within their families, but they generally cannot close the divide by themselves. Parents need the help of schools, nature organizations, city planners—and each other.

14. Scared Smart: Facing the Bogeyman

WHEN MY SONS were younger and wished to play in the canyon behind our house, swing on the rope, or explore the seasonal creek that winds through the eucalyptus grove, I preferred they explore the canyon with friends, not alone, and that they take their cell phone. They resisted taking the phone, but they knew that submitting to my vigilance was the price of their liberty.

As they grew, I tried to compensate for what was, at times, unfounded fear. I emphasized to them the importance of their experience in nature. I took them on hikes in the Cuyamaca mountain forests or the Anza-Borrego desert, and let them run ahead while I purposefully remained just at the edge of sight and sound. I put them deliberately in nature's way. I took my older son with me on research trips for books: we went fly-fishing for sharks off San Diego's coast; we rode with Mexican cowboys to Baja's Rio Santo Domingo. There, we caught and released genetically rare trout, and I watched as Jason scrambled over boulders along the lost river, almost out of earshot—but never out of sight.

The trick for me has been to offer controlled risk.

Today, I take Matthew, my younger son, to the Sierras; or we glide in a skiff on the bay a few miles away, across the flats, and he watches stingrays scatter like bats; or to the giant in-shore kelp forest, richly populated with fish larger than men. Over the edge of the boat, peering down into vertigo-inducing columns of water and light between the waving strands of giant kelp, Matthew sees into the beating heart of Earth. I watch him from the other end of the boat; in his absorption, he might as well be miles away.

Perhaps these trips make up for some of the freedom they do not have, and at least partially meet their need for solitude in nature. I hope so, and I believe that nature is one of the best antidotes to fear.

We know that parks generally build social cohesion. The Trust for Public Land, a national nonprofit that works to conserve land, argues that access to public parks and recreational facilities "has been strongly linked to reductions in crime and in particular to reduced juvenile delinquency."

Park design that incorporates a more natural environment can make children safer by changing adult behavior—specifically, by encouraging adults to supervise children. Trees and grass do more than decorate the landscape. For example, in the midst of a public housing complex in inner-city Chicago, greenery enhances children's creative play and encourages the presence of adult supervision. In 1998, the journal *Environment and Behavior* reported that in sixty-four outdoor spaces at a Chicago housing development, almost twice as many children (ages three through twelve) played in areas that had trees and grass than played in barren spaces, and their play was more creative. This complex has fifty-seven hundred residents and is in one of the ten poorest neighborhoods in the nation.

From a policy standpoint, "the findings about more play are exciting, because play in general has important implications in children's development," according to Frances E. Kuo, co-director of the University of Illinois Human–Environment Research Laboratory, which conducted the study.

The implication for safety was also important. The investigation found that children's access to adult supervision was doubled in areas with vegetation. Something there is about a tree. Such studies determine how large numbers of people behave, but what about the individual child?

Modern life narrows our senses until our focus is mostly visual, appropriate to about the dimension of a computer monitor or TV screen. By contrast, nature accentuates all the senses, and the senses are a child's primal first line of self-defense. Children with generous exposure to nature, those who learn to see the world directly, *may* be more likely to develop the psychological survival skills that will help them detect real danger, and they are therefore less likely to seek out phony danger later in life. Play in nature may instill instinctual confidence.

Hyperawareness in Nature: Instilling Instinctual Confidence

In many of my conversations with parents and their children, the issue of self-confidence came up, and my notebooks offer anecdotal evidence that nature does build self-confidence in children. Janet Fout's daughter, Julia, talks about it. Julia is a student at George Washington University; she majors in International Affairs with a specialty in Security and Defense. Recently, Julia took the officer candidate test. She is choosing a career that will certainly require her to face fear and uncertainty. Mother and daughter agree that nature, with a little help from her mother, helped shape Julia's self-confidence:

> When Julia was very little, when we went outdoors, rather than telling her to "be careful," I encouraged her to "pay attention"—which doesn't instill fear, but works against fear. Of all the times we were together outdoors, we never encountered any creatures (outside of some humans) that made either of us fearful. I hope that I taught her to use good judgment. For instance, when climbing around on rocks, it isn't prudent to put your fingers into a crevice that you haven't first examined.

I tried to instill in her a healthy respect for other living creatures, teaching her that, like most humans, animals were territorial, and were just out there doing what we were—trying to survive. Whether she encounters a growling dog in D.C. or a cougar in the wild, my advice is the same: back away slowly and don't run. Providing her with opportunities to be a "wild child," I believe, helped her hone her natural instincts for survival, not only for life in the woods, but life in the big city. Humans are sometimes the most dangerous creatures and the most difficult to read. I've always taught her about the important survival skill of listening to gut feelings—somewhat different than psychological survival skills. If you get an "uh-oh" feeling, it's real, and if you want to stay safe and survive, listen to it!

Julia agreed that childhood experiences in nature had made her a stronger, more observant, safer adult:

You asked what lessons I learned from nature, but first I must share what lessons I learned from my mother. Believe it or not, I was so comfortable in nature that my mother had to curb my behavior. Once, she was within seconds of dragging me to the hospital to test for parasitic infection when I told her I had been drinking from the creek near our house. I was seven and had stolen the litmus paper she used in her scientific work. I knew that the water had a safe pH reading and thought nothing of a luxurious drink. I knew which plants tasted good —in addition to which plants tasted good and would make me sick. There were firmly imposed restrictions—most memorably: Don't ever climb a one-hundred-foot rock face without a rope; it will give your mother a heart attack. This was followed closely by: Don't urinate in the backyard. However, all of these things are secondary and not particularly pertinent to my adult life (although I'm sure everyone appreciates that my mother broke me of personally fertilizing the garden). Nature awakened in me a kind of hyperawareness, which I encounter in very few people.

Julia's use of the word "hyperawareness" is instructive. Usually hypervigilance—behavior manifested by always being on guard and ready to fight or flee—is associated with trauma in childhood. But the hyperawareness gained from early experience in nature may be the flip side of hypervigilance—a positive way to pay attention, and, when it's appropriate, to be on guard. We're familiar with the term "street smart." Perhaps another, wider, adaptive intelligence is available to the young. Call it "nature smart."

John Johns, a California father and businessman, believes that a child in nature is required to make decisions not often encountered in a more constricted, planned environment—ones that not only present danger, but opportunity. A stronger adult emerges from a childhood in which the physical body is immersed in the challenge of nature. Organized sport, with its finite set of rules, is said to build character. If that is true, and of course it can be, nature experience must do the same, in ways we do not fully understand. A natural environment is far more complex than any playing field. Nature does offer rules and risk, and subtly informs all the senses.

"Intuitively, I believe my kids are better equipped to detect danger because of their time in nature," says Johns. "They've all had adrenaline-thumping whitewater experiences and spent moonless nights burrowed into their sleeping bags, imagining all manner of evils outside. Whatever neurons were firing then and whatever coping/adaptive responses they practiced now put them at some advantage in the world." He wonders if this is one of the primal reasons he and his wife have taken their children on so many nature excursions. "We just seldom think about it in those terms, that we're helping our kids sensitize themselves to the world. But we sense it."

Leslie Stephens, the Southern California mother who chose to live on the edge of a natural canyon, says her family made that decision in part because of the beauty there, but also because her children would be more likely to develop self-confidence, at their own speed, in such an environment. She says:

I think fondness for wild places is best nurtured when children are young. Otherwise they are off-put by it, afraid of it, and even more strangely, somehow not curious about it. I see this reaction repeatedly in other kids and adults that I meet and get to know. They don't feel comfortable in nature. They're a little paranoid of going out and exploring it.

Mothers in this neighborhood have asked me if I am, perhaps, foolish about my boys' safety. They want to know why I allow my boys to run in our canyon unsupervised. What about the dangers, they ask? They are afraid of "scary people" down there and coyotes (in the middle of the day, no less), and of course, snakes. I haven't seen a snake down there in twelve years, but custodians kill them over at the middle school playground regularly. Yes, there are dangers. I could tell you about the time my youngest son and his best friend stepped on the same rusty nail. Only boys could manage something so awkward and painful. The way they screamed made me think a snake had bitten them. This required a trip to the emergency room and a tetanus shot. But other than that, my kids' injuries and their friends' injuries have occurred playing organized sports. I think that's where the danger is: kids egged on to be ever more aggressive in order to win, win, win. The wilderness provides an environment for a child's interior life to develop because it requires him to remain constantly aware of his surroundings.

The Most Important Thing Parents Can Do

I am not suggesting that spending time in nature inoculates children against danger—certainly no scientific research supports that theory. But I do contend that nature-play offers residual safety benefits, and that some of the conventional approaches we take to protect children are less effective than we believe them to be. Parents can do other things, as well, to lessen the fear.

During a wave of national stranger-danger fear, CNN's Paula Zahn asked Marc Klaas what we can do to protect our kids. Like most of us,

Klaas would have preferred never to think about the question. In 1993, on a moonlit night, his twelve-year-old daughter, Polly, was snatched from her Petaluma, California, home and later murdered. Klaas went on to become a familiar face on television, a voice for missing children. Politicians paraded him as a poster-father for California's Proposition 184—the "three strikes" law. Vote for it, he and they said, and you'll be preventing future murders of children like Polly.

Just before the balloting, however, Klaas changed his mind. The law, he had concluded, would fill already bulging prisons with pot smokers and poachers, and the deeper root of child endangerment was something that that particular law wouldn't reach. When Zahn asked him for parental advice, he said, yes, we need to realize that if kidnappers can "get those children out of their bedrooms, every child in America is a child that is at risk." But, he added, "we have to dispel this whole notion of stranger-danger and substitute some other rules." Parents and children do have power. Children "should trust their feelings," he said. "They should fight abductors. They should put distance between themselves and whatever is making them feel badly. And then certainly they should also understand that there are certain kinds of strangers that they *can* go to."

Others have made this point. Don't just tell your kids about evil; teach them about good—teach them to seek out adults who can help them when they feel threatened. Teaching appropriate trust is more difficult than teaching fear, but just as important. As Klaas said, "Kids want the information that's going to enable them to protect themselves. What we have to do as parents is get over our fears and address the issue and talk to the kids." Such advice doesn't really apply to those occasions when children are snatched from their homes, but those instances are exceedingly rare. In an increasingly agoraphobic society, parents are most fearful of the potential out there—down the street, at the mall, in the canyon behind the house.

So how do we adapt without locking our kids away from the richness of community and nature?

Klaas offered one suggestion. "I would say that one thing that we should really seriously consider for children that are ten years of age and over is to get them their own cell phone so that we can have 24/7 contact with them at all times. And I'm not shilling for any cell phone company. I truly believe that this is one of the answers that we're seeking."

Several years ago, during another wave of stranger-danger hysteria, I asked David Finklehor, the University of New Hampshire sociologist I cited earlier, what he considered the most important thing parents could do to protect their children. He touched on something at the core of the bogeyman syndrome. "There are an awful lot of programs out there today trying to teach personal safety to children," he said. "But I honestly think the most important thing a parent can do is to have a good, supportive relationship with the child, because a child who has good self-esteem, good self-confidence, a closer relationship with the parents, is much less likely to be victimized. Our studies show that. Predatory people are not as likely to mess with them, because the predator senses that these are kids who will tell, who can't be fooled or conned. The studies show that most kids who are victimized are also emotionally neglected, or they come from intensely unhappy families, or suffer other deprivations."

So there is one key to facing the bogeyman, not necessarily related to nature. The time we give our children builds their self-esteem and self-confidence, and this gives them armor they can take with them the rest of their lives. The most important protection we can give them is our love and our time. If curing the bogeyman syndrome were as simple as a five-step program (beyond the usual law-enforcement bromides), the cure might look something like this:

- Spend more time with your children; educate them about the human dangers, but in the context of building self-confidence, sensory awareness, and knowledge of the many people they can trust.
- Increase the amount of positive adult contact that your children receive from good adults.

- Know your neighbors: reinvest in the life of the block and the surrounding community; encourage your children to know trustworthy adults in their neighborhoods.

- If your child is going beyond your visual contact, encourage him or her to play with a group of peers rather than alone. (Unfortunately, solitary experience in nature must sometimes be discouraged, if the alternative is no nature at all.)

- Employ technology. Tracking bracelets may be overdoing it, but a cell phone can be a life preserver. Just as children once carried Swiss army knives into the woods, today they should carry mobile phones.

As a parent, I must admit, even the act of making such a list feels inadequate and unsatisfying. On the one hand, I resist the idea that solitude is a luxury; on the other, I must be honest about the fact that my own fear is one of the reasons that my boys have not enjoyed as much physical freedom as I did when I was young. Still, I know it's time to put fear in its place: to acknowledge that what happens to any of us is beyond our absolute control, and that 98 percent of what can go wrong never does. The 2 percent factor is no small thing. Nature, however, is part of the solution. Let me offer here an unconventional thesis, a sixth step: *To increase your child's safety, encourage more time outdoors, in nature. Natural play strengthens children's self-confidence and arouses their senses—their awareness of the world and all that moves in it, seen and unseen.*

Although we have plenty of reasons to worry about our children, a case can be made that we endanger our children by separating them too much from nature, and that the reverse is also true—that we make them safer, now and in the future, by exposing them to nature.

Assessing Ice; Discovering Beauty

Ideally, a child learns to negotiate both city and country. Mastering each environment builds the senses and common sense. Is there something special about the experience in nature, at least a quality that sharpens a young person's senses? Wonderful possibilities await researchers wanting to explore that unknown frontier. Surely the width and depth of nature, the added mystery—the catalogue of sounds and smells and sights—is larger than the relatively short and known list of urban stimulations. In the city or suburb, much of our energy is spent blocking sounds and stimulants. Do we actually hear the honking of cabs—do we want to? In a forest, our ears are open—the honking of geese overhead enlivens us, and when enlivened, human senses grow and develop.

Some parents see another connection—between positive nature-risk and openness to beauty. In New Hampshire, David Sobel consciously uses nature to teach his daughter safety. He calls it "assessing ice":

> This experience is a rite of passage. I am trying to teach her the process of assessing thin ice, literally and metaphorically. We go out on the ice together and assess the structural integrity of the ice: what's risky and fun, and what's too risky. Through these experiences, I help her begin to be able to assess situations. Whether this began consciously or intentionally on my part, that's the effect. Crossing the ice, I teach her to read cracks, the ways of figuring out ice thickness and texture, to see the places where there is current—this is where ice is thick; this is where it is thin. I teach her how you must spread out when you have to cross really thin ice, to carry a stick with you, all of these intentional ways of assessing risk on the ice and being prepared.

A child could gain the same kind of experience and ability to assess a dangerous environment in a city, riding a bus or a subway. But Sobel, as an expert on nature's role in education, suggests that nature's life-instruction provides a mysterious and probably irreplaceable quality. He believes that the kinesthetic original experience of risk-taking in the natural world is closer to the natural organic way we've learned for millennia, and that the other experiences don't reach as deeply.

Listening to him, I wondered about this unnamed intensity of learning and hyperawareness that we detect in nature, but cannot prove. Is this quality, perhaps, linked simply to beauty, to those natural shapes and musical sounds that draw our souls to nature? Sobel thought about that question for a moment, and then said, yes, that made sense to him. He said he often cites a quote from a woman who narrowly survived California's 1989 Loma Prieta earthquake, one that killed at least sixty-two people and injured another thirty-seven hundred. This woman believed that the earthquake, far from destroying her life, saved it. She had been combating a borderline psychological state at the time, and then the earthquake came. She said later that the process of coming to terms with this massive natural act was more effective than any of the therapy she had received. Something about that experience shook her back to earth. "The phrase that stood out, from what she said," recalled Sobel, "is the diagnosis she came up with for herself. She said she had suffered from a 'distance from beauty.' That idea has become a part of me. I know when I am suffering from that distance from beauty. The solution for me is to find my way back to a closeness with nature."

He is determined that his daughter not suffer from this distance, that she find nature, that she walk in beauty, and that she understand the ice. Though self-confidence and awareness can come from experiencing nature, the generations do not go to nature to find safety or justice. They go to find beauty. Quite simply, when we deny our children nature, we deny them beauty.

15. Telling Turtle Tales: Using Nature as a Moral Teacher

Let Nature be your teacher.
— WILLIAM WORDSWORTH

FOR MY FAMILY, spring brought tornadoes and turtles. Just as the twisters roared up from Oklahoma and crossed over to the hills of eastern Kansas and western Missouri, the box turtles began their migration. The blacktop roads and cement highways would be dotted with spinners, crawlers, and splotches. Spinners were what we called those turtles that, while traveling to turtle Mecca, took a glancing blow from a tire, flipped over, and spun like tops. Crawlers and splotches were . . . self-explanatory.

Each year, my parents would load my brother and me into the Dodge and ride the road to save the turtles.

When we saw a spinner or a crawler, my father would brake the car and my mother would jump out, white blouse fluttering in the wind, shoot across the pavement—sometimes dodging cars—and grab the turtle. Often she would race back to the car with a turtle in each hand. She would deposit these lonesome travelers on the backseat floor mat, at my brother's and my feet. As we rode along on this mercy mission, we would collect as many as a couple dozen turtles.

Then my father would turn the wheel and head back home, weaving to avoid the new waves of crawlers and spinners.

The saved souls were deposited in what we called "the turtle pit" at the base of the backyard, under the shade of a hedge. Beyond the hedge were cornfields, and beyond those fields woods that went on forever (at least in my imagination). Under the hedge, my father dug a pit, lined it with chicken wire, pushed dirt back over the wire mesh, and then folded a flap of chicken wire over the top of the pit. He weighted the wire at the edges with stakes and rocks. Into the pit went the crawlers and the spinners. Each summer, I spent hours under the cool shade of the hedge, on my belly, peering into Turtle World. I fed berries and lettuce to the turtles, studied the patterns of their shells, the veined colors of their faces, the way they bobbed their heads, the way they defecated.

A hefty old turtle named Theodore was my favorite. He was a circumspect turtle. At first frost, I would lift the flap of wire and pick the turtles up and walk down into the brown, crackling cornfield and release my summer friends. Except for Theodore, who hibernated in our basement. One spring, Theodore did not awaken. I cried and wrapped him in toilet paper and gave him a decent burial near Turtle World. My mother attended the funeral.

I often think about the crawlers and spinners that would have been splotches, and sometimes I wonder if other parents cruise for box turtles in the spring, their children in the backseat, still in their pajamas.

Today, some folks would frown at a boy collecting turtles. But unless a child is collecting endangered species, the aggregate of good outweighs the damage to nature. Turtle collecting (and later, collecting snakes, which lived temporarily in a terrarium in the garage) offered me a hands-on experience with nature, and it was one of those acts that brought my family together. Biologically, we are not that many generations removed from the hunting and gathering family, in which each member of a family or clan had important work to do. That may give turtle-collecting undue weight, but I do remember that strange and wonderful feeling on turtle road, and I felt it, too, when my parents and brother and I fished together, because then we were whole.

The Case for Fishing and Hunting

For reasons that have more to do with emotion than reason, I don't hunt, nor do I encourage my boys to hunt—and they are appalled at the idea that others hunt. I acknowledge that there is slim moral logic dividing hunting and fishing, but I am prejudiced in favor of fishing as a way for children and adults to experience something beyond the voyeurism that sometimes passes for nature experience. In *A River Runs Through It*, Norman Maclean writes, "In our family, there was no clear line between religion and fly fishing." In my childhood family, there was no clear line between carp and the garbage can. Like many folks, I come from a family obsessed with fishing, but we weren't snooty about it. In fact, we leaned toward carp, which, unless you know how to cook them, are inedible. We heard rumors that some people knew how to tenderize them with a pressure cooker. So, my father, being a chemist, experimented with this technique. A vague recollection of an explosion and flying carp pâté sticks in my mind.

To my delight, both my sons understand the healing qualities of nature. Matthew, sixteen, has claimed fishing as his own medicine, and I suspect it will help him thrive during the remainder of his teenage years and the rest of his life.

Fishing is, by far, not a solely male activity. Women comprise the fastest growing segment of fly-fishing. "I almost hate to call it fishing," says Margot Page, who lives in Vermont and calls herself a "fishermom." A well-known fly-fisher, she's passing the fishing tradition on to her daughter. "I'd rather call it water treatment. Yes, it's about the line and these wild flashes of light you see in the stream, but it's really the water that we go to and the water we've always gone to. When you become more familiar with the creatures that inhabit water, you are drawn to see them, to connect somehow. But it starts with the water."

What's the appropriate age to begin a child's fishing experience? "Around five years old, but generally not before," says Hugh Marx, who offers a kids' fishing clinic at a lake near San Diego. "In the beginning, parents of small children do the fishing and kids do the reeling." Don't start a child out with sophisticated fishing techniques and gear, he advises. A child introduced to fishing this way may get so frustrated that fishing loses its appeal. The best policy is let them start with a cane pole, not a hundred-dollar rod and reel. "Let children appreciate the simplicity of fishing. At least if they become angling elitists later on, they can't say they were always one."

Begin with the non-glamour fish, he suggests. Crappie, carp, bullhead catfish—and most important, bluegills and other types of sunfish—any pan fish that make a kid's heart jolt when the bobber goes under. Bend down the barbs on the hooks for safety: this also makes it easier to release fish unharmed. Speaking for the fish, I recommend catch-and-release, although taking a few fish home to clean and eat can be a valuable lesson about the source of food.

For my older son, Jason, fishing has value chiefly as a way to spend time with his family, in nature. But Matthew definitely has the fishing gene. He started his angling career at age three, fishing in the humidifier in his bedroom. A few years ago, I asked him to help me with an article about fishing and kids. The piece was published in the *Chicago Tribune* and several other newspapers. His advice is still good:

Fishing Tips for Parents from Matthew Louv (age 12):

1. Fish with your kid.
2. Let your kids go fishing, even if you don't want to take them.
3. Let your kids buy supplies and tackle. That's half the fun of fishing.
4. If your kids are young, take them to a place where fish are easy to catch and are small.
5. Let kids fish as long as they want. Let them get obsessed.
6. Let the kids go off and do their own thing. It can get to be incredibly annoying and/or frustrating if there's an adult standing over them barking orders.

7. At least pretend to act excited when your kid catches a fish. It can quickly ruin a day of fishing if the kid feels you don't want to be there, and he's just dragging you down.
8. If you know how to fish, don't give your kid too much unsolicited advice, although it can be helpful if the kid is young.
9. Let your kid teach you how to fish; participate in the fishing. This can be quality bonding time.
10. Remember that fishing and spending time with family is just as, or more important than, homework.
11. Have fun; that's the entire point of going fishing in the first place.
12. And whatever you do, DON'T LET YOUR KID THROW ROCKS IN THE WATER!

Today's families are more likely to be confronted with moral questions, ones seldom asked in past decades, about children's traditional hunting-and-gathering interaction with nature. These questions come with the territory of the third frontier—and reflect the changing relationship between humans and other animals. In 2000, People for the Ethical Treatment of Animals (PETA) declared fishing "the final frontier of animal rights." The organization has targeted its anti-fishing campaign specifically at children. Activists have handed out anti-fishing fliers to children as they left schools; others protested at a Brooklyn children's fishing derby, holding up signs that effectively accused the children of being killers. In 2000, Dawn Carr, anti-fishing campaign coordinator for PETA, and Gill the Fish, a six-foot-tall piscatorial partner dressed in a fish-suit, attempted to visit dozens of schools around the country. "Only one school let us in," reported Carr. Undeterred, she and Gill stationed themselves just beyond school property. There, they passed out literature and told kids about the evils of fishing.

One PETA anti-fishing commercial features young Justin Aligata, who is a vegetarian, animal rights activist, and Boy Scout. "Scouting has taught me that Scouts should not harm the environment or animals in it. That is why I don't think there should be a fishing merit badge," he says. "Scouting is all about doing what is right and making a positive difference in the world—that is exactly what I am doing by helping PETA speak up for fish."

Even without PETA's opposition, fishing is slipping as a pastime among young people. Some 44 million Americans still fish regularly, but the age of anglers is rising, and the fishing tackle industry is concerned about a drop in some states in the number of young people fishing. "Every kid grows up with a mountain bike; it used to be a fishing pole," says *Sports Afield* editor John Atwood.

Hunting is another traditional way that young people first interacted with nature. In 1997, states issued approximately 15 million hunting licenses, about a million less than the previous decade. (Interestingly, women are responsible for maintaining hunting's numerical viability; the number of women hunters doubled in the 1990s, to 2.6 million.) In 1998, after a spurt of school violence by young people (some using hunting rifles), essayist Lance Morrow wrote, "Sometimes a society makes a tectonic shift, some great half-conscious collective decision. That happened with smoking, which was once, remember, a glamorous ritual of romance and adulthood. . . . It may be happening now with hunting."

Yes, there are alternative hands-on ways for children to experience nature, but when people who love nature argue for the end of hunting and fishing, without suggesting options equaling or surpassing the importance of those experiences to children, they should be careful what they wish for. By any measure, the destruction of nature caused by hunting pales in comparison to the destruction of habitat by urban sprawl and pollution. Remove hunting and fishing from human activity, and we lose many of the voters and organizations that now work against the destruction of woods, fields, and watersheds.

At the center of the fishing controversy is this question: Do fish feel pain? Without delving into the scientific controversy, suffice it to say that the answer to that question depends on your definition of pain and suffering; the answer is not as clear as it may seem. Certainly, the definition is not settled. Those children who do fish (or hunt) in the future will do so under a growing cloud. Yet, in an increasingly de-natured world, fishing and hunting remain among the last ways that the young learn of the mystery and moral complexity of nature in a way that no videotape can convey. Yes, fishing and hunting are messy—even morally messy—but so is nature. No child can truly know or value the outdoors if the natural world remains under glass, seen only through lenses, screens, or computer monitors.

Fishing also offers generational connection. In a world in which children seldom follow their mothers and fathers into the family business or the parents' professions, fishing is an avocation, a craft, a calling that a parent can deliver to the next generation. For so many families, fishing serves as glue that binds the generations, even if fishing fades.

My son Jason, twenty-two, now lives in Brooklyn and works in Manhattan. He spends hours exploring the city's neighborhoods and parks and along the water's edge. One evening, when I visited him in New York, we took a four-hour hike through Central Park. We stood for a long time on a bridge over the arm of one of the park's ponds, staring into the opaque, green water, stilled by evening calm. We watched a fifty-something man with a ponytail make his way through the undergrowth to the shore and cast across the water. Suddenly a bass grabbed the lure, exploded into the air and tail-danced across the water. Jason and I both laughed with surprise, and I suddenly missed the many hours we fished together when he was a little boy.

After a while, Jason said, "You know, Dad, when I walk through the older neighborhoods, with the old brick and all that organic change, I sometimes get the feeling I had when I was a kid exploring the canyon behind our house."

It pleases me that Jason finds forms of nature beneath the surfaces, where others may see none.

Wildcrafting and the Shift from Taking to Watching

For families not attracted to fishing or hunting, wonderful alternatives exist. One is wildcrafting, a term that originally meant gaining skill and knowledge about wilderness survival, but has come to be used more specifically as the hunting and gathering of plants in their wild state, for food, herbal medicines, or crafts.

This isn't your mother's leaf pressing, but a sophisticated interaction with nature, requiring patience, careful observation, and a cultivated knowledge of species identification. Wildcrafting also comes with its own set of ethical issues. *Utne* magazine, in an article on wildcrafting entitled "The Guerrilla Gatherers," pointed out that wildcrafting in protected wilderness areas is technically illegal. Wildcrafting organizations council parents and children to ask themselves such questions as: Are you collecting in a fragile environment? Is the plant rare, threatened, or endangered—or are such plants near enough to be damaged? Is wildlife foraging the stand? Is the stand growing, shrinking, or staying the same size? John Lust, in *The Natural Remedy Bible*, advises that wildcrafters "harvest where the plant appears to be thriving, as that is where we will be able to find the strongest plants," and to "be sure to leave enough so that the plant can easily recover its growth."

Careful wildcrafting, he argues, can be practiced "in such a way as to aid the growth of wild plants by judicious thinning and pruning." Wildcrafting's value is enhanced because it presents the ethical issues inherent in childhood hunting and gathering. Responsible wildcrafting connects children to nature in a direct way, helps explain the sources of food, and teaches them the basics of sustainability.

An even less invasive activity is wildlife viewing. Some folks watch raccoons in the backyard; others take trips of hundreds of miles to see a single bird species. Unfortunately, the number of Americans participating in traditional forms of recreational wildlife watching decreased between 1991 and 2001, from 76 million in 1991, to 66 million in 2001, according to the U.S. Department of the Interior's "National Survey of Fishing, Hunting, and Wildlife."

One branch of wildlife watching is growing. *World Watch* reports, "Birding has become one of the continent's fastest growing outdoor pastimes." Birding has traditionally been a hobby for mature adults. In contrast to some other outdoor activities, birding may be gaining ground among some groups of young people, according to *Birding* magazine. Part of this growth is due to the advent of compact field guides, and advances in camera technology make birding easier than in the past. Digital cameras dramatically reduce the cost of experimental photos of worms, beetles, and small feet. In 2001, the percentage of birders between sixteen and twenty-four years old increased from 10.5 to 15.5 percent of bird watchers; but the percentage of birders between twenty-five and thirty-nine actually fell from 31.8 to 24.3 percent. *Birding* surmised that "the busy family-rearing years of twenty-five to thirty-nine years old do not permit as much involvement in birding as they did a few years ago."

For a child who is primarily an audile learner, or who has poor eyesight, birding could be an especially wonderful way to experience nature. Little Teddy Roosevelt, with his poor eyesight as a child, could imitate hundreds of birdcalls, and did so even as an adult.

Birding does not need to be an elaborate or expensive endeavor. *Mothering* magazine offers some useful advice:

> Don't rush to the library for a book; let your young scientist learn to see and record the information firsthand. . . . Make a list or chart to note down the same observations for each different type of bird. In this way, your child will learn to rely on firsthand observations and knowledge building. . . . Learning about birds might lead your youngster to take an interest in other earth sciences: Why not help your child plant several rows of beans in the garden using different composts and fertilizers, or watch and compare three different types of

trees budding? The goal is to encourage your youngster to observe, question, and answer.

Is wildlife watching the twenty-first-century expression of our urge to hunt? *World Watch* associate editor Howard Youth offers a more complex explanation: "When only a few hundred members of a species remain, those last members may ironically attract thousands of humans who paid little attention when the species was common: witness the crowds that gather to observe captive pandas, gorillas, or California condors."

Nature journaling is also a useful tool for young people. The great naturalist writers John Muir and Aldo Leopold kept nature journals. Beginning at age eleven, Bill Sipple, an ecologist with the Environmental Protection Agency, kept a journal—now two volumes totaling over twelve hundred pages. Early explorer Henry Rowe Schoolcraft trekked across the Ozarks in 1818, and later published a detailed account of his journey. His journals depict a different landscape from what we see today. He vividly described the lush expanses of prairies and his encounters with herds of elk and bison. For more than 150 years, New England anglers have been keeping fishing logs and fishing diaries—and the ecological record kept in these logs are now key to the protection of wild trout streams.

Outdoor journaling is something a family can do together, and it offers reason and focus for being in nature. Linda Chorice, assistant manager at the Missouri Conservation Department's Springfield Nature Center, points out that journaling demands no special equipment, only a pad of paper or spiral notebook, several pencils, and a pencil sharpener. "While your journal may never be published as a historical document, it will serve as a personal record of your outdoor experiences, allowing you to accurately relive your memories each time you open its cover," she says.

All of these activities can teach children patience and respect for the other creatures on the planet, even if the lessons take a little time to accrue.

It's Not the Internet, It's the Oceans

Not long ago, I learned how one father, Robert F. Kennedy, Jr., exposed his kids to nature—through catching, releasing, and watching. Kennedy made his name as an environmental lawyer working with Riverkeeper, an organization that was created to protect the New York City watershed and that has helped bring the Hudson River back from its watery, polluted grave. One of Kennedy's most notable accomplishments was the New York City watershed agreement, which he negotiated on behalf of environmentalists and the city's watershed consumers to ensure the purity of the city's water. As the chief prosecuting attorney for Riverkeeper, the president of the Waterkeeper Alliance, and a senior attorney for the Natural Resources Defense Council, Kennedy has worked on environmental issues throughout the Western Hemisphere. In his spare time, he likes to take his five young children scuba diving in the Hudson. He does something called "buddy diving."

Kennedy and one of his children descend to the bottom of the river and sit next to a favorite large rock, sheltered from the current. He will hold his child around the shoulders or waist (for the child's security, and also to feel the child's breathing) and the two of them will pass the mouthpiece back and forth. They sit down there, next to that rock, embraced by the underwater foliage that dances in the current, and watch the fish go by: the aggressive bass and whiskered catfish, tropical fish released from aquariums (angel fish, especially, and sometimes sea horses), and even an occasional native sturgeon—monstrous, prehistoric, and graceful. For Kennedy, watching the fish go by is a way to distance himself from the pressures that come with his name; it is also a metaphor for how we can experience nature with our children.

As part of my research for an earlier book, I went fishing with Kennedy. I took my sons along in a small boat off the California coastline. And as we fished, Kennedy told me of his earliest experiences as the family's "nature child," as he called himself, and how those experiences shaped his fathering. "I spent every afternoon in the woods when I was growing up," he said. "I loved finding salamanders, crayfish, frogs. My room was filled with aquariums, *filled,* from when I was six years old. And it still is today. I have a 350-gallon aquarium, and I have aquariums all over my house." From the Hudson, he and his kids catch catfish, eel, bullheads, sturgeon, striped bass, perch, largemouth, bluefish, sturgeon, and trout—and bring them home live and keep them in their aquariums.

As we headed out to sea, Kennedy spoke passionately for the reconnection of children to nature. "We're part of nature, and ultimately we're predatory animals and we have a role in nature," he said, "and if we separate ourselves from that, we're separating ourselves from our history, from the things that tie us together. We don't want to live in a world where there are no recreational fishermen, where we've lost touch with the seasons, the tides, the things that connect us—to ten thousand generations of human beings that were here before there were laptops, and ultimately connect us to God."

We shouldn't be worshipping nature as God, he said, but nature is the way that God communicates to us most forcefully. "God communicates to us through each other and through organized religion, through wise people and the great books, through music and art," but nowhere "with such texture and forcefulness in detail and grace and joy, as through creation," he said. "And when we destroy large resources, or when we cut off our access by putting railroads along river banks, by polluting so that people can't fish, or by making so many rules that people can't get out on the water, it's the moral equivalent of tearing the last pages out of the last Bible on Earth. It's a cost that's imprudent for us to impose upon ourselves, and we don't have the right to impose it upon our children."

A swell lifted the boat and the gulls followed us, and the city began to disappear behind us in a haze. "Our children ought to be out there on the water," said Kennedy. "This is what connects us, this is what connects humanity, this is what we have in common. It's not the Internet, it's the oceans."

PART V

THE JUNGLE BLACKBOARD

It is not the language of painters
but the language of nature which one should listen to. . . .
The feeling for the things themselves,
for reality, is more important than the feeling for pictures.

—VINCENT VAN GOGH

16. Natural School Reform

*Teaching children about the natural world should be treated
as one of the most important events in their lives.*

—THOMAS BERRY

THE CONCEPT OF environment-based education—known by a
number of names—is at least a century old. In *The School and Society*,
John Dewey advocated immersing students in the local environment:
"Experience [outside the school] has its geographical aspect, its artistic
and its literary, its scientific and its historical sides. All studies arise from
aspects of the one earth and the one life lived upon it." Far from radical,
experiential education is at the very core of this older educational theory, an approach developed long before videotapes presented ring-
necked snakes to the classroom. While environmental education focuses
on how to live correctly in the world, experiential education teaches
through the senses in the natural world.

Support for nature in education was given an added boost by Howard
Gardner, professor of education at Harvard University, who in 1983 developed the powerful theory of multiple intelligences. As described
in an earlier chapter, Gardner proposed seven different intelligences
in children and adults, including linguistic intelligence, logical-
mathematical intelligence, spatial intelligence, bodily-kinesthetic
intelligence, musical intelligence, interpersonal intelligence, and intrapersonal intelligence. More recently, he added naturalist intelligence
("nature smart") to his list.

Fueled by this theory, and others, a nascent movement for what might be called natural school reform grows steadily—and, though still relatively small, is long overdue.

In America, software companies hawk computer-learning programs to parents of two-year-olds. By the second grade, most American children have already spent years in preschool and have been introduced to the rigors of testing. Lora Cicalo—a well-educated, hard-driving professional—is appalled at the stress felt by her daughter and her classmates, as their elementary teacher prepares them for California's STAR (Standardized Testing and Reporting) program. "The teacher must teach everything from how to properly fill in the answer bubbles (i.e., don't put an X through them or make a mark outside the outline of the circle) to how to keep pace with the rest of the class in the timed test," she said. "The kids worry about how they will look to the adults placing so much emphasis on this test. Remember, these children are only seven years old. Why are we putting all this pressure on them?" To improve schools, right? Maybe.

While Americans push kids to the competitive edge, Finland's educational system is headed in exactly the opposite direction. In a 2003 review by the Organization of Economic Cooperation and Development, Finland outscored thirty-one other countries, including the United States. Finland scored first in literacy and placed in the top five in math and science. The United States placed in the middle of the pack. "Finland's recipe is both complex and unabashedly basic," the *New York Times* reports. "Some of the ingredients can be exported (its flexibility in the classroom, for example) and some cannot (the nation's small, homogenous population and the relative prosperity of most Finns, to name two)."

By the standards of some American educators and policymakers, Finland's approach seems counterintuitive. Finnish students don't enter any school until they are seven years old—practically senior citizens in America. Finland offers no special programs for the gifted student, and spends less per student on education than the United States. While requiring educators to meet national curriculum requirements, Finland gives them wide leeway in how they teach. And Finnish educators believe in the power of—get this—play. In the United States, meanwhile, the trend is toward dropping recess. But at a typical school in the Suutarila district of Helsinki, students "pad about in their socks. After every 45-minute lesson, they are let loose outside for 15 minutes so they can burn off steam," according to the *Times*. Finland also encourages environment-based education, and has moved a substantial amount of classroom experience into natural settings or the surrounding community. "The core of learning is not in the information . . . being predigested from the outside, but in the interaction between a child and the environment," states Finland's Ministry of Social Affairs and Health. I'm sure American educators could teach Finland a thing or two about education. But what if we adopted at least two Finnish traits—greater social respect for teachers and an enthusiasm for environment-based education?

Lauren Scheehan, founder and faculty chair of the Swallowtail School in Hillsboro, Oregon, believes many people—including techies from deep in the Silicon Forest—are looking for more balance in both their own and their children's lives.

"We believe computer skills should be postponed in the classroom until high school," she says. "They can still use computers at home or play video games at their friends' houses; that world isn't closed to them." But Swallowtail gives students a break from "the electronic impulses coming at them all the time, so their sensory abilities are more open to what's happening naturally around them." The point, Scheehan says, is to create "a moral foundation of freedom of choice, instead of being totally dependent on electronic media." Several Intel employees send their children to the school. These parents value technology, says Scheehan, "but they understand that there are aspects of being a human that aren't inside a computer."

So far, Swallowtail is the exceptional school. But that could change. Bucking the status quo, an increasing number of educators are committed to an approach that infuses education with direct experience, especially of nature. The definitions and nomenclature of this movement are tricky. In recent decades, the approach has gone by many names: community-oriented schooling, bioregional education, experiential education, and, most recently, place-based or environment-based education. By any name, environment-based education can surely be one of the antidotes to nature-deficit disorder. The basic idea is to use the surrounding community, including nature, as the preferred classroom.

Real World Learning

For more effective education reform, teachers should free kids from the classroom. That's the message from Gerald Lieberman, director of the State Education and Environmental Roundtable, a national effort to study environment-based education.

"Since the ecosystems surrounding schools and their communities vary as dramatically as the nation's landscape, the term 'environment' may mean different things at every school; it may be a river, a city park, or a garden carved out of an asphalt playground," according to the Roundtable's report, "Closing the Achievement Gap." The report was issued in 2002, but has been largely ignored by the education establishment. The Roundtable worked with 150 schools in sixteen states for ten years, identifying model environment-based programs and examining how the students fared on standardized tests. The findings are stunning: environment-based education produces student gains in social studies, science, language arts, and math; improves standardized test scores and grade-point averages; and develops skills in problem-solving, critical thinking, and decision-making.

- In Florida, Taylor County High School teachers and students use the nearby Econfina River to team-teach math, science, language arts, biology, chemistry, and the economics of the county.

- In San Bernardino, California, students at Kimbark Elementary School study botany and investigate microscopic organisms and aquatic insects in an on-campus pond and vegetable garden, and in a nearby greenhouse and a native plant arboretum.
- In Glenwood Springs, Colorado, high school students planned and supervised the creation of an urban pocket park, and city planners asked them to help develop a pedestrian mall and park along the Colorado River.
- At Huntingdon Area Middle School in Pennsylvania, students collect data at a stream near the school. Teacher Mike Simpson uses that data to teach fractions, percentages, and statistics, as well as to interpret charts and graphs. "I don't have to worry about coming up with themes for application problems anymore. The students make their own," says Simpson.

David Sobel, who describes place-based education as a focus on "learning directly within the local community of a student," did an independent review of such studies, including one by the National Environmental Education and Training Foundation, which reported findings similar to Lieberman's. When it comes to reading skills, "the Holy Grail of education reform," says Sobel, place-based or environment-based education should be considered "one of the knights in shining armor." Students in these programs typically outperform their peers in traditional classrooms.

For example, at Hotchkiss Elementary School in Dallas, passing rates of fourth-graders in an environment-based program surpassed by 13 percent those of students in an earlier, traditional class. The Texas Education Agency's Division of Student Assessment called Hotchkiss's gains "extremely significant" when compared to the statewide average gain of 1 percent during the same period. Achievements in math are similar. In Portland, Environmental Middle School teachers employ a curriculum using local rivers, mountains, and forests; among other activities, they plant native species and study the Willamette River. At that school, 96 percent of students meet or exceed state standards for math problem-solving—compared to only 65 percent of eighth-graders at comparable middle schools. Environment-based education can amplify more typical school reform efforts. In North Carolina, raising standards produced a 15 percent increase in the proportion of fourth-graders scoring at the "proficient" level in statewide math scores. But fourth-graders at an environment-based school in Asheville, North Carolina, did even better—with a 31 percent increase in the number of students performing at the proficient level.

As an added bonus, the students in these programs demonstrate better attendance and behavior than students in traditional classrooms. Little Falls High School in Little Falls, Minnesota, reported that students in the environment-based program had 54 percent fewer suspensions than other ninth-graders. At Hotchkiss Elementary, teachers had once made 560 disciplinary referrals to the principal's office in a single year. Two years later, as the environment-based program kicked into gear, the number dropped to 50. "Both the principal and teachers attribute these decreases in behavioral problems to students' increased engagement in learning," according to Lieberman.

Sobel tells a charming story of a physics teacher at one school who was teaching mechanical principles "by involving students in the reconstruction of a neighborhood trail where they had to use pulleys, levers, and fulcrums to accomplish the task." On what the school calls Senior Skip Day, when seniors are free to skip any classes they want, one of the students told the physics teacher, "I want you to know, Mr. Church, that I skipped all the rest of my classes today, but I just couldn't miss this class. I'm too committed to what we're doing to skip this." With such indications that this kind of school reform works, why aren't more school districts considering it? That's a question unlikely to appear on any standardized test.

Proponents of experiential or environment-based education have established the Association for Experiential Education to support professional development, theoretical advancement, and evaluation of experiential education worldwide. The association now has approximately two thousand members in over thirty-five countries. A handful of organizations have made the leap from words to action. Among the oldest and best known is Foxfire, headquartered in Mountain City, Georgia. Its Foxfire Approach to Teaching and Learning originated in a program intended to teach basic English skills to high school freshmen in rural Georgia. These classroom experiences led to the student-produced *Foxfire Magazine* and a series of books on Appalachian life and folkways. Now three decades old, Foxfire offers teacher and student programs focusing on culture more than nature—but nature permeates the work, which offers information on everything from snake lore to wild plant foods to bear hunting.

Other active organizations include the venerable National Wildlife Federation and the Roger Tory Peterson Institute of Natural History in Jamestown, New York. Teachers at schools using the Peterson Institute's curriculum attend summer training. Upon their return to the classrooms, Peterson-trained teachers lead their students in a study of the square kilometer surrounding their building.

After a decade of publishing such writers as Gary Paul Nabhan and Robert Michael Pyle in *Orion* magazine, the Orion Society, a Massachusetts-headquartered nonprofit, "decided to help put some of these words into practice," writes environmental writer and frequent *Orion* contributor Will Nixon. Orion now gives nature education fellowships to teachers, including a summer workshop and grants to pay for field trips, sketchbooks, day packs, "or other items that schools with tight budgets can't afford."

Nixon quotes one Orion fellowship recipient, Bonnie Dankert, an English teacher at Santa Cruz High School: "I used to take student groups on trips to the California deserts or the High Sierras. We read literature about these places and studied the flora and fauna. We had some wonderful experiences." But, she confessed, she had never considered taking shorter excursions to the coastal mountains and Monterey Bay close to the school. She had assumed that her students knew and loved the area; she was wrong. Her students told her that they didn't feel connected to the place in which they lived; on a field trip to a state forest close to the school, Dankert discovered that 90 percent of the class had never been there. "They knew about it, but they had never been up there, sitting under a redwood tree and imagining what the scene looked like one hundred years ago," she told Nixon.

Dankert dropped the road trips and began teaching more locally, at Monterey Bay. She emphasized local authors. For example, while reading John Steinbeck's novel *Cannery Row*, Danker asked a local marine biologist to lead the students on a field trip to the tide pools in Monterey Bay, which Steinbeck had explored. In addition to helping the students learn about natural science, Dankert's students discussed the meaning of "community"—because one of Steinbeck's characters had described a tide pool as a metaphor for the community of life. And, wrote Nixon, the trip helped the class form its own community. "One kid had never taken off his baseball cap," Dankert remembered. "His eyes were always in shadow. Afterwards, he took off his cap and started interacting."

Another Orion fellow, a teacher at the junior high school in Homer, Alaska, helped organize a program that allowed eighth-graders to finish regular classes three weeks early; during that time, students studied a nearby glacier, learning glaciology, marine biology, botany, and cultural history. "This isn't memorizing information for a test," the teacher told Nixon. "When you sit in silence in front of a glacier and see the glacial pond, the dirt of the glacial moraine, the succession of plants from the lichens to the climax forest, and you write and sketch what you see, you make a bond with that moment. This experience becomes part of you."

James and the Giant Turnip

An increasing number of parents and a few good schools are realizing the importance and the magic of providing hands-on, intimate contact between children and nature as a larger part of a child's education. Some teachers come to interdisciplinary place-based education on their own, with no institutional support besides a sympathetic principal. Most current progress in education, in fact, comes from iconoclastic individuals, including the principals, teachers, parents, and community volunteers who chart their own courses. Committed individuals and service organizations can accomplish a great deal.

One creative elementary school teacher, Jackie Grobarek, describes what she called her "butterfly theory" of teaching, based loosely on meteorologist Edward Lorenz's theory that very small inputs at the beginning of a system's evolution are amplified through feedback and have major consequences throughout the system. (One interpreter popularized Lorenz's theory by calling it the "butterfly effect," wondering if the flap of a butterfly wing in Brazil could set off a tornado in Texas.) Grobarek describes the kind of hands-on experience with a payoff not always immediately visible:

> Schools are nonlinear systems and small inputs can lead to dramatically large consequences. Our students this summer have raised earthworms, plants, and caterpillars and released the emerged butterflies. Because the students' "babies" needed food, they also learned that the worms would eat garbage, the plants would thrive on worm castings, and that the butterflies required specific plants to eat, and other plants on which to lay their eggs. Many of these things were identified on our school grounds and in our canyon. They realized that our canyon, which had become an unattractive nuisance and trash pit in the neighborhood, was actually a wonderful habitat. It is filled with wild fennel, which is the host as well as food plant for the giant swallowtail butterfly. We are now working as class teams, and this week alone have hauled almost four Dumpsters of trash out of the area. Will this

improve their reading and math scores? Maybe, but I feel that this experience will change them in ways that tests may not be able to measure.

Sometimes, the catalyst is a principal with vision. At Torrey Pines Elementary School, near where I live, a committed young principal and his students adopted a nearby canyon. "We get the classes down here touching, tasting, smelling, tracking. It's hard to get twenty-six kids to be quiet, but we do it," said Dennis Doyle, the principal. He believes that encouraging more hands-on experience with nature is a better way to introduce children to science than relying just on textbooks. In fact, he explained, during the nineteenth century, nature study, as it was called, dominated elementary school science teaching. Now that nature study has been largely shoved aside by the technological advances of the twentieth century, an increasing number of educators have come to believe that technically oriented, textbook-based science education is failing.

At Torrey Pines Elementary, sixth-grade classes were scoring poorly on the hands-on portion of a science test given nationwide by the National Teachers Association. So Doyle and his staff decided on a radical tactic. They would restore the canyon behind the school to its natural state to create an outdoor classroom and nature trail. The idea was to help kids experience the kind of intimacy with nature that many of their parents enjoyed, and to improve science education—to make it immediate and personal.

On their forays into the canyon, work teams of kids, teachers, and parents ripped out the plants not native to the area, including pampas grass and Hottentot fig (commonly known as ice plant). Spanish sailors probably brought Hottentot fig to California. It is an edible and hardy plant rich in vitamin C, useful in the prevention of scurvy, explained a docent from nearby Torrey Pines State Park, who had teamed up with the school. Many people believe the Hottentot fig, a ground cover, prevents soil erosion, but, because of weighty water content in finger-like leaves, the plant can pull down a steep embankment. In this canyon, for this fig, the jig was up. The students returned the canyon habitat to native plants, including Torrey pines, yucca, cacti, and chaparral. The schoolchildren grew seedlings in their classes for later replanting.

One weekend, thirty parents worked in the canyon alongside the kids. Half of the parents were from wealthy nearby neighborhoods, the other half from the less affluent neighborhoods from which some of the students were bused. They hacked away at the pampas grass with machetes, all pushing and pulling together. "That kind of experience binds people together more than any formal integration program," Doyle said.

Doyle tries to keep the kids' canyon forays as relaxed as possible, and his adult view of nature minimized. As we walked through the canyon behind the school one day, he asked the kids questions, but didn't give the answers.

"Look at these twigs," said a boy named Darren. "It looks like one twig is dead, but one is alive."

"Why do you say that?" asked Doyle.

Darren launched into an elaborate and erroneous theory.

"That's an interesting theory."

Darren trailed after Doyle, excitedly checking other twigs. In this special classroom, imagination was more important than technical precision.

IN 1999, I MET a remarkable woman named Joan Stoliar. She lived in Greenwich Village with her husband, appeared to be in her sixties, had battled two types of cancer, and often traveled the streets of New York, with her high heels and fish-shaped earrings, astride her Lambretta motor scooter. A few months before cancer finally claimed her life, I accompanied her on a visit to a classroom at Intermediate School 318 in Brooklyn, where a cluster of seventh-graders attended four hundred trout fingerlings. The students hovered over the aquarium, set up to replicate a piece of trout stream.

For decades, Stoliar was one of the grande dames of the tweedy, traditional New York fly-fishing culture. She was probably the first woman to join the old, distinguished Theodore Gordon Flyfishers club. She talked the club into sponsoring New York State's trout-in-the-classroom program—with the help of Trout Unlimited, the National Fish and Wildlife Foundation, Hudson River Foundation, and Catskill Watershed Corporation.

Such programs—which began in California—have been springing up around the nation over the past decade. Their goal: to enliven biology and to connect kids to nature. The New York effort matches city kids with country kids, in what Stoliar called "a social experiment in creating sensitivity at both ends of the water tunnel." Several hundred students in ten inner-city New York schools and eight upstate schools work together to raise the trout and replant streams.

"This program gives city kids an appreciation for nature, but also teaches them about the source of their drinking water. They become watershed children," she said. In October, each school received several hundred fertilized brown trout eggs from the state's Department of Environmental Conservation; the hatchery director even gave the kids his home number in case anything went wrong. Students placed the eggs in tanks designed to re-create the habitat of a trout stream.

In Brooklyn's eight-foot piece of stream, a pump pushed water over rounded rocks and aquatic plants, and routed it through a chiller to keep it at a steady forty-nine degrees. Above the water, in a canopy of screening, insects hatched, rose, and fell. A "trout-cam" sent magnified images of the fish to an adjacent TV. The students cared for the trout and checked water temperature and pH level and other factors that can kill the eggs or fish. Stoliar called what the kids were learning "instant parenting."

In January of that year, the kids reported their progress on their class Web page: "We saw a caddis fly larvae eating a dead trout [and] we found a large fry with a trout tail sticking out of its mouth—it probably ate a smaller fish. Lot of dining action! About 42 fish have died in 1999 but we still have over 400 fish." As the trout grew, the rural and urban kids traded letters and e-mail about their progress. "We hope they remain friends for years, and maybe even fish in the same streams together someday," Stoliar said.

Each year, if the delicate trout survive until spring, the kids are bused north to a stream in the Catskills, where they meet the rural students, and together they release the fish into the wild. An eighth-grader named LaToya told me, "Up there you don't smell anything like toxic waste. I never saw a reservoir before. It was so beautiful, so clean."

ONE MORNING I visited the private Children's School in La Jolla, where teachers, parents, and kids were hard at work on a garden, following the guidelines of a famous expert on gardening who would visit shortly. As the students waited for Mel Bartholomew's arrival, I asked the fourth-, fifth- and sixth-graders in teacher Tina Kafka's class what they thought of gardening.

"I think the lettuce you buy at the store tastes better than the lettuce you get from a garden," said James, a skeptical eleven-year-old. "At the store they wash it real well. They've got those spray nozzles going all the time." James is new to gardening; the school's is his first. Matt, ten, offered his own critique of gardening. "The problem I have with gardening is it's not improving, not like technology, not like TVs and computers. All these old wood gardening tools haven't changed in decades." Speaking like a true child of the twenty-first century, he added, "Tools should improve." James and Matt are typical of many youngsters today, particularly the ones who live in Southern California housing tracts with their square-foot backyards. It's tough for a garden to get a kid's attention, unless it's on CD-ROM.

In an effort to change that, Kafka and her co-teacher, Chip Edwards, helped their students create a garden based on Bartholomew's approach. Bartholomew, now a retired civil engineer and efficiency expert, wrote *Square Foot Gardening* several decades ago. The best-selling book was the basis for a long-running Discovery Channel series on cable TV. People who use his system eschew traditional rows, which made sense for plowing, in favor of square-foot blocks, which lend themselves to more personal care. Gardeners can easily reach the plants in each cluster for planting or weeding. This approach also seems to make more sense for kids, whose arms and reach are shorter. It reduces gardening to a more manageable scale and increases the chance for success. "I ate some lettuce from our school garden," said Brandon, ten. "I washed it and put some salad dressing on it, and it tasted better than the lettuce you get from the store."

A classmate, Ben, eleven, added, "I like the radishes out of our garden a lot better. The ones from the store are too spicy." And Ariana, ten, reported how a gopher attacked a turnip she grew in the school garden. "He hollowed it out!"

I turned to James. "Would any turnip that touched a gopher's lips touch yours?" "No!" he answered in horror.

Just then, Bartholomew arrived. Bartholomew, who lives in Old Field, New York, is a tall, lanky man with a mustache, thinning hair, and the kindest of eyes; he was accompanied by his sister, Althea Mott, of Huntington Beach. The two of them founded the Square Foot Gardening Foundation, which promotes the therapeutic value of gardening. They visit libraries, nursing homes, churches, and schools.

"Our goal is to have gardening included in every school curriculum," he explained. "We're writing programs for all grade levels and all seasons. We want kids to communicate with other gardening kids around the country, first by letter, but eventually through the Internet. We also hope they'll take gardening home and involve their families." Wearing jeans and ready to garden, Bartholomew headed out back to the class garden. The kids (including James and Matt, who now seemed particularly eager) moved confidently to their tasks, to weeding and watering. Bartholomew hovered over them, smiling, asking them gently about their crops.

Kafka, who stood to one side, said, "For us, the garden has been much more than simply planting vegetables and taking care of them. It's been a bonding experience. When we go to the garden as a class at the end of the day, there is a strong feeling of shared joy and peace no matter how hard the day has been." She described how, one drizzly Monday morning, the students arrived to find that skateboarders had vandalized their garden. "We decided to focus on renewing our garden rather than on whodunit," said Kafka. After the vandalism, the students named their garden "Eve's Garden," after one of their fellow students, who had left the school and whom they missed.

Bartholomew looked proudly at the students working together. "It's so important for kids to understand where their food comes from," he said. Suddenly James announced, "My turnip is ready. It's a *big* one."

"James and the Giant Turnip," someone said.

"Drum roll!"

James grunted and pulled on the turnip until it came loose from the soil. He held it up proudly for all to see, and brushed the dirt from it. Then he held the turnip close to his ear. He knocked on it to see if it was hollow. And he grinned.

Ecoschools

Ideally, school nature programs will go beyond curriculum or field trips: they will involve the initial, physical design of a new school; or the retrofitting of an old school with playscapes that incorporate nature into the central design principle; or, as described earlier, the use of nature preserves by environment-based schools.

The schoolyard habitat movement began in the 1970s, stimulated by environmental education programs, such as Project Learning Tree and Project WILD, and a successful national program in Great Britain called Learning through Landscapes. At least one-third of Britain's thirty thousand schoolyards have been improved by this program, inspiring a similar program in Canada called Learning Grounds, and a major Swedish program, Skolans Uterum. By 1996, more than forty or-ganizations were involved in natural school-grounds enhancement, ac-cording to a survey by the U.S. Fish and Wildlife Service, one of several major agencies with traditional wildlife conservation missions working in this area. Some organizations, which originated in environmental ed-ucation, have also forged links with science and education departments of universities, museums, and conservation organizations. The Na-tional Wildlife Federation, with its Schoolyard Habitats certification program, is a leader in encouraging the creation of hands-on, outdoor learning opportunities that cannot be duplicated in the traditional class-room setting.

Mary Rivkin, a professor of early childhood education at the Uni-versity of Maryland, Baltimore County, and one of the most thoughtful and prolific academics working in this arena, cites the biophilia hypo-thesis, as well as the work of attention-restoration researchers Stephen and Rachel Kaplan, particularly their work on "nearby nature" and its wide range of benefits for children and adults. Many preschools "have excellent outdoor play spaces because early childhood teachers have a long and sturdy tradition of having plants and animals accessible to chil-dren and incorporating outdoor play into their daily activities," accord-ing to Rivkin. She describes the typical greening efforts and the ideal: "Schools usually start with small projects, although some schools do major work, especially in new construction." They might begin with butterfly gardens, bird feeders and baths, tree planting, or native plant gardens. Moving on to larger projects, they can create ponds, nature trails, or restore streams. Ecologically valuable projects are valued over beautification. Pump-operated or natural streams can offer water play. "Dirt and sand must be for digging as well as planting; clay can often be found for making things. Some plants must be for picking," she advises. "Seeing such things is only part of learning about them. Touching, tast-ing, smelling, and pulling apart are also vital. Shrubs and trees for climbing are the real thing . . ." Assuming a secure perimeter around the schoolyard, children also need private spaces: bushes, tall grass, a cluster of rocks. "A circle of 6-foot pines is a forest to young children."

As Rivkin points out, the task of helping the 108,000 schools in the United States "green their grounds" is daunting, even with the widening web of institutional support, including conferences sponsored by the American Horticulture Society, the North American Association for Environmental Education, the Society for Ecological Research, the Brooklyn and Cleveland Botanical Gardens, and others. Increasingly, preschools and child-care facilities are housed in office buildings, a trend that undermines the burgeoning schoolyard habitat movement. And in public-school settings, "the bleakness of asphalt and close-mown grass in outdoor areas presents a major challenge to outdoor nature experiences." Nonetheless, the schoolyard habitats movement "is literally gaining ground."

There is another movement that tends to ebb and flow during bad and good economic times: the ecoschool, which is a school initially designed for and dedicated to using nature studies as a touchstone in its curriculum. The concept has been popular for decades in Europe. There are 2,800 ecoschools in the United Kingdom and Scotland. The concept attracts Dave Massey, regional coordinator of the California Regional Environmental Education Community, a new state office. Massey says school districts should protect every square inch of natural landscape adjacent to schools, not only for environmental reasons, but also for educational gain. He recommends, "We [need to] put some thought into the planning of every new school so that the surrounding nature is available and used." As an elementary-school principal, Massey prized a stream near his school as an outdoor lab: "I had kids out there twice a week, studying the cottonwoods, planting native plants."

At the cutting edge of ecoschool thinking are foundation-to-roof "green" schools, constructed with, say, compacted straw bales and plaster, an increasingly popular low-cost alternative for building highly insulated walls. The school itself becomes a lesson in ecology.

Toward an Interconnected Nature Education Movement

To suggest that ecoschools, schoolyard greening, or experiential education programs are representative of a major movement would be misleading, but the numbers are increasing, and a major movement is possible —and not just in the United States and other post-industrial countries.

Among the challenges the potential movement faces: the need for more coordination and links between diverse organizations, initiatives, and individual schools. These links would encourage greater collaboration and, with luck, political power. There is a push now under way to further document the connection between academic achievement and environment-based education. As "happy and proud" as Lieberman is about the findings of his study, "it's not enough. We need other people doing more studies—and more in the classroom."

As could be expected, place-based education increases students' sense of stewardship and environmental consciousness and adds to their sense of attachment to place. Yet, Lieberman detects a curious resistance to environment-based education from some quarters of the environmental movement. He believes that some of these organizations see the young primarily as message-delivering instruments. "If you ask most environmental groups what the purpose of environmental education is, they'll say it's a great way to get their messages to adults."

Environmental organizations do have a vital role to play in outdoor education. For example, the Sierra Club's popular Inner City Outings (ICO), a community outreach program, provides low-income, inner-city youth with trips to the wilderness. The Sierra Club's San Francisco Bay chapter established the first ICO group in 1971. In 2002, forty-six Sierra Club chapters led eight hundred trips for fourteen thousand children. That's an impressive beginning. But, as of this writing, for all ICO programs in the United States, only two paid positions exist—a national coordinator and an assistant. Volunteers provide the backbone of the movement. Most ICOs operate their outings on budgets of less than seven thousand dollars a year and depend on such companies as REI to donate or loan equipment, tents, and hiking gear.

A survey by the U.S. Fish and Wildlife Service reveals that more than forty organizations are working to encourage the development of schoolyards "as places to directly inform children about their natural heritage and engage them in its preservation," according to educator Mary Rivkin. But the United States lags behind Great Britain, Canada, and Sweden in this area; much more remains to be done.

Fortunately, even in the face of economic hard times and so many trends that move children away from nature, many individual teachers, parents, and organizations around the world, particularly in Canada, Great Britain, the Scandinavian countries, and the United States, continue to work for more nature in the classroom, more focus on "nearby nature," greener school grounds and even new designs for ecoschools. In addition, the experiential learning movement and its ancillaries are working to better document the relationship between environmental education in schools and stewardship behavior.

What else would help? Schools could begin to build significant relationships with nature centers, environmental organizations, and bird sanctuaries, rather than using them for one-shot visits. Instead of waiting for a turnaround in school spending, such organizations could band together to hire part-time environmental educators to work in classrooms, organize parent/teacher/student activities, and help teachers learn how to integrate school grounds and nearby parks, woods, fields, or canyons into the core curriculum. Ultimately, such efforts lead to more effective education. "'Behavior leads to behavior' is one of our maxims," says Lieberman. "For a long time we talked about knowledge leading to behavior; instead, we believe that behavior leads to behavior." What about the pure joy of being in nature? "Pure joy? Not in the curriculum," he says, laughing. "We advocate for joy, but certainly haven't tried to measure it."

Higher Education, Ecological Literacy, and the Resurrection of Natural History

David Orr, professor of environmental studies at Oberlin College and founder of the Meadowcreek Project, a conservation education center, calls for a new environmental literacy requirement at the college level. Orr argues that the ecological crisis is rooted in the way we educate future generations. The dominant form of education today "alienates us from life in the name of human domination, fragments instead of unifies, overemphasizes success and careers, separates feeling from intellect and the practical from the theoretical, and unleashes on the world minds ignorant of their ignorance." In other words, today's practices help create the know-it-all state of mind, and the accompanying loss of wonder.

Orr calls for a new approach to education to promote "ecological design intelligence" that could, in turn, create "healthy, durable, resilient, just, and prosperous communities." He asks educators and students this elemental question: Do four years in college make "graduates better planetary citizens or does it make them, in Wendell Berry's words, 'itinerant professional vandals'? Does this college contribute to the development of a sustainable regional economy or, in the name of efficiency, to the processes of destruction?" He envisions the kind of education reform—or reformation—that would fully acknowledge the social and biological alienation from the natural world, and the necessity of the healing of that division to the survival of the human race.

Orr proposes that colleges set a goal of ecological literacy for all students, so that no student would graduate without a basic comprehension of:

- the laws of thermodynamics
- the basic principles of ecology
- carrying capacity
- energetics
- least-cost, end-use analysis

- how to live well in a place
- limits of technology
- appropriate scale
- sustainable agriculture and forestry
- steady-state economics
- environmental ethics

Such a focus on ecological reality is essential at the college and every other educational level, but its implementation carries the risk of promoting joyless ideology. A sense of wonder and joy in nature should be at the very center of ecological literacy.

For this type of reform to take place in a meaningful way, there will need to be a rebirth of natural history in the academy. In an earlier chapter, Paul Dayton offered his obituary for natural history. The professor of marine ecology argues that natural history has been "expelled from the ivory tower," and that biology undergraduates at many universities are not taught classic botany or zoology. The prevailing patent-or-perish approach in the sciences has left many first-year graduate students with little or no knowledge of major phyla, or of the life-history biology of the very organisms they study.

In a scathing paper for the journal *Scientia Marina*, Dayton and associate professor Enric Sala argue that some students are taught ecology using textbooks based almost entirely on molecular biology and theoretical population biology. "This prevailing attitude denies students the sense of wonder and sense of the place fundamental to the discipline. Worse, there are ecologists who have never seen the communities or populations they model or speculate about, and who could not identify the species composing these communities. This is like having the illusion of conducting heart surgery without knowing what a real heart looks like." The study of ecology has moved from the descriptive to the mechanistic, and research support has shifted from "individualized small science to very large integrated research programs where the players have small roles well defined by the group," rewarding "group mentalities more than individual creativity." They write:

> Without a sound formation on natural history, we risk producing narrow-minded ecologists. Naturalists are closer to poets than to engineers, and it is the intuition based on first-hand experience and common sense that produces the better leaps of thought. We should imprint on our students the importance of intuition, imagination, creativity, and iconoclasm, and prevent restricting them with the braincuffs of rigid assumption frames and techniques, if we are to revitalize an ecological science that is more than ever becoming a stronghold of fundamentalism.

By that, Dayton and Sala mean the fundamentally narrow vision of science. When I asked Dayton how such a revolution—or counterrevolution—might be organized, he said, "I am sure that there are some wonderful naturalists who are also molecular biologists. I am not sure I have met many, but they are there. And for sure that is true of taxonomists." Still, he worries that his fellow natural historians do not understand the stakes involved. Universities cannot find teachers to teach such classes because so few now know the fundamentals of biology and natural history. How do we reverse this trend? I again urge parents, primary and secondary educators, environmental organizations, and policymakers to weigh the meaning of this loss to education, to creativity, and to the natural environment. The associations of remaining natural historians must help lead the crusade. The survival of their own profession is linked to a larger cause: the reconnection of the young with nature.

An environment-based education movement—at all levels of education—will help students realize that school isn't supposed to be a polite form of incarceration, but a portal to the wider world.

17. Camp Revival

For decades in San Diego, the school district has operated a sixth-grade camp in the nearby mountains. Generations of kids have spent a week during the school year among the pines. Over the years, however, this camp's central purpose has shifted from a pure nature experience; it has become, primarily, a race-relations retreat with nature used as backdrop. Still, this camp continues to give some children their first or best experience in nature. Myra, now in ninth grade, describes her time at sixth-grade camp:

> I haven't truly experienced nature much. My family is not one that believes in camping or spending time in the outside world, even though my parents were brought up in a rural society. For the most part, I spend my time at home. The only time I can remember having lived in nature, in the open, was in sixth grade on the camping trip to Palomar. There, I felt truly comfortable, being among few people and walking down paths that weren't paved. . . . Sure, the food was bad and the cabins were uncomfortable, but the walks and hikes were interesting and fun. I truly belonged somewhere in the scheme of things. . . . Sometimes, I feel like I just want to get away from the world, so I dwell in nature through my thoughts and memories.

As with so many young people, the modern world is sometimes too much with Myra. How can we overestimate children's need for respite from CNN, school stress, or family tensions? Camps have their own pressures, but the healing quality of nature is always there, just beyond the screen door, and then, as Myra experienced, those memories remain, like time-release capsules of medication.

Clearly there's more to the camping experience than tents and bug bites. The *nature* experience at these camps could be lost if nature camps allow their mission be become diluted, if they attempt to please everyone all the time. Race-relations and other cultural/political programs at camps across the land are important attempts to imagine a gentler, better world. These are important discussions in a democracy, but childhood is short. If we make those issues our sole priority, another generation—or more—could enter adulthood without significant experiences in nature. The great worth of outdoor education programs is their focus on the elements that have always united humankind: driving rain, hard wind, warm sun, forests deep and dark—and the awe and amazement that our Earth inspires, especially during our formative years.

The social context of camp is important. "The best camps are creating the best of what existed in the 1940s—a sense of shared purpose" says Mary Pipher, clinical psychologist, family therapist, and author of *Reviving Ophelia*. But the direct experience in nature is the most important aspect of the camp experience.

Adults who enjoyed early camp experiences often tell stories about practical jokes and latrine hazards, but they can also describe transcendent moments—and the importance of building self-confidence in situations of controlled risk. Ann Pearse Hocker, who later became a photographer for CBS (often doing her work in dangerous conditions), recalls the sense of independence and responsibility that summer camp in Colorado taught her:

> I learned about caution. Once we were on a training hike for Longs Peak and an electrical storm drove us down early. We passed a couple of hikers stuck at the boulder field on the way down. The woman

had wedged her leg between two boulders and couldn't get out. The rain was pounding and the lightning was below us. We had to run straight down the power line easements and skip the trail, which was full of switchbacks. Met the ranger on his horse on the way up to rescue them. The lightning was so bad on the way down that I felt buzzing in my braces and had to hold my mouth with my hand. We were wet and a bit scared but also felt powerful when we got to the bottom and the safety of the old blue bus. It was a vivid lesson on how nature plays hardball if you aren't prepared when you go into the back or high country, and I never forgot it. I made mistakes sometimes but the basis of respect was well laid.

Why the Investment Makes Sense

According to Andrea Faber Taylor's and Frances E. Kuo's analysis of the literature, "Some of the most exciting findings of a link between contact with green space and developmental outcomes come from studies examining the effects of outdoor challenge programs on children's self-esteem and sense of self. . . . It is interesting to note that four studies included longitudinal measures and found that participants continued to report beneficial outcomes long (up to several years) after their nature experience."

Studies of outdoor-education programs geared toward troubled youth—especially those diagnosed with mental-health problems—show a clear therapeutic value. The positive effect holds true whether the program is used as an add-on to more traditional therapy or as therapy in and of itself; it can even be seen when outdoor programs are not specifically designed for therapy. Studies over the past decade have shown that participants in adventure-therapy programs made gains in self-esteem, leadership, academics, personality, and interpersonal relations. "These changes were shown to be more stable over time than the changes generated in more traditional education programs," according to Dene S. Berman and Jennifer Davids-Berman, in a review of such programs for the Clearinghouse on Rural Education and Small Schools.

Camping programs have been used to facilitate emotional well-being since the early 1900s. According to one study, an increase in self-esteem was most pronounced for preteens, but was positive across all ages.

Outward Bound USA is the nation's leading nonprofit adventure-education organization. It serves and supports four wilderness schools, two urban centers, and a primary and secondary school program. The organization's programs emphasize personal growth through experience and challenge in the wilderness. With more than five hundred thousand alumni, Outward Bound USA programs enlist more than sixty thousand young people and adults each year. An analysis of ninety-six studies published between 1968 and 1994 concludes that Outward Bound programs stimulate the development of interpersonal competencies, enhance leadership skills, and have positive effects on adolescents' senses of empowerment, self-control, independence, self-understanding, assertiveness, and decision-making skills, according to Judith A. Boss, a lecturer in philosophy at the University of Rhode Island.

Camp experiences are also highly beneficial for children with disabilities. Between 1994 and 1995, the National Survey of Recreation and the Environment conducted a national study of 17,216 Americans. A 2001 analysis of that data, focusing on people with disabilities, found that their participation in outdoor recreation and adventure activities was *equal to or greater than* that of people without disabilities. Other studies show that people with disabilities participate in the most challenging of outdoor recreation activities; they seek risk, challenge, and adventure in the outdoors just as do their contemporaries without disabilities.

Researchers have also found that people with disabilities gain enhanced body image and positive behavior changes from their camp experiences. One study of fifteen residential summer camp programs with specialized programs for children with disabilities—including learning disabilities, autism, sensory disabilities, moderate and severe cognitive disabilities, physical disabilities, and traumatic brain injury—revealed that participating children demonstrated improved initiative and self-direction that transferred to their lives at home and in school.

A strong public argument for the expansion of camps and outdoor education can be made based on the restorative power of nature; the connection to health is a more marketable idea than is nostalgia for s'mores and campfires. We need, in essence, a camp revival.

Here is a plan for an alternative future: the institutions that care for children—churches, synagogues, Scouting organizations, recreation programs, businesses, conservation and art groups—should form partnerships to build a new arm of public education. Every school district in America should be associated with one or more wildlife-and-childhood preserves in its region. Creating and nurturing such places would be far less expensive than building more brick-and-mortar science labs (though we need more of those, as well) and more needed than the purchase of the newest generation of soon-to-be-obsolete computers. These preserves could also become the focus of higher education's recommitment to natural history. And they should produce added impetus for a nationwide review of liability laws.

Such nature-education preserves could be part of a new kind of school reform.

Childlife Preserves

One example of the potential for new outdoor-education preserves is on Washington's Bainbridge Island, where Debbie Brainerd and husband Paul Brainerd, former owner of the major software company Aldus, bought 255 acres and turned it into the nonprofit Puget Sound Environmental Learning Center, which the *Seattle Post-Intelligencer* called "a $52 million, 255-acre layout that melds the adventure of Tom Sawyer's island with space-station technology and wilderness serenity." Debbie Brainerd calls it "a magical place for learning," particularly for low-income, underserved urban youths; it is a place where youths and teachers can stay for several days, using "all five senses to learn science, math, art, writing, technology and culture—and how subjects can be linked," according to the *Post-Intelligencer.* An energy-efficient student dorm, called the "Birdsnest," is made of hand-hewn wood and includes a "mud room." Museum-donated fossils are imbedded in rock fireplaces. But children spend most of their time outdoors, exploring. This nature-focused learning center has been called "the world's most innovative center for environmental education." Though not every community has benefactors like Debbie and Paul Brainerd, a proliferation of smaller-scale child/nature preserves is possible and practical—given the high cost of brick-and-mortar classrooms.

The future of education, said Candy Vanderhoff, is in the outdoors. I walked with her as she headed through the cool woods down a little ravine and watched students spread out in solitude, writing, listening. Vanderhoff is an architect whose side specialty is indigenous shelters. Her personal goal is to photograph and catalogue South Sea island huts before they fade away forever. Several years ago, she found her way to Tijuana, Mexico, to help internationally respected artist James Hubbell create a school of earth and stone and tiles. In 2001, Hubbell urged her to take a lead role in a program for teenagers at Crestridge Ecological Reserve, a 2,600-acre parcel of mountainous land near El Cajon, California—the same place I visited with the boyz of the woods.

Crestridge is a new kind of park—part day camp, part nature preserve—a type that some communities across the country are creating and a model for what others should create.

Here, a partnership of several organizations, including Granite Hills High School, a conservation organization called the Back Country Land Trust, and Hubbell's company have joined forces. At the time of my first visit, Hubbell and his son Drew were planning to construct "a nature kiosk at the head of the trail, a gate of sorts, a way to break out of one pattern and enter another," as James put it. Construction will be "sustainable," said Vanderhoff. Biodegradable. Recycled.

Later in the day, we hiked through the tangle of oaks and joined a half circle of students under an oak old enough to have sprouted when Lewis and Clark were scouting real estate. The kids sat on granite boulders pocked with wrist-deep acorn grinding holes created long ago by the Kumeyaay Indians. The group listened to Larry Banegas, founder of Kumeyaay.com, a Web site that tells the history of his people. Raised on the nearby Barona reservation, Banegas teaches what he calls "traditional knowledge." He explained to the kids that the Kumeyaay "weren't nomadic; they lived part of the year in the mountains and part of the year at the beach," and were far from passive players in the wilderness. Among other techniques, they employed fire to open the chaparral canopy and allow the growth of plants used for food and medicine. They also created dams to trap river sediment, raising the water table and creating new wetlands for watercress and wild celery and lettuce. These manipulations of land and water contradict the Eden myth: that the Indians lived in a wilderness untouched by human intervention. What Banegas was saying lends weight, instead, to controversial new theories about the pre-Columbian Western Hemisphere: that it was much more populated and sophisticated than we have generally believed.

I wondered: What message will the students take home about human involvement in nature? Will they learn that humans have always shaped nature in order to sustain it, in order to survive? This question is at the heart of the future of environmentalism.

Later that morning, I mentioned a pet peeve to Vanderhoff. By the understandable rules of nature preserves everywhere, no kid will be allowed to build a tree house or fort on Crestridge Ecological Reserve—despite the fact that many of us, including environmentalists, first learned to engage nature by building forts in the woods. What happens when kids can no longer do that, when what remains is under glass?

Vanderhoff thought about this for a while, then went to her car and returned with a book about California Indian survival techniques. She pointed to an illustration of a hut, a Kumeyaay shelter framed in willow and covered by brush and tulles. "There!" she said, smiling. "That's what kids could build here. Wouldn't that be terrific?"

That it would.

TODAY'S YOUNG PEOPLE ARE, as we've seen, growing up in America's third frontier. This frontier has yet to completely form, but we do know the general characteristics. Among them: detachment from the source of food, the virtual disappearance of the farm family, the end of biological absolutes, an ambivalent new relationship between humans and other animals, new suburbs shrinking open space, and so on. In this time of quickening change, could we enable another frontier to be born—ahead of schedule?

PART VI

WONDER LAND: OPENING THE FOURTH FRONTIER

. . . we have not merely escaped from something

but also into something . . . we have joined the greatest of all communities,

which is not that of man alone but of everything which shares with us

the great adventure of being alive.

—JOSEPH WOOD KRUTCH

18. The Education of Judge Thatcher: Decriminalizing Natural Play

SOMETIMES IT SEEMS that Mark Twain's Tom and Huck should pack it in—come home from the woods, plug in Becky's PlayStation 2, and master the new Grand Theft Auto video game. If Becky's father, Judge Thatcher, were to review the bizarre legal framework today covering children, recreation, the environment, and landowner liability, he might be puzzled by the phalanx of legal restrictions and homeowners' covenants—which come from the left and the right—that favor electrical outlets over just about every form of natural play.

Asked for legal advice on this matter, the judge might log on to LexisNexis, the online legal database, and study up. Likely, he would seize on the one apparent bright spot in our legal structure: the so-called "recreational use" statutes adopted by many states in recent years.

"Ah, potential satisfaction!" he might mutter.

These laws were established to encourage landowners to allow people to recreate on their open land. For example, California Civil Code section 846 is calculated "to balance the need for increased recreational area with the concern of landowners regarding liability to entrants who use private land for recreation." The statute states that a property owner "owes no duty of care to keep the premises safe for entry or use by others for any recreational purpose or to give any warning of hazardous conditions. . . ." In other words, a landowner who permits people to recreate on his property is not required to guarantee their safety. The statute does not limit liability, however, in cases of "willful or malicious failure to guard or warn against a dangerous condition or for injury suffered in any case where permission to enter for the above purpose was granted for a consideration other than the consideration."

"Whatever that means," Judge Thatcher might say, crossing his eyes.

Also, the statute does not protect landowners from being sued by "any persons who are expressly invited rather than merely permitted to come upon the premises by the landowner." The statute doesn't mention children specifically; that application is up to case law. But here's one way to interpret the wording: a parent who invites kids to use the property or supervises their play (or whose own child invites another child over to play) is more vulnerable to lawsuit than a parent who doesn't know who is on the property—or a parent who says "okay," in a generalized fashion and looks the other way.

At this point, Judge Thatcher might sit back, adjust his spectacles, and conclude that he had slipped into another universe, not just another century.

True, different attorneys can look into this statute and tell different futures. Ultimately, liability is determined by the interpretation of a particular court, and the courts have been inconsistent, to say the least. For example, in 1979, a California judge in Santa Clara Valley ruled that the recreational use statute did not protect a property owner. In this case, a girl fell while riding her bike across a bridge on private property. Since she was not "recreating," the landowner was found liable. Got that? In another case, however, a landowner was granted immunity when a child was injured climbing a tree on his property.

"Go forth and figure!" Judge Thatcher might exclaim.

Upon further contemplation, he might well consider leaving the bench to become a trial attorney. Scratching his muttonchops, he would begin to think—about Tom painting that fence, from a public sidewalk?—And about that incident at the cave—with his very daughter! Who owned that cave?

"Why, the very idea!" he might say. "Becky, come here. Right now. I want to ask you a few questions . . ."

Natural Tort Reform, and Other Remedies

As a powerful deterrent to natural play, fear of liability ranks right behind the bogeyman. One goal in the fourth frontier should be a nationwide review of laws governing private land and recreation, especially involving children. This review process should be public; it should invite parents, children, and experts on child's play and others to offer testimonials. And it should be done with the goal of protecting both the child's safety and the child's right to play in natural settings. It should focus on reducing the anxiety of parents and children—and the fear of lawyers that, even if only subconsciously, adds to modern barriers separating children from natural play. As part of this conversation, community associations should review their covenants to decide where they stand on the criminalization of nature play. Public governments should do the same. This issue is not only a question of the letter of the law, but also the spirit.

In the public domain, part of the solution is a change of official attitude. Many of the restrictions on kids' play, particularly the environmental rules designed to protect nature, are rational, if applied with a sense of proportion. For example, rather than serving citations, or chasing kids away without explanation, park rangers could focus on nature education, teaching families and the young how to enjoy the outdoors without being destructive. Many rangers are doing these things already—when they are not understaffed and overwhelmed by other duties. But let's be realistic. As long as cities continue to overdevelop housing tracts and underdevelop parks and other sites for natural play, our regional parks and beaches will be crushed by demand, necessitating ever more stringent enforcement. The ultimate remedies aren't to lift the restrictions on endangered habitat, but to create or preserve more natural places to play—including the vacant lots and ravines and backyards of our own neighborhoods—and to reduce private vulnerability to lawsuits and fines.

One way to confront the litigious barriers to natural play is to create more naturally landscaped public parks and more heavily insured private play spaces. These would be, essentially, legally protected, natural play reservations—something like the Crestridge Reserve. Environment-based education expert David Sobel proposes the creation of what he calls "environmental sacrifice zones." Play reservations, if you will. "It's good to have streams where kids can dam and obstruct the ecosystem; the nature of that play is more important, and worth it to the environment in the long term," he says. "Kids aren't supposed to play on the dunes, because that creates erosion, which undermines the foundations of houses along the shore. But some dunes ought to be accessible for dune play, even though a bit of damage might occur as a result. When I say that, people roll their eyes. You can make that same argument about tree houses, which undeniably damage the tree, but that occasional damage to a tree is not as important as what children learn when playing in that tree."

Even with the creation of many such play areas, families and neighborhoods will still face an array of laws, regulations, and private restrictions on outdoor play; but options exist.

A private neighborhood could potentially overcome liability issues by following the lead of the SkatePark Association of the USA, a group started by a Santa Monica mom in 1996. Let's say a skate park joins the organization. The fee is currently $40 a year for private parks and $120 a year for city parks. Individual skaters sign up for a nominal fee. In return, the skater receives $100,000 excess medical coverage while in a sanctioned park or anywhere else, and $1,000,000 liability insurance in the park. This arrangement suggests interesting possibilities for more natural play: the Sierra Club or some other major environmental organization could someday offer a similar group insurance policy.

Another option is that every family, with or without children, consider increasing its liability insurance coverage. The American Insurance Association suggests that a standard homeowner's insurance policy will cover liability for, say, a tree-house accident, but homeowners should still check their coverage. The typical homeowner policy carries on-site accident coverage of only $100,000. Some insurance experts recommend buying extra liability insurance. The price of an umbrella policy, providing $1 million worth of coverage, to accompany a homeowner policy, is, in fact, modest—usually about $200 a year; add another $50 and gain an extra million in coverage. Some umbrella policies will cover empty lots, too. The problem here is if the bar is set at $1 million, someone's going to sue for $2 million. Where, short of tort reform—or a fortified system of peer review to stop nuisance lawsuits—does it end?

Don't Give Up

The legal tangle of outdoor play will be one of the most difficult challenges in the fourth frontier. But to encourage a host of other positive changes to take place, the barriers of a litigious society must be lowered.

"In the past, if a child or teen broke an arm on the sidewalk, in a neighbor's yard, or at the school yard, Dad's insurance would pay the bills," says Jim Condomitti, a father who lives in Escondido, California. "Our parents accepted responsibility for our accidents, careless behavior, or deliberate actions. Today, as seven-figure monetary awards dance in our heads, we open the Yellow Pages and search for attorneys who can fish in the deep pockets of a school district, a city, or an insurance company."

In many cases, the litigious bark may be worse than the bite. Condomitti found this out when his community began to crack down on playing ball in the street. (Such play may not involve nature, but at least it's based on direct rather than simulated experience and it's outdoors.) Condomitti pored over the vaguely worded legal codes of several municipalities, and found few if any legal grounds to ban such play, unless children actually block or impede the flow of traffic. "Parents and kids shouldn't give up so easily," he says. The good news is that they don't have to.

Bad law can be rewritten; protections from litigation strengthened; new types of natural recreational areas invented—and even new kinds of cities and towns created, where nature is welcome and natural play the norm—for children and adults.

19. Cities Gone Wild

Julia Fletcher, Janet Fout's daughter, moved from West Virginia to Washington, D.C., to attend George Washington University. She operates a refreshment cart at the Kennedy Center and sometimes takes it to the roof terrace, where she finds the view of the Potomac River calming. Early one evening, she noticed a man there with his two young children. The girl and boy were paying close attention to their father, who was watching a circling raptor.

"It's not a turkey vulture," he said, "but you're close. What else could it be?" The kids looked heavenward again.

"A hawk," pronounced the boy.

"Warmer," replied Dad, "but what kind of hawk?"

"A white-headed hawk?" inquired the daughter.

"Nope. What kinds of hawks are near the water?"

As Julia tells this story, she was about to burst with the answer when the son said:

"One that eats fish?"

"Exactly. It's an osprey," their father said. "Now, how can you identify it next time?"

At this point, Julia moved on with her work, but continued to think about the conversation. Because her mother took time to explore nature with her, she identified with the children and their questions. "And I was heartened that even in a city like Washington, there were other children who would grow up like I did," she says. "Until that moment, all evidence of this had been to the contrary, since no one I know at the university can identify an osprey. Nature in the city is nature at her most tenacious—in some ways that makes it my favorite kind of nature."

Today, a growing number of ecologists and ethicists are challenging the assumption that cities have no room for wildlife. Some would have you imagine your city as a "zoopolis." That's the word—rhymes with "metropolis"—that Jennifer Wolch, a professor at the University of Southern California and director of the Sustainable Cities Project, uses when she imagines areas in cities transformed into natural habitats through land-planning, architectural design, and public education.

To most people, that would seem like a stretch. Just listen to our language: We talk about "empty land" at the urban fringe (far from empty, it teems with non-human life), and "improving" land (grading and filling and topping it with Jiffy Lubes). Most urban theory ignores non-human species. So do even the most progressive architecture schools, even as those graders keep scraping the hills. Yet, says Wolch, a zoopolis movement, though poorly documented, is emerging in many U.S. cities, often for practical reasons. For example, conventional landscaping produces biologically sterile, water-dependent environments. This has led some cities in arid regions to encourage native plant species, which need less maintenance and contribute to wildlife habitat.

Central to this notion is the psychological need for biophilia—the life-enhancing sense of rootedness in nature. Daniel Botkin, president of the Center for the Study of the Environment, in Santa Barbara, asserts that "Without the recognition that the city is of and within the environment, the wilderness . . . that most of us think of as natural cannot survive." John Beardsley of the Harvard Design School expresses the same hope for a new kind of urban and suburban landscape in which our children and our children's children could one day grow up:

We need to hold out for healthy ecosystems in the city and the suburbs; we need to insist that culture—however much it might flirt with simulation—retain a focus on the real world, its genuine problems and possibilities. At the mall or the theme park, what does this mean? Can we imagine a mall that is also a working landscape, that is energy self-sufficient, that treats its own wastewater, and that recycles its own materials? Can we imagine a theme park that is genuinely fun and truly educational and environmentally responsible all at once? I don't see why not. We have created the "nature" we buy and sell in the marketplace; we should certainly be able to change it.

Preserving islands of wild land—parks and preserves—in urban areas is not enough, according to current ecological theory. Instead, a healthy urban environment requires natural corridors for movement and genetic diversity. One can imagine such theory applied to entire urban regions, with natural corridors for wildlife extending deep into urban territory and the urban psyche, creating an entirely different environment in which children would grow up and adults could grow old— where the nature deficit is replaced by natural abundance.

Growing the Zoopolis Movement

The notion of zoopolis is not as new or utopian as it might sound. In the 1870s, the "playground movement" valued urban nature more than swing sets or baseball fields; nature was presented as a health benefit for working-class Americans, particularly their children. This movement led to the nation's largest urban parks, including New York's Central Park. Closely associated was the "healthy cities" movement in the early twentieth century, which welded public health to urban design, even codifying how many feet parks and schools should be from a home.

Then other forces interceded. Cities continued to build a few large urban parks in post–World War II development, but usually only as an afterthought—and these were increasingly less natural and more attuned to organized sports and the threat of litigation. Neither children nor wildlife have been of much concern to urban planners in recent decades. Arguably both were given more consideration in the early part of the twentieth century. Since then, playgrounds and parks have not kept up with population growth in most cities (in terms of acreage covered). At the same time, these public spaces have become increasingly domesticated, flat, lawyered, and boring—and designed without taking wildlife into consideration. Wolch has noted how the debate about sprawl does not concern itself with wildlife; the new urbanism tends to define sustainability as a question mainly of energy resources, transportation, housing, and infrastructure.

In the recent past, even nature writers ignored the nature within urban or suburban realms. "As recently as 1990, you could read all 94 writers and 900 pages collected in the *Norton Book of Nature Writing* and barely comprehend that most people spent most of their lives in cities," reported the *Los Angeles Times*, in a glowing article about one of the prophets of this urban-nature movement, naturalist Jennifer Price, author of *Flight Maps*. In that book, Price argues that, "You cannot expect to preserve wilderness or endangered species unless you think about how to make the places where most people live sustainable." This movement goes far beyond the traditional focus on parks and reaches toward a new definition of urban planning, architecture, and the restoration of that which has been lost. The *Times* describes a "vast and probably unstoppable conglomeration of community groups, architects, urban planners, engineers, writers, bureaucrats and politicians that is now out to restore the river [the Los Angeles River system] to something more than a ditch."

Times are changing. Wolch talks about "re-enchanting the city" by bringing animals back in. Her views are steeped in a philosophy of animal rights; in fact, she may view the primary beneficiaries of a renaturalized city as being the animals themselves. "Agreement about the human/animal divide has recently collapsed," she writes. "Critiques of post-Enlightenment science have undermined claims of human-animal discontinuity, and exposed the deeply anthropocentric and androcentric roots of modernist science. Greater understanding of animal thinking and capabilities now reveals the astonishing range and complexity of animal behavior and social life, while studies of human biology and behavior emphasize the similarity of humans to other animals. Claims about human uniqueness have thus been rendered deeply suspicious."

Some of us, myself included, are less comfortable with a total rearrangement of the relationship. We're not quite ready to pass laws requiring equal housing for possums. Nonetheless, we do acknowledge that a de-natured urban or suburban environment is not good for children or the land. Rather than some kind of polemical realignment, what we seek is simply a reattachment. Even a truce would be progress.

Cities and suburbs are still wilder than we think, with deeper roots than we know. In 2002, the *New York Times* reported that remnants of virgin forests still stand in the Bronx and Queens—a 425- to 450-year-old, 75-foot tulip tree in Queens is the oldest living thing in New York City; in Pelham Bay Park, in the Bronx, according to the *Times*, "rare birds and vegetation flourish among trees that have been growing since the 1700s." Just as we, counterintuitively, must now plan unstructured time and supervise opportunities for solitude for the young, we must now also manage our urban regions as if they were wildlife preserves. "Where we have a large opportunity for gain is to see that people and animals coexist in a lot of areas. The largest unmanaged ecosystem in America is suburbia," writes wildlife biologist Ben Breedlove, a noted designer of sustainable communities.

Indeed, the peculiar and growing proximity of wild animals and urban/suburban dwellers is one of the defining characteristics of the time, ironic because this is occurring even as young people disengage from nature. The urban/suburban influx of wild animals could stimulate a rethinking of who lives in the city, and why. Wolch writes: "The fast-expanding metropolitan edge brings a wide range of species—including predators—into back yards and public spaces, much to the consternation of residents unfamiliar with their behavior and unprepared for their presence. . . . The presence of wild animals thus often triggers public debate and conflict, lawsuits over wildlife-related injuries, contested hunts and extermination efforts. In short, what do you do with a mountain lion in the middle of Santa Monica?" As she points out, the destruction or domination of nature is unpopular or unacceptable with much of the public, "yet the arts of coexistence with wild animals remain unfamiliar."

According to Wolch, the growing public awareness that "conventional landscaping produces biologically sterile, resource-intensive environments, [is] leading some cities to pass regulations emphasizing native species to reduce resource dependence and create habitat for wildlife." She also points out that there is a growing number of grass-roots struggles in urban regions focused on the protection of specific wild animals or animal populations, and on the preservation of urban canyons, woodlands, wetlands, and other wildlife habitat. Even as science commodifies the bodies of humans and other animals, Wolch and others have detected a growing public sensitivity to wild animals as beings in their own right.

Landscape urbanism is one conceptual framework for such thinking. Ruth Durak, director of the Kent State University Urban Design Center, offers this definition:

> Landscape urbanism is a call to turn urban design inside out, starting with open spaces and natural systems, to structure urban form instead of buildings and infrastructure . . . The idea of landscape urbanism reorders the values and priorities of urban design, emphasizing the primacy of the void over built form and celebrating indeterminacy and change over the static certainty of architecture. It recalls nature's restorative cycles and tries to put them back to work in the city.

Another, more popular, term gaining cachet is green urbanism, an approach that goes beyond the current American vogue of the "new urbanism"—which has, until recently, focused less on urban ecology than on building somewhat better suburbs—even beyond the sustainable-cities movement, which is focused more on energy concerns. In fact, a green urbanism movement is growing quickly, particularly in Western Europe.

Green Urbanism: The Western European Example

Huck Finn has left the territories and gone to the Netherlands. That must be him in the photograph, that boy on a wooden raft, poling his way down a stream-like canal with banks of reeds and willows in Morra Park, an ecovillage in the city of Drachten.

You won't often see that kind of scene in today's America. Here, people still "tend to think that true nature can only be found on the pristine, remote extremities of civilization and that these places have little to do with the everyday human world," writes William McDonough, a visionary architect from Charlottesville, Virginia, and a leading American proponent of sustainable, regenerative community design. Oddly, such thinking raises hives on both the thick hide of mass developers and the prickly skin of some environmentalists. Mass developers want to give us one option and call it choice. Some environmentalists grump: *Why, if people start thinking they can regenerate nature in cities, they'll use that as an excuse for suburban sprawl.* That may be a legitimate concern but, as McDonough puts it, dominant urban/suburban design is "so impermeable to nature [that] it is all too easy to leave our reverence in the parking lots of national parks."

By contrast, cities and suburbs in parts of Western Europe are becoming more livable and loveable by protecting regenerating nature. There's Huck, happily on the water, in Morra Park, as evidenced in Timothy Beatley's book *Green Urbanism: Learning from European Cities*, cited earlier. In Morra Park's closed-loop canal system, storm-water runoff is moved by the power of an on-site windmill, and circulated through a manufactured wetlands where reeds and other vegetation filter the water naturally—making it clean enough for residents to swim in.

A similar Dutch development called Het Groene Dak (The Green Roof) incorporates a communal inner garden, "a wild, green, car-free area for children to play and residents to socialize," writes Beatley. At a similar suburban ecovillage in Sweden, "large amounts of woodland and natural area have been left untouched." To minimize impact on nature, homes are built on pillars and designed "to look as though they had been lowered out of thin air."

He describes an astonishing array of European green-city designs: cities with half the land areas devoted to forest, green space, and agriculture; cities that have not only preserved nearby nature, but reclaimed some inner-city areas for woods, meadows, and streams. These neighborhoods are both denser and more livable than our own. Nature, even a suggestion of wildness, is within walking distance of most residences. In contrast to "the historic opposition of things urban and natural," he writes, green cities "are fundamentally embedded in a natural environment. They can, moreover, be re-envisioned to operate and function in natural ways—they can be restorative, renourishing and replenishing of nature."

"Greenroofs" are increasingly common. Covered by vegetation— native grass or even trees—such roofs provide protection from UV rays, clean the air, control storm-water runoff, aid birds and butterflies, and cool homes in summer and insulate them in winter. The higher initial cost of such a roof is outweighed by its longevity. From above, the green looks like an expanse of fields. Increasingly, architects incorporate construction requirements for "greenwalls" of ivy and other plants, which naturalize a building and prevent graffiti.

Designers are creating "often quite wild and untamed" green spaces, says Beatley, while increasing human population densities. This is promoted not only by architects, but also at the urban planning level. In Helsinki, Finland, for example, an extensive system of green space extends in a mostly unbroken wedge from the center of the city to an area of old-growth forest north of the city.

About one-quarter of the land area in Zurich, Switzerland, is in forests. Granted, much of this space was grandfathered into these cities by the conversion of old royal estates to public use, but green urban activists didn't stop there. Many cities are restoring streams and creeks previously tamed by concrete or routed underground. Zurich's goal is to uncover and restore forty kilometers of urban streams and line them with native trees and vegetation.

A web of bikeways and lanes connects all neighborhoods and major destinations in the city of Delft, Netherlands. One plan in the Netherlands calls for capping a two-kilometer stretch of highway with an eco-roof for pedestrian, bicycle, and wildlife connections.

Another trend is the creation or purchase of urban farms. The city of Göteborg, Sweden, owns sixty farms at its fringes, some open to the public—including pick-your-own berry and vegetable farms, a visiting or petting farm for children, and another offering a riding stable for people with disabilities. Small areas of pasture, livestock, and farm buildings are even being sited at the core of new housing clusters.

Schools, too, are being transformed. Zurich is redesigning its schools, breaking up concrete surfaces around the buildings and planting trees and grass. Through a system using mirrors, students in the classrooms of one school can see and monitor the solar voltaic system and the life of the greenroof. Proponents say such design goes beyond aesthetics; children and adults in these more natural settings concentrate better and are more productive.

In his campaign to encourage such green urbanism in the United States, Timothy Beatley is increasingly interested in its impact on children. During the years he and his wife lived in the Netherlands, they were struck by how free the children were—how they were less endangered by traffic, how they could ride public bikes and public trams, and get around on their own. They were impressed by the increasing number of new developments that include wild places specifically for kids to play—where they could dig, or build a pond or build a little fort. "The fear just wasn't there," he says. "We also noticed that there was less resentment toward parents—we seldom heard kids saying, 'Oh, my Mom won't let me go anywhere.' Maybe part of this is cultural; you see fewer commercial messages to kids there. But a lot of the reason is design. Now that we're back in the U.S., and have small children of our own, we're much more aware of the importance of creating a different way of living, one more connected to nature."

While many Americans may consider such ecotopian thinking bizarre, even threatening, green urbanism in Western Europe proves that an alternative urban future is possible and practical, and has given hope to pioneers in American cities who agree with McDonough that cities should be "sheltering; cleansing of air, water, and spirit; and restorative and replenishing of the planet, rather than fundamentally extractive and damaging." Who knows? If such thinking spreads, Huck might even come home to the territories.

The Return of Green America

Two decades ago, I visited Michael Corbett where he lived, in the future. Corbett and his wife, Judy, had bought seventy acres of tomato fields in the college town of Davis, California, in 1976. There, they built Village Homes, the first fully solar-powered housing development in America, and one of the modern world's first examples of green urbanism.

As Corbett escorted me around this two-hundred-home neighborhood, I was struck by the inside-out nature of the place. In Village Homes, garages were tucked out of sight; homes pointed inward, toward open green space, walkways, and bike paths. In a typical planned community, then and now, you find martially trimmed postage-stamp yards and covenants that prohibit or restrict variables on the developer's original theme. At Village Homes, I saw a profusion of flowers and vegetable gardens. Grapevines on roofs thickened in the summer, providing shade, and thinned in the winter, letting the sun's rays through. Residents were producing nearly as much edible food as the original farmer had. Instead of a gate or wall, orchards surrounded this community. Corbett's teenage daughter, Lisa, elaborated: "We've got a group of kids called 'the harvesters.' The orchards are set aside for the kids; we go out and pick the nuts and sell them at a farmer's market at the gazebo in the center of the village."

As we walked through the development, Corbett stopped at the far edge. Shielding his eyes from the sun, he pointed beyond the almond trees at the periphery and across the street, to a condominium development that was not part of Village Homes. Its surfaces were almost entirely white stucco, glaring in the sun. A small child pumped his tricycle slowly across a white cement parking lot. "Look at that kid over there," Corbett said. "He's kind of limited where he can go, isn't he? Where's he going to go?"

Recently, I asked Corbett if he had any observations about the behavior of the young people who had grown up at Village Homes or about their parents. "The parents loved it here because their kids were easy to watch; there was no through-traffic, so it was safe. The kids really got involved with the gardens, and harvesting the fruit from the orchard. They developed a respect for where food came from. The junior high kids were particularly interested in gardening—they started gardening on their own. This was less true of the high school kids. Interesting—not once in twenty years have I seen the kids who live here throw a tomato or fruit at anyone else."

Not once?

"Not once. Kids from outside Village Homes did it, but our kids chased them out."

By nearly every measure, Village Homes succeeded. From the time Village Homes was launched, people lined up to move in. Among them: liberals, conservatives, libertarians (including economist Milton Friedman's daughter); this was never a counterculture commune. In 2003, a professor of Environmental Science at University of California, Davis, told CBS's Charles Osgood that the typical Village Homes resident's energy bill was a third to a half that paid by residents in surrounding neighborhoods. Developers and architects from around the world visited Village Homes. And as the years passed, similar eco-communities started springing up across parts of Western Europe, where green design is now considered mainstream.

But in one crucial way, Village Homes did not succeed. In America, no commercial developer, to Corbett's knowledge, has replicated the Village Homes concept, a fact that deeply disappoints him. He places some of the blame on the exterior cosmetics of his own design. And the morning is young. The influence of urban naturalists and environmentalists is on the increase, particularly in the Northwest. The naturalist and nature writer Robert Michael Pyle praised Portland urban naturalist Mike Houck for launching an effort to involve the arts community in refreshing the cities and devoting himself to urban stream restoration. "When streams are rescued from the storm drains, they are said (delightfully) to be 'daylighted.' We are finally discovering the link between our biophilia and our future," writes Pyle. Portland's international "Country in the City" conference pushes for urban ecological diversity and encourages the dedication of urban Northwesterners to the wild salmon.

Timothy Beatley reports an array of U.S. experiments in green urbanism. The city of Davis now requires new developments to be connected to a greenway/bikeway system that extends through the city. "An important objective is that elementary schoolchildren be able to travel by bike from their homes to schools and parks without having to cross major roads," according to Beatley. In Oregon, Portland's Greenspaces program calls for the creation of a regional system of parks, natural areas, greenways, and trails for both wildlife and people. A 1997 study by Portland State University students identified a third of downtown Portland's roofs that could be converted to greenroof design. Such conversions could potentially reduce the volume of combined sewer overflow by up to 15 percent and achieve a huge savings for the city.

Numerous studies have shown the economic benefits of green space; for example, some show how adjacent housing benefits from small neighborhood parks. If the green space is well designed, the public gains a higher return on their property tax, adding value to the neighborhood and increasing the net return to the tax rolls. These economic incentives should encourage us to move away from the flat, green parks (which are underused by children, who prefer the rough edges to the flat green) toward a more natural pocket-park design. Indeed, such better-designed areas must be part of a reinvention of the way we live—part of the physical creation of zoopolis.

A good example of zoopolis is Oregon's famous trail system, known as the Loop, which encircles the Portland metro area. A century ago, when the system was conceived, the plan was for a 40-mile series of trails. Today, the system is 140 miles long and still growing. The Loop connects parks, open spaces, and neighborhoods. From it, other trails radiate out and connect to county, state, and federal recreation areas.

Green architecture slowly is gaining popularity in the United States. In San Bruno, the new Gap office has a greenroof of native grasses and wildflowers, "which undulates like the surrounding green hills," according to *Architecture Week*. The roof reduces sound transmission by up to fifty decibels and provides an acoustic barrier to nearby air traffic. In Utah, the new twenty-thousand-seat Conference Center for the Church of Jesus Christ of Latter-day Saints is capped by a greenroof. In Michigan, designers of a Herman Miller furniture factory constructed a wetlands system for collecting and treating storm-water runoff. According to Beatley, the most ambitious green building at this time may be the new Adam Joseph Lewis Center for Environmental Studies, at Oberlin College in Ohio. The building was designed to be off the power grid. It treats its own wastewater and generates power through a combination of Southern orientation, rooftop photovoltaics, geothermal pumps, and energy conservation. Carpet tiles, when replaced in future decades at the end of their useful life, will be recycled. As one designer put it, the Oberlin building "comes closest to achieving the metaphor of a structure functioning like a tree."

The Robert Redford building, a retrofitted structure built in 1917 that houses the Natural Resources Defense Council's office in Santa Monica, California, is another good example. The building uses about 60 percent less water than most other buildings because its roof captures rainwater; its floors are made of bamboo, a fast-growing substitute for traditional hardwoods. The carpets are hemp. Toilets flush with rainwater and urinals use no water, because of a special filter that extracts waste.

Surprisingly, one of the best examples of what the future could hold is the city of Chicago. Under the leadership of Mayor Richard Daley, the city is reclaiming its 165-year-old motto, "City in a Garden," by launching an impressive campaign not just to preserve open space, but also to re-create wildlife habitat, greenways, stream corridors, and other natural land, thereby adding to its existing seventy-three hundred acres of parklands. Daley's goal: make Chicago the greenest city in the nation. Inspired by rooftop gardens in Germany, Daley insisted that the new, thirty-thousand-square-foot roof of City Hall be designed as a rooftop garden to help insulate the building, absorb excess storm water, help prevent sewer flooding, and act as a giant air purifier.

"The garden has already yielded some promising results. During an August heat wave, surface temperatures in areas of the garden were between 86 and 125 degrees Fahrenheit, 40 to 70 degrees less than the temperatures of the black-tar roof of the adjoining Cook County building," reports Nancy Seegar, in *Planning*, the publication of the American Planning Association. This roof cost about twice as much as a conventional roof, but is expected to last twice as long. As with other roofs of this type, energy savings pay for the maintenance cost. More than twenty thousand plants representing 150 different species grow in the garden, and it even claims two beehives and four thousand non-aggressive honeybees; the beekeepers harvested 150 pounds of honey during the first year. Future harvests will be packaged and sold at the city's Cultural Center. The bees are expected to forage for nectar in nearby Grant Park.

Among the city's other accomplishments: some three hundred thousand trees planted since 1989. The municipality has also restored twenty-eight miles of boulevard gardens, and turned twenty-one acres of underused city land and abandoned gas stations into pocket parks and seventy-two community gardens. In time, there may be two hundred such gardens. One of those once-blighted lots is now the "El Coqui" garden, named after a tree frog native to Puerto Rico; the garden serves as a classroom for a nearby elementary school. On Chicago's Southeast Side, the city has established the Calumet Open Space Reserve, with four thousand acres, including wetlands, forests, and prairies. In Kane County, in the far western Chicago region, a Farmland Protection Program will buy farmland or development rights to farmland.

At the same time, Chicago has developed one of the best renewable-energy rebate programs in the nation. A growing network of bike paths connects neighborhoods, parks, and business districts. An excellent mass-transit system means owning a car in metropolitan Chicago is no longer a necessity. Chicago has also developed a five-year plan to generate 20 percent of its electrical power from renewable energy sources and to retrofit existing public buildings. This is no Lone Ranger adventure, but a collaboration of 140 public and private organizations working under the banner of the Chicago Wilderness coalition. Commercial outlets are following Chicago's public lead. For example, a new Target store, located on a redeveloped site, will have its own rooftop garden.

The greening of Chicago has even received praise from conservative columnist George Will, who quotes Daley extolling the virtues of flowers. "Flowers calm people down," says the son of the first Mayor Daley, who was beloved by many locals, but whose baton-wielding police force cracked the heads of 1960s flower children and political protesters.

This latest mayor's inventiveness, in fact, is in step with the rebirth of an older Chicago ethic. "Everyone is entitled to a home where the sun, the stars, open fields, giant trees, and smiling flowers are free to teach an undisturbed lesson of life," wrote the great Chicago landscape planner, Jens Jensen, in the 1930s. The city's original planners called for a metro park system "developed in a natural condition." The initial result: the city's park system and two hundred thousand acres of forest preserves surrounding the city. The 1909 Plan of Chicago called for "wild forests, filled with such trees, vines, flowers, and shrubs as will grow in this climate. . . . There should be open glades here and there and other natural features and the people should be allowed to use them freely." This century's Chicago plan, then, is no love child or wild-eyed radical act (this is big-shouldered Chicago, remember, not California), but a rational response to decades of urban de-naturing. One wonders how we strayed so far from life-affirming visions. Clearly, it's not too late to find our way back.

Perhaps the most moving representation of green urbanism was offered in proposals from several architectural firms to green part of Ground Zero at the World Trade Center site in New York City. The proposals provided "ample proof of the power of landscape to transform a scarred and haunted place," according to the *New York Times*, which published the results. Designers offered ideas to turn the crater into a tree nursery, "a memorial arboretum—a large sunken garden of extraordinary tree specimens, flowers and wildlife from all over the world." Trees germinated there would be carried along "the same routes once traveled by daily commuters from the World Trade Center on their way home," to be planted in neighborhoods and parks throughout the city. That serious consideration is given to such ideas in these uncertain times speaks well of Mike and Judy Corbett's own farsighted vision, which they struggled to realize in that tomato field so many years ago.

Reinventing the Vacant Lot: Green Urban Design for Kids

Until recently, the new urbanism and the sustainable cities movement have paid insufficient attention to the needs of children. There has been little in the way of research related to urban design and the environment of childhood, according to educator Robin Moore, president of the International Association for the Child's Right to Play. Notable exceptions have addressed the issue of traffic, worldwide, and its negative effects on childhood. For example, in cities where traffic has severely restricted children's freedom to roam, new urbanism initiatives favor traffic-calming speed bumps and pedestrian-friendly shopping and residential areas. Such efforts help, but are seldom, if ever, coordinated with efforts to increase the urban child's access to nature. Even so-called "green developers" show little interest in integrating children and wildlife. Biologist Ben Breedlove points to 273 publications and software that allow easy, functional wildlife habitat design: "Virtually none of these manuals and related techniques is in use, because architects, planners and regulators control the 'natural habitat.'" Future urban design should not only meet the human needs of road capacity and smooth traffic flow, but also, as Breedlove maintains, meet the needs of nature, with provisions for wild animal mobility and life cycles.

The preservation of natural areas in an urban region does not necessarily mean that children will be exposed to more nature. For example, the *San Francisco Chronicle* describes, as the Bay Area's version of the Thirty Years' War, the long crusade to transform most of the East Bay shoreline into a state park "has found itself halted just short of its goal—torn by a civil war among different visions of what the park should be." The most striking clash, according to the *Chronicle*, has been between Bay Area residents who want more playing fields and groups "appealing with equal passion for endangered hawks, migrating ducks and other wildlife." Arthur Feinstein, co-executive director of the Golden Gate Audubon Society, calls the park "one of our last hopes for our children to understand that there is a natural world."

The good news about the Bay's Thirty Years' War is that a major urban park is at least being contested by those who envision it as a future site of playing fields and those who envision it wild, as a place of direct experience. Children's access to nature is at the center of that debate; hopefully, this and other future parks will emphasize opportunities for children to get their feet wet and their hands dirty. Yes, we need playing fields and skateboard parks, but put them where they belong, on already urbanized land—on multi-use school sites, for example. Prize the natural spaces and shorelines most of all, because once they're gone, with rare exceptions they're gone forever. In our bones we need the natural curves of hills, the scent of chaparral, the whisper of pines, the possibility of wildness. We require these patches of nature for our mental health and our spiritual resilience. Future generations, regardless of whatever recreation or sport is in vogue, will need nature all the more.

We are now seeing small but significant examples of innovation and commitment to child-friendly green design. The city of Austin, Texas, purchased a farm, renamed it Pioneer Farms, and turned it into a living history museum. "Kids can go out there, learn about agriculture, pet the animals," says Scott Polikov, a Texas town planner and attorney. "It's more akin to a zoo, but at least it's a farm that kids can visit regularly." The Montessori organization is reviving the idea of "farm schools," by tapping into the founder's original vision of adolescent students spending part of their year operating a working farm. In Kansas City, Missouri, Randy White and Vicki Stoecklin of the White Hutchinson Leisure and Learning Group offer their help to neighborhoods or businesses interested in designing outdoor children's play spaces—discovery play gardens. "There is a sense of wildness about a discovery play garden," they write. "Children's discovery play gardens are very different than landscaped areas designed for adults, many of whom prefer manicured lawns and tidy, neat, orderly, uncluttered landscapes. Discovery play gardens are much looser in design because children value unmanicured places and the adventure and mystery of hiding places and wild, spacious, uneven areas broken by clusters of plants."

Educator David Sobel wants to reinvent the vacant lot. He campaigns for new partnerships of educators, environmental groups, landscape architects, and developers to protect natural areas, or playscapes, for children. As he points out, developers often leave aside land—slices of property not large enough to be playing fields, not conveniently enough located to be pocket parks, but just fine as islands of wildness. Sobel's vision is to claim these stray patches as playscapes and incorporate such natural features as ponds with frogs and turtles, berry vines to pick, hills to sled, bushes and hillsides for hiding and digging. Unrealistic? A growing number of planners and educators are creating wonderful playgrounds, such as one in Central Park in Manhattan, where kids can climb rocks to the top of a granite outcrop with a spiral slide carved into its side (and mud at the bottom). At a Sunnyvale, California, play area next to wetlands, kids are encouraged to dig for fish fossils.

The concept of so-called adventure playgrounds originated in Europe after World War II when a playground designer studied children playing in "normal" asphalt and cement playgrounds—and found they preferred playing in the dirt and lumber from the post-war rubble. The concept is well established in Europe, and a few adventure playgrounds have been built in this country, including ones in Berkeley, Huntington Beach, and Irvine, California. The Huntington Beach Adventure Playground is a previously empty lot where kids created their own play environment in the past. Today, on the lot, children seven and up can still play in the mud and build forts. The playground includes a small pond with rafts. A rope bridge leads over the pond to the "zip line," a tire swing that runs down a cable. There is also a water slide, which is simply a slot in a hill covered with plastic that lands kids in muddy water at the bottom. The Irvine Adventure Playground also offers organized outdoor and nature activities such as campfire building and cooking outdoors, astronomy, and gardening. At Irvine's adventure playground, new kids must complete a safety course before they can take up hammer and nails and build a fort; an adult must accompany kids under age six. These playgrounds may not offer much solitude, but they do emphasize direct experience with natural elements.

Such efforts will gain credibility as the new research in the restorative quality of nature becomes better known, especially the compelling studies that show the link between outdoor play in green settings and Attention Deficit Hyperactivity Disorder.

Healthy Planning for Children and Other Living Things

During the next decade or two, a crush of city and county master plans will be newly drawn or updated, determining the future of our open space. All over the country, creators of these plans and the public that advises them will have an opportunity to consider whether the veins of nature and wildness will be as important as the arteries of transportation to the future of our neighborhoods. Rather than accept a parcel-by-parcel, park-by-park approach, we need to call for broad, regional strategies—and for new ways to form them.

William B. Honachefsky, one of the pioneering scientists who first championed the link between environmental sustainability and local land-use planning, argues that, on the surface, municipal land-use practices would appear to minimize environmental damage, through building regulations and site-specific environmental impact statements and local ordinances that control storm-water runoff, soil erosion, vegetation removal, and steep-slope construction. "While these are certainly well-intentioned additions, there is a dark side to their application," according to Honachefsky. "Collectively, they perpetuate a system of segmented reviews, analyses, and mitigation that is the antithesis of the way natural systems actually function."

One answer to this fragmented, piecemeal approach is what Will Rogers, president of the Trust for Public Land (TPL), a private conservation group headquartered in San Francisco, calls "greenprinting"—an approach to urban ecology that is catching on around the country. Greenprinting uses traditional real-estate techniques and entrepreneurial conservation methods to identify and protect open space, creating a blueprint for the public conservation process. When TPL works with a city or region, "We ask [people what] they want their community to look like in fifty years," says Rogers. He calls such proactive planning "taking conservation out of the emergency room." Instead of reacting to sprawl, planners get ahead of the wave.

Although preserving vistas and watersheds and protecting wildlife habitat in an urban environment are worthy goals, human health provides another reason for preservation, one that doesn't get enough attention. For example, preserving open space could be essential to solving the crisis of childhood obesity. A 2001 report by the Centers for Disease Control and Prevention found a connection "between the fact that [typical sprawl] makes no room for sidewalks or bike paths and the fact that we are an overweight, heart disease-ridden society." The authors assert that children are particularly at risk, citing a South Carolina study showing that students are four times more likely to walk to schools built before 1983 than to those built later.

One way to address that challenge is to accelerate the protection of disappearing open space through a national greenprinting movement. Such efforts are taking hold in Seattle; in Chattanooga, Tennessee; in Atlanta; in Stamford, Connecticut; and along the East River in Brooklyn. In recent months, Jacksonville, Florida, the city that "used to smell like pulpwood and Puppy Chow," according to the *Orlando Sentinel Tribune*, "has become the poster community for 'greenprinting' in Florida." In these cities, TPL leads a four-step greenprinting process that includes "visioning" by government and private organizations, extensive public conversation, an investigation into how to pay for land, and finally the identification of the targeted land. As a result, Jacksonville voters approved a half-cent sales tax to set aside open space. Some cities, counties, and private conservation groups prefer to buy development rights from landowners, especially farmers—who are then "paid" to farm rather than sell to developers.

Environmental designers and biologists such as Ben Breedlove argue for a far larger urban eco-management system—the kind of computer-driven, digital system that's been in use for about eighteen years by the U.S. Fish and Wildlife Services' Habitat Evaluation Process (HEP). This system assesses conditions of wild habitat, yet can be applied to already developed areas (say, neighborhoods in need of suburban redevelopment) and project optimum configuration of that area.

"That's going to be increasingly important, because we're not going to be able to buy large land tracts in the future," Breedlove says. "You can aggregate groups of animals and their preferences in the landscape. . . . For large groups of species there is not a particular competition between humans and animals for terrain. Where there is, you can deal with landscaping, you can deal with lot sizes and basically accommodate many of those species, too."

The problem with such visionary plans is that they are often either used to push for changes that the authors did not intend or they end up gathering dust on the shelves of planners, professors, and journalists. Critics typically say such visions never stick because no one bothers to come up with a long-term plan, with teeth, that details how to get there from here.

What we really need, in addition to the long view, is a simple, central organizing principle. The best planning guide may be hidden in the folds of one of those prescient urban plans from the past. In 1907, John Nolen, a father of American urban planning, offered four guiding principles. Future development should:

1. Conform to topography
2. Use places for what they are naturally most fit
3. Conserve, develop, and utilize all natural resources, aesthetic as well as commercial

4. Aim to secure beauty by organic arrangements rather than by mere embellishment or adornment.

Today that set of principles might be boiled down to a single focus: *respect the natural integrity of place*. We may not be able to agree on the definition of "quality of life," but we all know a natural horizon when we see it. Because of what we now know about the relationship between children and nature, we can appreciate the added importance of that integrity.

Reimagining One Urban Region

I can imagine San Diego as a potential prototype. My city already markets itself as a nature designation for tourists. Why stop with the famous zoo and the beaches? Why not market all of San Diego as the nation's first zoopolis?

"That could be an exciting campaign," Pat Flanagan told me. Until recently, Flanagan was director of Informal Education at the San Diego Natural History Museum. "Where we could really design for urban wildlife would be to increase the number of pollinating birds and insects— including butterflies," she said. "By planting so many non-native plants and scraping the hills, we're depleting the native nectar plants; we're interrupting the flow of hummingbirds coming north from Mexico in the spring." She suggested that the natural history museum replicate the "forgotten pollinators campaign" conducted by Tucson's Arizona–Sonora Desert Museum, which works to repair pollination corridors. Imagine the San Diego museum and zoo selling packets of indigenous seeds of pollinating plants. Every garden in San Diego "could contain a palate of plants that would not only be beautiful to look at but would provide nectar, and roosting and nesting sites for animals—as well as protective cover."

Local school districts currently offer studies on rain forests and global warming—but fail to focus on their home region's own rich array of indigenous species. In the new zoopolis, our schools would use surrounding natural environments as classrooms. In a city with so much sunlight, with such fair weather, natural playgrounds should be the rule.

In the surrounding city, the practitioners of green urban design could flourish. Landscape architect Steve Estrada, president of the San Diego chapter of Partners for Livable Places, suggests that one way to protect endangered species is to create *new* territory within the urban space: "Some of our endangered birds love willow trees. Why not plant great swaths of indigenous willows in the city—instead of palms—as new nesting areas?" New neighborhoods should contain continuous patches of local vegetation, like the English hedgerows that have for hundreds of years remained abundant with wildlife. "These days, we're focused on smart growth for people," he says. "Why not smart growth for animals?" He also imagines the presence of native plants and animals where people can't miss them—in the malls. Mike Stepner, former city architect and dean of the New School of Architecture, believes that animal- and plant-related design questions should be incorporated into architecture and planning curricula.

Organizing a new urban/suburban approach to nature, it seems to me, requires an early focus on a symbolic, tangible, and reachable goal.

San Diego, for example, is blessed with a unique topology, laced with canyons that are home to an extraordinary array of plant and animal life. Steadily, almost imperceptibly, these canyons have been chipped away to accommodate sewer-access roads, expensive homes, bridges, roads, highways, hot tubs. In recent months, in my role as a columnist for the *San Diego Union-Tribune*, I suggested that what my city needs is a San Diego Urban Canyonlands Park. The political protection of these canyons depends on our ability to see each as part of a single, named, public resource. Response was enthusiastic, and progress is being made. Beyond stopping the encroachments, the San Diego Park and Recreation Department's deputy director for open space hopes that San

Diego will someday "find a way to connect the canyons, not only by the trails in the canyons, but by designated bikeways and walkways between them—a whole system."

To achieve this, however, the public must see the currently isolated canyons (or, in other cities, other disconnected natural areas) as something large and singular. For that to happen, the biological, educational, psychological, and spiritual value of open space must be clear. Its economic value must be clear, too. Recently, American Forests, the nation's oldest nonprofit citizens' conservation organization, estimated that San Diego's urban forest removes 4.3 million pounds of pollutants from the air each year, "a benefit worth $10.8 million annually." The canyons and other natural urban land also serve to control and carry storm water runoff. By preserving "green infrastructure," as American Forests calls it, we avoid massive public investments in man-made infrastructure.

The most important value is generational. Before her death, community college biology professor Elaine Brooks championed the canyons not only for their unique ecologies and their beauty, but for their psychological and spiritual value to future generations—whose connection to nature is now threatened. "There is a canyon within a reasonable distance of nearly every school in the city," she pointed out. What an exciting prospect, she said—a network of natural libraries for teaching children about the region's rare and fragile ecosystems—and about themselves. It is not too late to tie these ribbons of chaparral and sage, to offer this gift to the future. Nor is it too late for other cities across North America, and the world, to become green zoopolises in their own right, and in their own ways.

Overly idealistic? Perhaps. But this is worth repeating: Over a century ago, some of the world's greatest cities faced a choice not unlike what we consider today, a choice between urban health and pathology. The healthy cities movement of that time resulted in the first wave of great urban parks, including Central Park. Our generation has a similar opportunity to make history.

Joni Mitchell had it right: "They paved paradise/And put up a parking lot." But perhaps, in the near future, we could add a line of hopeful epilogue to that song: *Then they tore down the parking lot/And raised up a paradise.*

20. Where the Wild Things Will Be: A New Back-to-the-Land Movement

When going back makes sense, you are going ahead.
—Wendell Berry

ON A SUMMER MORNING, *a nine-year-old girl wakes to the sound of the Smiths' rooster. She watches dust fall in the rays of sunshine in her room.*

She remembers that yesterday was the last day of school. She grins, throws on her jeans and T-shirt and canvas shoes, grabs her paperback copy of her favorite Maurice Sendak book, and stuffs it in her day pack. Her parents are still asleep. She tiptoes down the hallway, stops at her brother's doorway long enough to tie the laces of his shoes together, grabs a package of graham crackers from the kitchen, and rushes out into the sun.

She runs along the path of the common green, past her family's garden and onward. She hears the periodic hum of the central cogeneration plant, and the whirring of the new windmills at the edge of the village. As she passes the Smiths' house, with its roof of low grass and flowers, the rooster races across the path. Elaine chases it a few feet, flapping her elbows, then trots down a winding side path to the creek—a waterway that runs through the village. She knows that this is recycled rainwater cleaned by the natural filtration of vegetation, but she does not think about this: she considers the rings in the water. She sits down on the bank of the stream and waits. By now, her parents are probably up; her mother is usually at her computer before her father, because her father likes to climb up on the green roof and stand in the grass and sip his coffee, and watch the sun move higher on the horizon.

The girl sees the first head pop up. Then another. She sits perfectly still. The frogs' eyes appear above the surface of the water and watch her. She takes off her shoes and drops her feet in the water, and the frogs flee again. She moves her toes in the mud. She wonders if her brother has discovered his shoes, and she smiles. . . .

A Better Way to Live

If we hope to improve the quality of life for our children, and for generations to come, we need a larger vision. We can make changes now in our family lives, in classrooms, and in the organizations that serve children, but in the long run, such actions will not seal the bond between nature and future generations. As we have seen, a new kind of city—a zoopolis—is possible. Yet no matter how designers shape it, any city has limits to human carrying capacity—especially if it includes nature. Children in the future will still grow up in residential areas outside of cities. The current models for that growth are unsatisfactory; they include suburban sprawl at the edges of cities and buckshot development in rural areas. Both separate children from nature.

When seen through the prism of green urbanism, however, the future of the small town and rural life is exciting. Children who grow up in a new Green Town will have the opportunity to experience nature as the supporting fabric of their everyday lives. The technology and design principles for the widespread creation of Green Towns already exist, and an incipient back-to-the-land movement is emerging. You and I may not live to see the day when Green Cities and Green Towns are the norm, but the imagining and creation of them can be the great work of our children and their children. We can offer them a head start.

The full pursuit of such promise will require a forgiving definition of the wild. The poet Gary Snyder has said, "A wilderness is always a specific place, basically there for the local critters that live in it. In some cases a few humans will be living in it too. Such places are scarce and must be rigorously defended. Wild is the process that surrounds us all, self-organizing Nature . . ." Self-organizing nature must surely be preserved whenever possible, but, for the purposes of reintroducing future generations to nature, we cannot stop there. In truth, the nature that shaped so many of us was seldom self-organizing—at least not in the pristine way that Snyder suggests.

Many Americans still do live in rural areas, and those who grew up in what remains of the farm country share a memory—often idealized—of that life. Before she died, my friend Elaine Brooks, who took such good care of the last natural open space in La Jolla, described the landscape of small-town western Michigan, where she had spent her childhood summers on her grandparents' farm: "There was always a sense of being places where no one had quite been before, wandering the farm. Many years later, revisiting the farm long after it had been sold, I walked back into some woods that had not been a part of my grandparents' farm, to discover the remains of an old house that I had never seen before." The skeletal house was only a few hundred feet from the sandy valley where she and her cousin had played. "But we had never ventured beyond my grandfather's wire fence. The land seemed wild to us, but it had been tamed a hundred years before." During her occasional trips back to western Michigan to visit relatives, Elaine found that she could easily re-create this illusion of wildness. As time passed between visits, she found that she had to drive farther to get away from houses; there were more homes salted back in the woods, now that the convenience of snowblowers and dune buggies and snowmobiles made it easier to live away from town. But still, even in the small towns, it was easy to go for a walk and find patches of woods and streams that blotted out the evidence of human habitation.

Open land is still accessible and natural play is still possible in many places in America. We have seen that accessibility to nature isn't everything. Even in areas of the country where residential neighborhoods are still nestled in woods and fields, parents express puzzlement because children tend to prefer to connect with electrical outlets. But location does count. If future generations are to rediscover nature, where will they find it? In the past, children found nature and exploratory freedom even in the densest inner-city neighborhoods—in vacant lots, weedy alleys and waterfronts, even rooftops. However, urban infill (building on remaining open space in existing neighborhoods, as a trade-off for protecting outlying green belts) is reducing even that space.

When cities get denser through infill, parks are often an afterthought and open space is diminished. Such development is spreading quickly; it now dominates even the outer rings of most growing American cities and seeps into the most rural areas, creating an urban milieu that "screams human presence," as Elaine Brooks once put it. In such places, most original vegetation was eradicated long ago, so that occasional landscaping is the only living relief. Landscaping in such settings is merely an architectural element in urban design. This type of development is especially dominant in South Florida and Southern California—but almost everywhere in America, new residential developments are cut from this architectural and legal pattern.

We don't have to continue down this road. There is another possibility with long-term potential: the resettling of vast areas of rural America emptied in recent decades by the crash of agriculture and its supportive industries. We might call this "pro-nature" cluster development. In 1993, (the year that the Census Bureau stopped issuing farm-resident reports) author and *New York Times* Denver bureau chief Dirk Johnson pointed out that, a century earlier, Frederick Jackson Turner had declared the frontier closed based on a measurement by the Census Bureau that defined an area as "settled" when it had more than six people per square mile. As of 1993, though, in about two hundred counties on the Great Plains, population density had fallen below that frontier threshold. "While hardly anyone was paying attention, something quite extraordinary happened to a huge swath of the United States: it emptied out," Johnson wrote. "In five states of the Great Plains, there are more counties with fewer than six persons per square mile than there were in 1920. In Kansas, such counties cover more territory than they did in 1890. . . . Even the number of counties with fewer than two persons per square mile is on the rise."

Since then, the emptying of parts of rural America has only increased. The causes are complex; not the least of them the rise of corporate mega-farms and the bankruptcies among small farmers. But great stretches of land are now underpopulated. A few years ago, the governor of Iowa invited immigrants from other countries to resettle his state. Geographers at Rutgers University have called for the federal government to remove the stragglers and turn parts of the Great Plains into a wildlife park to be called Buffalo Commons. That specific event is unlikely, and the geographers have since amended their controversial proposal. But something akin to it could happen. The emptying of the plains, the notion of zoopolis, the new knowledge of our kinship with other animals — these trends suggest that the idea of frontier for future generations is not settled, and that future generations in this part of the world may well create a sensible way to distribute population. Permanent disconnection of the young and nature is not inevitable.

Indeed, while short-term relief is important at, for example, the family and school level, the long-term reconnection of future generations with nature will require a radical change in the way cities are designed, where population is distributed, and how those populations interact with land and water. Imagine, in a fourth frontier, a back-to-the-land movement unlike any in our history.

Such thinking should seem more familiar than grandiose, rooted as it is in Thomas Jefferson's agrarian vision, Thoreau's self-reliance, and the homesteading of the West. Its precedents include the middle-class "back-to-the-land" movement in nineteenth-century England. In the 1960s, a back-to-the-land movement in a number of Western countries attempted an ad hoc resuscitation of that vision as an act of rebellion against what was perceived as a materialist culture; that exodus may have attracted over one million people in the United States. While

remnants of that original migration remain, the 1960s agrarian movement neither succeeded nor failed, but, instead, evolved: into environmentalism, into a focus on sustainable communities, and into the
simplicity movement.

In the early 1980s, another trend seemed to be on the verge of changing the face of rural America. The 1980 Census showed that the nation's
population was less concentrated; in addition to the sprawl of the suburbs, more Americans were moving to rural areas than to high-density
older cities. With the advent of the personal computer, both farmers
and upscale information workers could suddenly imagine themselves
living in a new Eden, where the best of the rural and urban worlds could
be linked by modem. Some Americans realized that dream, but two realities intruded: one was that when people moved to small towns, they
generally brought their urban expectations and problems, including
suburban sprawl, with them; second, the city-to-small-town movement
proved to be a demographic blip. A few small towns were transformed,
but most continued to lose population—particularly in the Great
Plains. Certainly no back-to-the-land rush followed.

Yet, all the elements of desire remain, and a new literature of sustainable community design has since emerged. A new back-to-the-land
movement may be possible, considering the densification of suburbia
and its failure to deliver on its original promise of increased natural surroundings; new research showing the necessity of nature to health; and
a new realization that dramatic, visionary change will be necessary if tomorrow's children are to experience a direct connection to nature. The
green urbanism of Western Europe and parts of the United States helps
to point the way, by showing that the improbable is possible. We are no
longer talking about retreating to rural communes, but, rather, about
building technologically and ethically sophisticated human-scale population centers that, by their very design, reconnect both children and
adults to nature.

Brave New Prairie

The girl is glad that her family moved here from Los Angeles. Her memories of that city and its congestion and the smell of the air are beginning to fade. She did not even mind the long winter, when the snow built up in drifts and the wind blew the snow dry, so that even after the snow stopped falling from the clouds, the blizzard continued. She loved watching that from the window of her bedroom, surrounded by her books and drawing paper.

One night, her father woke her in the middle of the night and led her outside under the stars, and said, "Look." She saw lightning on the horizon, and the great river of light above. "Lightning and the Milky Way," said her father. His hands were on her shoulders. "Amazing." She liked the way he said that word, softly, without saying anything else until she was tucked back in bed.

Now she is up moving again, to the edge of the village. . . .

PROFESSOR DAVID ORR describes what he believes is a paradigm shift in "design intelligence" comparable to the Enlightenment of the eighteenth century. He calls for a "higher order of heroism," one that encompasses charity, wildness, and the rights of children. As he defines it, a sane civilization "would have more parks and fewer shopping malls; more small farms and fewer agribusinesses; more prosperous small towns and smaller cities; more solar collectors and fewer strip mines; more bicycle trails and fewer freeways; more trains and fewer cars; more celebration and less hurry . . ." Utopia? No, says Orr. "We have tried utopia and can no longer afford it." He calls for a movement of "hundreds of thousands of young people equipped with the vision, moral stamina, and intellectual depth necessary to rebuild neighborhoods, towns, and communities around the planet. The kind of education presently available will not help them much. They will need to be students of their places and competent to become, in Wes Jackson's words, 'native to their places.'"

Several years ago, I visited Wes Jackson at the Land Institute on the

Kansas prairie near Salina. An admiring *Atlantic* profile once described him as an intellectual descendant of Thoreau, and possibly as important. A recipient of a MacArthur Fellowship—the so-called genius award—Jackson established and served as chair of one of the country's first environmental studies programs at California State University–Sacramento. Restless by nature, and increasingly dismayed by what he considered the dead-end, anti-environment direction of agriculture, he and his wife, Dana, came home to Kansas and created the Land Institute, a research institution linked to the nation's Land Grant agricultural colleges and surrounded by hundreds of acres of native prairie grasses and plant-breeding plots. For over two decades, Jackson has been one of the most prominent voices arguing for the resettling of the Great Plains, albeit in an entirely new way. Some consider Jackson outrageously radical, the John Brown of rural America. (His great-grandfather rode with the abolitionist Brown.) He wants to emancipate the land and the rest of us along with it. His vision describes a world where families would return to a more natural existence, but avoid the mistakes of past back-to-the-land movements.

He claims that agriculture as we know it is a grand mistake, a "global disease," and that the plowshare may have destroyed more options for future generations than the sword. In his office overlooking rolling hills and fields of prairie grasses, he leans forward and says, "I'm trying to build a new agriculture that's based on the model of the prairie." Jackson, a large and imposing figure (described by one writer as a cross between the prophet Isaiah and a bison) adds, "But we can't stop there: we need a human economy based on the prairie, on nature." According to Jackson, the natural prairie of perennial grasses that once held the topsoil tight is now tilled regularly, loosening the soil, and as a result the nation's legacy of precious topsoil is floating downstream and turning to sediment. Streams and rivers throughout the Midwest run unnaturally muddy. Erosion is ripping away soil at a rate twenty times natural replenishment, even faster than during the Dust Bowl. By one estimate,

Iowa has lost half of its topsoil in the last 150 years. Kansas has lost a quarter. He sees much of the current emphasis on crop rotation as wishful thinking.

At the Land Institute, Jackson and his researchers are conducting ecological and genetic research to create prairie-like grain fields, what he calls a "domestic prairie for the future." Modern agriculture relies on annuals such as corn or wheat, which must be seeded every year, after the land is tilled, with resulting erosion. By contrast, the native prairie, with its perennial plants and deep sod and spreading root systems, doesn't lose topsoil; it builds it. The only problem is, the original prairie isn't particularly edible for humans.

Jackson's new domestic prairie would be a mix, a polyculture, of hardy perennials, some of them offspring of the natural wild grasses of the original prairie, which would produce edible grain. He hopes to produce high-yielding grains that will reproduce through their roots, and thereby withstand harsh winters and hold the soil in place. Jackson has little faith in genetic engineering; one mistake, he says, and we could suffer a disaster on the scale of ozone depletion. Through slower, traditional genetics research—the kind done in the larger world, not by physically manipulating DNA—he estimates it will take fifty years, maybe longer, to produce plants for a sustainable agricultural prairie. But some day, he suggests, this domestic prairie could yield nearly as much grain nourishment per acre as the average acre of Kansas wheat now produces, once energy costs are factored in. He can imagine this new prairie flourishing over most of the nation's cultivated land sometime later in this century, or perhaps the one after that.

But here's the catch: If the domestic prairie is really to sustain us, we'll eventually have to redistribute the population out across the country and live a kind of life that few of us can imagine today, a more radical life than back-to-the-land hippies had in mind. In Jackson's view, our great-grandchildren will live in farms or villages spread out across the land. Their distribution will be based on intricate ecological formulas, employing technologies at once familiar yet radically different from those of the 1990s—or the 1890s. Whether you view this future as a new Utopia or a rural gulag depends, he says, "on the limits of your imagination." He believes that no form of solar energy, including the domestic prairie, will produce enough energy to sustain us unless the population is redistributed. Later in this century, in his analysis, American settlement patterns will be determined by how many people the land in each particular bioregion can sustain. Cities will still exist, but will be downscaled, most with about forty thousand citizens. Outside the cities, the rural population will be triple what it was in 1990, but this population will be carefully distributed. For example, the plains of central Kansas will support about one family for every forty acres. In Iowa and some of the West, including the Sacramento Valley, each family will be supported by as few as ten acres. (Considering this possibility, a friend of mine says, "I know this place. It's called 'France.'")

These rural areas will sustain a new kind of farm and village life. People will live within square-mile communities; farm families will live on their own land but near each other, just outside the village, which is located at the center of this square. Several hundred to several thousand people (not everyone would be a farmer) would live in these new communities. The farmers working the domestic prairie will provide most of the protein and carbohydrates. Animals (including a winter-resistant cross between buffalo and cattle) will be raised in mobile pens wheeled around the unfenced landscape. This will eliminate the cost of repairing thousands of miles of fencing and allow wild species to migrate freely. People who live in the villages will spend part of their days raising vegetables, fruits, and animals in solar bioshelters. Energy needs will be provided by a variety of technologies, from passive solar installations to wind-powered generators to old-fashioned horsepower. For children, what an extraordinarily different environment—both futuristic and ancient—this would be.

Eco-exodus

The possibility of a return to wild prairie has precedent. As farming became concentrated in the Midwest and West, the small farms of New England faded. Between 1850 and 1950, thousands of square miles in New Hampshire, Vermont, and Maine that once were cropland became woodland. Like the remnants of an ancient civilization, forgotten stone farm fences disappeared into an overgrowth of pines and maples. Jay Davis, editor of the *Republican Journal* in Belfast, Maine, calls this period New England's "sleeping century." In a history of his county, Davis wrote, "As the fences of Waldo County knelt and fell and the trees stepped out to reclaim what had been theirs, and the mills decayed into the streams and the ridges were deserted, as people left and the survivors worked hard for a living, what emerged was, at least relatively, a twentieth-century wilderness."

How similar that sounds to the current condition of the Great Plains. In a 2004 *National Geographic* description of the depopulating of that region, John G. Mitchell described how, in some communities, the median age of residents is already creeping into the sixties. "In fact, grass appears to be staging a comeback on some public lands, too," Mitchell reports. "Fifteen national grass-lands embracing more than three and a half million acres are scattered across the Great Plains from North Dakota into Texas—a legacy acquired by the government after bankruptcies and foreclosures evicted thousands of unlucky homesteaders in the 1930s. It's enough to make a person wonder: When grass returns to the Great Plains, can buffalo be far behind?" In fact, the number of bison—now seen as a reasonable ranching alternative to cattle—has grown dramatically. In the northern Plains, banks now help ranchers switch from cattle to bison. Such change, as *National Geographic* points out, offers a "sweeping perception of what the Great Plains used to be—and might in some ways be again."

Could a new generation of settlers follow? We have seen at least one false start. In the mid-1970s, for the first time since 1820, rural areas began to grow faster, proportionately, than cities. Rapid growth is still occurring in small towns, especially those that have been anointed by major employers—say, an automobile manufacturing plant—or, more commonly, those on the metropolitan fringe, meaning within an hour's drive of a city. Housing is cheaper there, so gas prices be damned. But it's also true that in great stretches of rural and small-town America, the city-to-rural migration of the 1970s did not last. Economics was one reason; another was the fact that human beings are social animals. The buckshot urbanization of rural areas was simply too isolating. So today, sprawl rules, but the great migration to the farther reaches of America has yet to occur, and perhaps—as of now—that's for the best. Too often, small towns invaded by urban expatriates lose their character and physical beauty to overdevelopment.

Still, history is full of false starts, and it is shaped by waves that came and receded and then returned in greater force. In 1862, President Abraham Lincoln signed the Homestead Act, opening millions of acres to settlement. As of this writing, Congress is entertaining several bills similar in spirit; instead of offering land, one of the bills, which calls for a New Homestead Act, offers incentives for people willing to start businesses in those rural areas that have lost population over the past decade. The act provides tax and savings credits, seed money for start-ups, and repays up to half of recent graduates' college loans—no small offering to the 40 percent of student borrowers who leave college with debt payments higher than 8 percent of their monthly income. Other incentives to move out of major population centers will likely be more powerful, such as the spread of wireless computer services (currently, the country's largest regional wireless broadband network covers a 600-square-mile rural county, where the largest town has a population of only 13,200); the creation of a spate of regional airports serving smaller cities and towns; and a rising concern about terrorism in the larger cities.

Given these developments, families with children will continue to have several choices. They can, right now, move to a smaller city, such as Sioux Falls, South Dakota. "The single best thing about living here is that everything is easy," says sociologist Rosemary Erickson, who moved back to her native South Dakota from California in 2004. This was her second return; the first time was in the 1980s, when she operated her business from Davis, a hamlet a few miles outside of Sioux Falls. Sioux Falls is no small town, but it's far quieter and arguably much closer to nature than the heaving megalopolises on the coasts, and the prairie and farms Rosemary loved as a girl surround it. Sioux Falls, she points out, has become "amazingly diverse, with Sudanese refugees and all the rest," she says. "When I was a girl in Davis, there was only one black student." People in Sioux Falls by no means feel isolated from the world. While retirees comprise much of the migration back to her area of the country, Rosemary does know families that have moved to South Dakota so that their children could experience a quieter upbringing, including a more direct experience of nature.

Weather is probably the greatest disincentive, but surmountable through more sophisticated insulation—some of it being perfected by green engineers—and better weather forecasting, along with the new popularity of manufactured residential storm rooms. "We have tornado shelters in all big malls. A lot of people say, 'There's a tornado warning; lets go to the mall!'" Rosemary says, laughing.

So we have a choice about the kind of cities and towns we will build, about the way population is distributed, about the values we bring to such political and personal decisions. We could, in fact, someday create a smaller-scale way of life in those parts of America that are now losing population.

Green Towns in the Countryside

The dream of green towns in the countryside is rooted in a rich tradition. Ebenezer Howard, the most important historical figure in urban planning, was born in 1850, grew up in small towns in England, immigrated to America as a young man, and failed as a Nebraska farmer. Arriving in Chicago in 1872, the year after the great Chicago fire, he witnessed the rebuilding of that city. During his years in America, his reading of Walt Whitman, Ralph Waldo Emerson, and the American utopians helped shape his views on how a better life might be achieved through town planning. In 1898, he published *Tomorrow: A Peaceful Path to Real Reform*, later retitled *Garden Cities of Tomorrow*. His vision of what he called "town country" remains valid. The three magnets of social organization, he wrote, were the town, the country, and the town-country, the latter combining the best social and economic features, and avoiding the downsides, of the first two. Thus came the Garden Cities movement, in its various versions.

Howard's key idea was that groups of citizens would create a joint company to buy land in economically depressed agricultural areas and establish new towns with a fixed population of thirty-two thousand residents living on one thousand acres. Each town would be surrounded by five thousand acres of green belt. He expanded this idea into what he called the Social City: several Garden Cities linked by rail lines or highways. In the following decades, Howard's theories were sometimes put into practice, mainly in England and America, and influenced suburban development. The problem now is that many of the elemental green influences were lost along the way; instead of garden cities, we got gated cities. From the developers' viewpoint, fear sold better than green. Howard's "town country" concept never really blossomed, but in recent applications of New Urbanist thinking, the idea's time may have arrived. New Urbanism, a community design philosophy often associated with Smart Growth and controlling suburban sprawl, favors the return of such traditional features as front porches, backyard garages, multi-use buildings, and housing clustered near commercial service areas.

Of course, creating new green towns, ones that directly reconnect future generations to nature, isn't simply a town design challenge. Part of the dilemma is that such settlements, to be truly green, should be connected to employment centers by transportation mechanisms beyond just the automobile—eventually even beyond autos with hybrid engines. No single community design will suffice; numerous, simultaneous approaches will be required, including green-urban infill, green towns, increased public transit options, and greater use of telecommuting and teleconferencing.

Ebenezer Howard would recognize such a settlement as a new take on the town-country, the Garden City of the future. Plans or trial projects for such towns already exist—more rural versions of Michael Corbett's Village Homes project in Davis, California. For example, CIVITAS, a Vancouver-based, internationally recognized, multi-disciplinary land planning company, was engaged to create a visionary concept for the long-term sustainability of 325 acres of existing agricultural land known as the Gilmore Farms within an agricultural land reserve in Richmond, British Columbia. According to CIVITAS, the plan calls for two compact villages placed on existing farmland, organized around a series of public spaces including a market street; farmland around the villages would use intensive farming techniques and grow specialty crops: "The concept also provides an opportunity to develop nature preserve areas in the form of ecology parks, wildlife viewing, environmental studies and sanctuaries."

Another CIVITAS project, Bayside Village, in Tsawwassen, British Columbia, calls for an "ecological village: a small-scaled housing cluster with the ambiance of a cohesive country hamlet" with smaller "and more humane" road widths "than those in standard suburban subdivisions." Native plant species and landscaping will provide new habitat for songbirds within the residential areas. The ecological village single family residential neighborhood will be "set within vast areas of enhanced wildlife and bird habitat including cultivated agricultural fields, pastures, a nature park, a waterfowl marsh and a songbird buffer area adjacent to the foreshore."

A skeptic might contend that such new towns sound better on paper than they would prove to be in reality, and that they are, in fact, euphemistic Trojan-horse developments that could open the countryside to further sprawl. Considering the spotty history of planned communities and new town developments, the skeptic would have a point. But if the approach is not piecemeal, if green urbanism principles are applied with the force of law and green-town development boundaries set, the result could be positive, indeed. At the very least, such concept towns remind us that there is more than one way to build a town.

Let me return to why such futuristic thinking is important to the relationship between children and nature. In our family lives, and our schools, and in all the environments in which we now live, we can do much—right now—to encourage the nature-child reunion. But in the long run, unless we change cultural patterns and the built environment, the nature gap will continue to widen. Moreover, the goal of this prescription must be not only to maintain the current level of health, but to dramatically improve it—to create a far better life for those who follow. We can conserve energy and tread more lightly on the Earth while we expand our culture's capacity for joy. The writer Peter Matthiessen has said, "There's an elegiac quality in watching [American wilderness] go, because it's our own myth, the American frontier, that's deteriorating before our eyes. I feel a deep sorrow that my kids will never get to see what I've seen, and their kids will see nothing; there's a deep sadness whenever I look at nature now." Such sorrow is understandable on one level, but inappropriate given that long horizon of the possible, of the regenerative, of a new frontier.

No future is inevitable. Those children and young people who now hunger to find a cause worth a lifetime commitment could become the architects and designers and political force of the fourth frontier, connecting their own children and future generations to nature—and delight. Am I out on a limb here? Of course. But that, as the saying goes, is where the fruit is.

A.D. **2050**

The girl, whose name is Elaine, passes a row of public bicycles, and ducks under the branches of the pecan trees that ring the village. And suddenly she is in another world; she runs along the path through the knolls carpeted by wild onion, Indian hemp, columbine, and sky-blue aster—she knows the names of all these plants. She looks for tracks on the sandy path, and finds them: jackrabbit and quail. She places her hand over a coyote track, and compares the size of the toe marks to her own fingers.

She climbs one of the little knolls on hands and knees, holding her breath, and peeks over the edge, pushing aside milkweed. She sits in the grass and watches the sky and wonders if the clouds are moving or if she, on the earth, is turning. She reaches into her day pack and takes out her book. She lies back in the grass, and opens it, and reads:

"The night Max wore his wolf suit and made mischief . . ."

She feels the morning wind on her skin.

She hears bees.

A half hour later she opens her eyes and the clouds are gone. She sits up.

The light is different. On a ridge to the north, she sees one, two, now three antelope. "Pronghorn," she whispers, relishing the feel of the word. They slowly turn their heads in her direction. To the west, Elaine sees the little electric combines moving out to seed the native grain. And far to the east she sees the movement of dark shapes. "Bison," she whispers. "Buffalo." She decides she likes the word buffalo more, and says it again.

While she has slept, the world has changed.

Part VII

To Be Amazed

A child said What is the grass? fetching

it to me with full hands;

How could I answer the child? I do not

know what it is any more than he.

—Walt Whitman

21. The Spiritual Necessity of Nature for the Young

*To trace the history of a river or a raindrop, as John Muir would
have done, is also to trace the history of the soul, the history of the
mind descending and arising in the body. In both, we constantly
seek and stumble on divinity . . .*

— GRETEL EHRLICH

WHEN MY SON Matthew was four, he asked me, "Are God and
Mother Nature married, or just good friends?"

Good question.

During the course of researching this book, I heard many adults describe with eloquence and awe the role of nature in their early spiritual
development, and how that connection continued to deepen as they
aged. Many were committed to sharing that connection with their children, but faced challenges: how to explain the spirituality of nature —
or, rather, our spirituality *in* nature — without tripping on the tangled
vines of Biblical interpretation, semantics, and politics. These can be
real barriers to communicating the simple awe we felt as children as we
lay on our backs seeing mountains and faces in clouds. It also inhibits
progress toward a nature-child reunion.

There is a path out of this bramble.

Several years ago, a group of religious leaders that included a Protes-
tant minister, a Catholic priest, a rabbi, and an imam met in my living
room to discuss parenting. At that meeting, Rabbi Martin Levin, of
Congregation Beth-El, offered a wonderful description of spirituality:
to be spiritual is to be constantly amazed. "To quote the words of Professor Abraham Joshua Heschel, a great teacher of our age," he said,

"our goal should be to live life in radical amazement. Heschel would encourage his students to get up in the morning and look at the world in a way that takes nothing for granted. Everything is phenomenal; everything is incredible; never treat life casually. To be spiritual is to be amazed."

In the old texts, a child's spiritual life was assumed. Abraham began his search for God as a child. The Bible tells us that "God's glory above the heavens is changed by the mouths of babes and infants." Isaiah foresaw a future time when "the wolf shall dwell with the lamb, and the leopard shall lie down with the kid, and a little child shall lead them." Jewish mysticism describes the fetus as privy to the secrets of the universe—forgotten at the moment of birth. And in the Gospels, Jesus said, "Unless you turn and become like children, you will never enter the kingdom of heaven." The visionary poets William Blake and William Wordsworth, among others, connected the child's spirituality to nature. As a child, Blake announced that he had seen the prophet Ezekiel sitting in a tree (and he received a beating for it). He also reported a tree filled with angels who sang from the branches. Wordsworth's poetry describes the transcendent experiences of children in nature. In "Ode: Intimations of Immortality from Recollections of Early Childhood," he wrote:

> There was a time when meadow, grove, and stream
> The earth, and every common sight,
>> To me did seem
>> Apparelled in celestial light,
> The glory and the freshness of a dream.

Of course, there were those who considered such thinking sentimental claptrap. Sigmund Freud, an atheist, considered such mysticism a regression into what he called the "oceanic experience" of the womb. As Edward Hoffman wrote in *Visions of Innocence: Spiritual and Inspirational Experiences of Children*, "Freud regarded childhood as a time in which our lowest, most animalistic impulses are strongest." Children were, in Freud's view, instinct-driven vehicles for incestuous longings for self-gratification. So much for winged angels in the trees.

Carl Jung, Freud's closest intellectual ally, broke with him in 1913, and offered a view of the human psyche influenced by Eastern philosophy, mysticism, and fairy tales, among other influences. Jung believed that human beings become attuned to visionary experience in the second half of their life. "Late in Jung's career, though, he seemed to shift his position somewhat," according to Hoffman. In his autobiography, *Memories, Dreams, Reflections*, Jung even recalls how, at the age of seven or nine, he would sit alone on a boulder near his country home, asking himself: "Am I the one who is sitting on top of the stone, or am I the stone on which he is sitting?" However, other than such recollections about his own childhood, Jung had little to say about childhood spirituality. "In this respect," according to Hoffman, "he was unfortunately typical of the whole current of mainstream psychology and its therapeutic offshoots."

Even William James, who, as the founder of American psychology at the turn of the twentieth century, possessed a keen interest in religious experience, never really turned his attention toward the early years. Not until the 1960s and 1970s did the topic gain much interest, notably in Robert Coles's book, *The Spiritual Life of Children*. The narrower topic of nature's influence on childhood spirituality has been given shorter shrift. Ironically, much of the current work on the influence of nature on childhood cognition and attention is rooted in James's work.

Hoffman is one of the few psychologists to attend this area. A licensed clinical psychologist in the New York area, he specializes in child development. While writing a biography of Abraham Maslow (who created the famous Hierarchy of Needs in the late 1960s), he discovered that the preeminent psychologist shared Hoffman's view that even small children grappled with questions of a spiritual nature. Maslow died before he could elaborate on his findings. Hoffman pursued them, interviewing children and several hundred adults who described their spontaneous childhood experiences "of great meaning, beauty, or inspiration . . . apart from institutional religion." He writes, "Most fundamentally, it now appears undeniable that some of us (perhaps far more than we suspect) have undergone tremendous peak—even mystical—experiences during our early years. In this respect, conventional psychology and its allied disciplines have painted a badly incomplete portrait of childhood and, by extrapolation, of adulthood as well."

The reports he collected from children indicate (as do Coles's studies) that a variety of exalted or transcendent experiences are possible during childhood. Among the triggers are heartfelt prayer or more formalized religious moments; the result can be "a visionary episode, a dream experience; or simply an ordinary moment of daily life that suddenly became an entry point to bliss." Aesthetics can be a gateway, too: witness child composers such as Mozart and Beethoven. Most interesting, however, is Hoffman's finding that most transcendent childhood experiences happen in nature.

Testaments

Nature was the seed of Janet Fout's spirituality, and she has replanted it for her daughter. When Janet looks back on her childhood in nature, she sees it not only as the source of her environmental activism—her work protecting the mountaintops of West Virginia—but also as nourishment for her own spirit. Her favorite place to visit was a dairy farm run by her aunt and uncle. There, her imagination and spirit took flight.

Off she would dash—to the barn, the henhouse, a hillside, meadow, or creek to explore the rich, natural treasure trove that lay before her. Whether she was watching the birth of newborn kittens or mourning the loss of a baby bird found featherless and cold on the ground, nature provided Janet with ample opportunity to feed her curiosity about life and taught her about the inevitability of death.

"I still am awed by celestial happenings like comets, eclipses, and meteor showers," she says. "And as I gaze on these heavenly wonders, I somehow connect to the countless humans or human-like others who did the same eons before my birth. The infinite cosmos and its mysteries help me keep my life in perspective. More than ever, the commonplace of nature fills me with amazement—every bird feather with its one million parts. As a child, I found unfettered joy in nature and still connect with my deepest joy beside a flowing stream or beneath a canopy of stars." Janet says she senses something in nature beyond adequate description: "God longing for Him/Herself," she says. Her grown daughter, though she lives in a far more urban environment, senses this presence, too.

Joan Minieri worked for several years for an interfaith environmental organization in New York City. Nature informs her spiritual life and her commitment to others, even though she lives in a busy city. Minieri's testament underscores the need for urban nature, and more of it. Also a parent, she understands the necessity of parental enthusiasm for nature, and the need to be "intentional about nourishing it," as she says. Her spiritual life is rooted in Catholicism, though in recent years she has also been practicing Buddhist-inspired meditation, which cultivates refuge in silence. "As parents, Frank and I see it as our responsibility to bring our children to nature, just as my parents saw it as their responsibility to bring me to church," she says. "We teach our daughter, Alin, to pray. But connecting her with nature offers such an important touchstone and a context for her prayer, a place to learn about love and respect for all of life—to see, touch, and smell where it all comes from, and to understand why she'll be called to do her part to take care of things."

Minieri smiles and adds, "I hope that, as she grows, she will continue to so clearly and truly love bugs."

For other parents, the spiritual importance of nature is best described as an ethical issue. Some parents see an experience in nature as essential to their children in that regard. For example, fishing is a controversial topic to some people, but others see it as one way to introduce their children to ethical questions about conservation, our relationship with other animals, and life and death.

This certainly rings true for Seth Norman, one of the country's best fly-fishing writers. Norman introduced his stepson to fishing, an activity that offered a context for amazement—but at the same time taught his son *not* to romanticize or deify nature. When I asked him to describe his spirtual life in nature, he turned the question on its head. "Here's one idea I wish that I had encountered a lot sooner: the more often I see savagery in the wild—mixed in, of course, with everything beautiful—the more I appreciate people," he said. "Forests and deserts, I discovered to my vast confusion, were nothing like the Garden of Eden. Wild things killed wild things and there was no justice in the way this happened. To my surprise, people couldn't control much of this: it took me years to understand that my all-powerful father really couldn't save some of the orphans I brought home."

He also remembers asking some hard questions of God, as a child in nature. "I still do. Grasping the Grand Scheme is demanding for adults; for kids raised on Disney, it's simply shocking to discover that it takes a bunch of Bambis to feed a Lion King, and that Mowgli's wolves would eat Thumper and all his sibs. Eventually, most of us figure out that it's people, not nature, who create morality, values, ethics—and even the idea that nature itself is something worth preserving. We choose to be shepherds and stewards, or we don't. We will live wisely—preserving water and air and everything else intrinsic to the equations we're only beginning to understand—or we won't, in which case Nature will fill the vacuum we leave. She is exquisite, and utterly indifferent."

Nature introduces children to the idea—to the *knowing*—that they are not alone in this world, and that realities and dimensions exist alongside their own. John Berger, who was born in London in 1926 and now lives in the French countryside, is known as an art and film critic who writes eloquently about how human beings experience reality, how we *see.* In *About Looking,* he writes that our fellow animals first entered the human imagination as messengers and promises, with magical, sometimes oracular, functions. Living parallel lives, animals "offer man a companion different from any offered by human exchange. Different because it is a companionship offered to the loneliness of man as a species." The Hindus, for example, envisaged the Earth being carried on the back of an elephant and the elephant on a tortoise. Anthropomorphism, "the residue of the continuous use of animal metaphor," was central to the relationship between humans and other animals. But anthropomorphism fell into disrepute during the past two centuries as animals became used as raw material, as test subjects, their DNA combined with machines. As wild animals have gradually disappeared from our lives, "in this new solitude, anthropomorphism makes us doubly uneasy," writes Berger. Yet, never have so many households, at least in the richest countries, owned so many pets. "Children in the industrialized world are surrounded by [animal] imagery: toys, cartoons, pictures, decorations. No other source of imagery can begin to compete with that of animals," writes Berger. Though children have always played with toys made in the image of animals, "it was not until the 19th century that reproductions of animals became a regular part of the decor of middle class childhoods."

Over this time, the animal toys shifted from symbolic to realistic. The traditional hobby horse was first a rudimentary stick "to be ridden like a broom handle; in the 19th century, the symbolic hobby horse evolved into the realistic rocking horse, shaped as a close reproduction to a real horse, painted realistically, sometimes with parts made of real leather, and manes of hair, and designed to closely reproduce a horse's galloping. In the accompanying ideology, animals are always the observed. The fact that they can observe us has lost all significance." Or has it? Often when I would tuck my sons into bed, one of us would pick up a stuffed animal and make it speak: a cotton koala, a polyester monkey, a fabricated fish, each available for consultation, each of them with a name and character. Science may frown on anthropomorphism, but children do not: each decade, stuffed animals seem to populate more of the human environs; they appear in their rows and mounds in every corridor of every airport, in mall stalls, in zoos and museums and even fast-food restaurants. Berger writes that these playtoys "address our loneliness as a species, our powerful yearning, this spiritual hunger, which at its very core is a faith in the invisible." He adds, "Even as wildness fades from our children's lives they signal their hunger—or, perhaps more accurately, we sense their hunger. We come full circle, and nurture their souls with totems, with the anthropomorphic symbols of the parallel lives all around us."

Nearly every parent—even the most rational, who also speak with or for teddy bears—can report some spiritual moment in their own memory of childhood, often in nature. Or they can relate experiencing similar moments in their own children's early years. Yet the spiritual necessity of nature to the young is a topic that receives little notice. The absence of research may suggest a certain nervousness. After all, a child's spiritual experience in nature—especially in solitude—is beyond adult or institutional control.

Some religious institutions and belief systems resist and distrust the suggestion that nature and spirit are related. Suspicious of environmentalism as an ersatz religion, they perceive a creeping, cultural animism. This belief, which runs deep in American culture, is perhaps one of the least acknowledged but most important barriers between children and nature.

Suzanne Thompson is keenly aware of the impact of environment on human behavior. A few years ago, Suzanne, who is in her early fifties, looked around her rather sterile Southern California neighborhood and decided it was unsafe for kids. Their parents seldom ventured out except to go to work. This meant that children playing out front were more vulnerable to unsavory passersby, so she ripped up her front yard, built a courtyard with a river-rock wall around it, put out some Adirondack chairs, and announced to her neighbors that they could use the courtyard as a place to socialize. When I visited Thompson's neighborhood courtyard one early evening, her neighbors sat with their drinks and the kids sat on the wall or played out on the darkening grass. With her simple creative act, she recast the spirit of her neighborhood.

She loves spending time in nature and encouraged her daughter to do the same. But like many religiously conservative Christians, she is suspicious of any cultural emphasis on the spirit-nature connection and what she calls the "environmental agenda."

"The Lord created and placed humans in a garden with a mandate to enjoy it, manage it with authority, in subjection to the Creator," she says. At the core of the creation story, she believes, is the "truth that humans are made in the image of God, sharing some of the capacities unique to God, such as freedom to choose, creativity, authority over creation." Without an informed Biblical foundation, she believes, concern for the environment falls prey to sentimentalism; idolotry of nature; bioegalitarianism (which "elevates animals, devalues humans"); and biocentrism (which "disregards the Biblical notion that where human needs and non-human needs are in conflict, priority goes to meeting the human needs"). Thompson sees it as "essential for children to interact directly with nature before being presented with abstractions about its importance. It's not whether they will care. . . . it's also about why."

Yet, a new movement within environmentalism suggests that her faith and an intensified effort to protect nature, and expose children to it, are not at odds.

Faith-based Environmentalism, Science, and the Next Generation

We cannot care for God if we do not care for his creation. "The extent that we separate our children from creation is the extent to which we separate them from the creator—from God," says Paul Gorman, founder and director of the National Religious Partnership for the Environment, headquartered in Amherst, Massachusetts. In Gorman's view, "Any religious faith that acts as an accomplice to this separation is heretical and sinful. Many of us are coming to share this radical view." Radical, yes, but not fringe. Gorman's organization, formed in 1993, is an alliance of major Jewish and Christian faith groups and denominations. Its four founding partners include the U.S. Catholic Conference, the National Council of Churches of Christ, the Coalition on the Environment and Jewish Life, and the Evangelical Environmental Network. Gorman describes a growing, faith-based environmental movement—one that defies liberal or conservative stereotypes.

This coalition isn't new. In 1986, I visited Whatcom County, Washington, a heartbreakingly beautiful farming region steeped in Dutch religious traditions. There, Concerned Christian Citizens, a non-profit group, campaigned against abortion and for the environment. "We have the ethic of Christian stewardship," the organization's director, Henry Bierlink, told me. "The American attitude toward the environment has been shaped by the Biblical edict to 'subdue the Earth.' But we believe that God gave us the responsibility to care for the land, not subdue it, that we are only visitors on the land, and that we need to pass it on with care." Whatcom County's culture religiously walked its ecological talk. Many farmers there refused to sell their land to developers, and instead worked with the Trust for Public Land to protect their green pastures forever. In a cover essay for the magazine *Nature Conservancy*, Gorman describes how this ethic is spreading, especially since 1990, when Pope John Paul II suggested that Christians were morally responsible for the protection of God's creation.

Today, in Arkansas, when a synagogue celebrates Tu B'Shevat, the Jewish New Year of Trees, kids plant the seeds of native grasses. Meanwhile, Catholic bishops of the Pacific Northwest issue a pastoral letter declaring the Columbia River watershed a "sacred commons . . . a revelation of God's presence . . . [that] requires us to enter into a gradual process of conversion and change."

Some religious traditions might consider such talk blasphemous animism — nature worship. But in Raleigh, North Carolina, the *News and Observer* reports how one Baptist church's "environmental mission group" sells worm composting bins at the church's alternative Christmas fair and holds a "kids and nature connect" camp. Places of worship around the country now offer courses in Biblical ecology, where they teach the lessons of biodiversity to be found in Genesis. "The debate has moved on," Gorman says. "It would be understandable for some people to hear the language of dominion and see it as causal of a rapacious attitude. But human beings didn't need scripture to rape the natural world. Yes, it's important to think in terms of stewardship instead of domination, but I have always made the point that given the power of human agency over nature now, we have dominion whether we like it or not."

Just as many places of worship are going green, environmental organizations are increasingly likely to evoke the spiritual. The Nature Conservancy, for example, describes its land purchases as acts of redemption. The Trust for Public Land says it translates "the soul of the land into the soul of the culture." Bill McKibben, author of the 1989 environmentalist classic, *The End of Nature*, has since suggested an imaginary newspaper headline that would sum up our age perfectly: "'Humans Supplant God; Everything Changes.'" So what does it mean when Sunday school begins to sound like Ecology 101 and environmentalists (many of them church-allergic) begin to sound like street preachers? Good news for both.

We should not underestimate the power of this new synergy to shape the relationship between the next generation and nature.

Faith-based environmentalism can create strange bedfellows and powerful unions. In 2003, Gorman and a group of evangelicals launched the now-famous "What Would Jesus Drive?" campaign, directed against gas-guzzling SUVs. In 2002, the National Council of Churches and the Sierra Club sponsored a joint TV ad opposing oil drilling in Alaska's Arctic National Wildlife Refuge. (That same year, the Senate narrowly rejected drilling in the refuge.) Potentially, places of worship could be more important institutions than schools in connecting the young with the natural world. "More and more people of faith, as they grow in their awareness of the connection between nature and religion, are bringing nature into the discussion," says Gorman. "But you have to start with parents. First and above all is for parents to understand this connection itself. The future is not about designing curriculum. It's about awakening to creation. Kids have to feel that this connection is vital and deep in their *parents*. They see through us all the time. They know what is fake and feigned. As the connection becomes more vivid to us, our commitment to it becomes more authentic, and children respond to that authenticity. The most important thing is the *awakening*. That joy of awakening and discovery is what it's like to be a child." The recommitment to the spirit-nature connection must be that kind of process. "And it can be. And it's wonderful."

What would Gorman say to Suzanne Thompson about her fear of children worshiping nature instead of the God who created it? Reflect on Genesis: "The purpose of creation really is to bring us—children and all of us—closer to the creator. As a parent, you don't encourage children to experience nature because it's pretty, but because your children are exposed to something larger and longer standing than their immediate human existence," he says. Through nature, the species is introduced to transcendence, in the sense that there is something more going on than the individual. Most people are either awakened to or are strengthened in their spiritual journey by experiences in the natural world. "This is particularly true of personal spirituality, as opposed to theology—which is the work of churches, synagogues," says Gorman. "And certainly the Bible uses the language of nature. *The Lord is my shepherd, I shall not want. He maketh me to lie down in green pastures. He leadeth me beside clear waters. He restoreth my soul."*

The reconnection of spirit and nature is not solely the work of faith-based organizations. Many scientists argue that the practice and teaching of science must rediscover or acknowledge the mystery of nature, and therefore its spiritual aspect. In 1991, thirty-two Nobel laureates and other eminent scientists, including E. O. Wilson and Stephen Jay Gould, circulated an "Open Letter to the American Religious Community" expressing deep doubts about humanity's response to the environment. This document was part of what stimulated the creation of the National Religious Partnership for the Environment. The scientists wrote that scientific data, laws, and economic incentives are not enough; that protecting habitat is inescapably a moral issue: "We scientists . . . urgently appeal to the world religious community to commit to preserve the environment of the Earth." One of them, Seyyed Hossein Nasr, a professor of physics and religion at Georgetown University, argued, "If the world is just a bowl of molecules banging against each other, then where is the sacredness of nature?"

Gary Paul Nabhan, who is director of the Center for Sustainable Environments at Northern Arizona University and author of *The Geography of Childhood*, believes that his fellow ecologists are moving toward a deeper appreciation of the cohesiveness of living communities and beginning to recognize that science and religion share a core characteristic: both are humbling to human experience. Says Nabhan, "Science is the human endeavor in which we are frequently reminded how wrong we can be." If scientists rely only on reason, then "our work has no meaning. It needs to be placed in some spiritual context."

So does the environment. Children are the key. In 1995, the MIT Press published the results of one of the most extensive surveys of how Americans really think about environmental issues. The researchers were stunned by what they discovered. They noted an increased environmental consciousness observed in language (for example, a patch of land once referred to as a swamp was more likely to be called wetlands); and a core set of environmental values. "For those who have children, the anchoring of environmental ethics in responsibility to descendants gives environmental values a concrete and emotional grounding stronger than that of abstract principles," according to the MIT report. That environmental values are already intertwined with core values of parental responsibility was, the researchers asserted, "a major finding." A substantial majority of people surveyed justified environmental protection by explicitly invoking God as the creator, with striking uniformity across subgroups. "What is going on here? Why should so many nonbelievers argue on the basis of God's creation?" the researchers asked. "It seems that divine creation is the closest concept American culture provides to express the sacredness of nature. Regardless of whether one actually believes in biblical Creation, it is the best vehicle we have to express this value." If the MIT report is correct, spiritual arguments for the environment, seldom used by the environmental movement, will be far more effective than utilitarian arguments. In other words, arguing for the protection of a particular toad is less potent than calling for the protection of God's creation (which includes the toad). The consideration of the right of future generations to God's creation—with its formative and restorative qualities—is a spiritual act, because it looks far beyond our own generation's needs. This spiritual argument, made on behalf of future children, is the most emotionally powerful weapon we can deploy in defense of the earth and our own species.

God and Mother Nature

The coming decades will be a pivotal time in Western thought and faith. For students, a greater emphasis on spiritual context could stimulate a renewed sense of awe for the mysteries of nature and science. For the environmental movement, an opportunity arises to appeal to more than the usual constituencies, to go beyond utilitarian arguments to a more spiritual motivation: conservation is, at its core, a spiritual act.

After all, this is God's creation that is being conserved for future generations. For parents, this wider conversation will intensify the importance of introducing their children to the biological and the spiritual value of green pastures and still water.

Our families and institutions need to listen carefully to young people's yearning for what can only be found in nature. Psychologist Edward Hoffman believed that children under age fourteen do not have the capacity or language skills to describe their early spiritual experiences in nature. But my experience has taught me that children and young people have much to tell us about nature and the spirit, if we care to listen. Consider the tale one ninth-grader shared with me, about The Spot, as he called it, where he found his moment of amazement:

> As long as I can remember, every time I heard the word "nature" I thought of a forest surrounded by mountain peaks seen off in the distance. I never thought too much of this until one year when I was on a family vacation at Mammoth Mountain. I decided I would try and find a place that was similar to the place I have thought about since I was a kid. So I told my parents I was going to go on a walk. I grabbed my coat and I left.
>
> To my surprise, it only took about five or ten minutes to find The Spot. I stood there in awe; it was exactly how I imagined it. Dozens of massive pine trees were visible. Maybe one hundred feet from where I stood, snow lightly covered the ground; pine needles were scattered about. Out in the distance above the trees was a breathtaking view of the mountaintop. To my side was a small creek. The only sound I could hear was the trickling of the water (and the occasional car on the highway not too far behind me). I was in a star-struck daze for what seemed to be five or ten minutes, but that turned out to be two and a half hours.
>
> My parents had been looking for me because it was getting dark. When we finally met up, I told them I had gotten lost, for how could I share such an experience, such an overwhelming religious experience? This episode really made me think about the real meaning of

nature. I have come to the conclusion that one's idea of nature is also their idea of a paradise or a heaven on earth. In my case, I felt perfect when I was at The Spot.

Fred Rogers knew how to listen. A few years before he died, I interviewed him for my newspaper column. I took my son Matthew, who had just turned six. My son has always been ebullient and outgoing, but on this day, he was tense and silent. As I introduced him to Mister Rogers, I noticed that my son's upper lip was quivering. Rogers smiled and shook his hand. Later, he interrupted his conversation with the adults and sat down next to Matthew, who had pulled a book about rocks out of his little backpack.

"I love rocks, too," Mister Rogers said. He owned a lapidary machine, he said, which he kept in an outbuilding on his property because of its constant whirring. Matthew's eyes widened, because his own birthday present had been a lapidary machine to roll and polish the most beautiful rocks he collected. Rogers and Matthew leaned together over one of the pages of his book, whispering the secrets of stone.

I remembered that Rogers was an ordained minister, so I mentioned to him Matthew's theological question about God and Mother Nature. "Are they married, or just good friends?" When my son had said this, I had involuntarily laughed. Mister Rogers did not.

"That's a very interesting question, Matthew." He thought about it for a long moment. "Your mom and your dad are married and they've had two fine boys, and they're mighty important to those two boys, and I think that's one way we get to know what God and Nature are like, by having a mom and a dad who love us."

Maybe the statement wasn't exactly politically correct (what about single parents?), but it worked for Matthew. Then Mister Rogers said something so quietly that only my son could hear, and Matthew smiled.

Later, as everyone prepared to leave, Mister Rogers sat down next to Matthew and said to him, "Will you let me know, as time goes by, what answer you find to your question?"

22. Fire and Fermentation: Building a Movement

At first light, my wife, Kathy, woke up and walked outside to get the paper. She felt a wave of heat and looked up. The sky was amber and black and foul.

"Something's wrong," she said, shaking my shoulder.

Four hours later, we were driving out of Scripps Ranch as a blazing orange thing with its single burning eye stared down at our cul-de-sac. Our van was packed with the past — photo albums and children's drawings, our kids' baby clothes, pictures pulled from the walls. Binkley the Cat, in a cardboard box, harmonized with the sirens. "How can this be happening? The rug pulled out like this," Matthew, our now-teenage son said, the words choking in his throat. He was stunned, incredulous. He was sure that his world would end in flames. "It's okay," I answered, in a poor attempt to reassure him, "Think of it as an adventure. Hey, I grew up with tornadoes. We did this kind of thing every spring."

"Well, I didn't," he said. And he was right to say that.

We drove east and north, keeping the rising cloud of smoke in our rearview mirror. The traffic was bumper-to-bumper. Forty minutes later, we pulled into a parking lot at a freeway-side Hampton Inn, near the ocean. The hotel was offering price-breaks to evacuees. The lobby was filled with dazed San Diegans and their pets. People gathered around a large-screen television, holding their hands to their mouths in disbelief.

Three blocks from our house, the fire stopped, reversed, and the wind blew it back over the backcountry.

By the time the largest fire in Southern California history was over, in October 2003, two dozen people died, more than two thousand homes were burned to the ground, and the Cuyamaca forest—the place in my county to which I was most attached—was gone. The fire burned so hot that boulders the size of houses exploded. Trees estimated to be eight hundred years old were turned to charcoal.

Some of the special places offering nature programs for children that you have read about in these pages were destroyed or damaged as well. Candy Vanderhoff, the architectural designer who for two years had devoted herself to the establishment of Crestridge Ecological Reserve— the mountainous land where high school students confronted the wonders and peculiarities of the backcountry—reported that most of the reserve was burned away.

Vanderhoff and other Crestridge volunteers had spent weeks constructing an educational kiosk at the entrance to the preserve. The kiosk, designed by artist James Hubbell and made primarily of biodegradable straw bales, was also destroyed as the firestorm roared through Crestridge. All that remained were twisted fingers of burnt oak and blackened boulders pocked with the acorn-grinding holes of ancient Kumeyaay.

Jim Hubbell's family compound, nestled in the chaparral and oak thirty miles to the east, was burned as well. He had spent forty years creating structures—sculptures, really—of concrete, adobe, stone, wood, wrought iron, and glass. Over the decades he added a flourish here, a piece of glass that caught the light there. The buildings weren't built as much as grown from the land. Over the years, thousands of visitors came for day visits to soak up the spirit of Hubbell's creation. The fire incinerated much of the compound; the deer that moved like ghosts are gone.

Still, Hubbell—a gentle, aging man whose hands shake with palsy—believes in seeds, in rebirth.

A few weeks after the fire, Jim and his wife, Anne, were back on their land, planting possibilities and reattaching themselves. Not long ago, I received a letter from Jim that perfectly described poet Gary Snyder's reference to the spirit of *natura*—birth, constitution, character, course of things—and beyond natura, *nasci*—to be born:

> This year good work will grow out of the ashes, just as green grass grows out of the ashes of the burnt chaparral, for along with the destruction came something unexpected. As we looked at our land, we discovered an emptiness that held a beauty not previously perceived. Boulders, once hidden, were revealed, placed as if in a garden. There were quiet places for reflection. The hard soil, scorched by the fire, was now soft and yielding to the foot. The undulations of the land were all visible. This emptiness, this new space, holds an excitement for us. It is a gate into a world only partly glimpsed. Our task is to walk through and discover where the gate leads.

I relate this story as metaphor. When we contemplate the unraveling relationship between children and nature, we might consider it a fire going through, and only that. We look forward to renewal.

Time to Plant

Healing the broken bond between children and nature may seem to be an overwhelming, even impossible, task. But we must hold the conviction that the direction of this trend can be changed, or at least slowed. The alternative to holding and acting on that belief is unthinkable for human health and for the natural environment. The environmental-attachment theory is a good guiding principle: attachment to land is good for child and land.

We can be encouraged by the recent past.

Those of us who came of age in the 1950s and 1960s remember a time when people thought little of tossing an empty soda can or a cigarette butt out a car window. Such habits are now the exception. The recycling and anti-smoking campaigns are perhaps the best example of how social and political pressure can work hand in hand to effect societal change in just one generation. We can apply the lessons of these earlier campaigns. One perspective comes from Michael Pertschuk, cofounder of the Advocacy Institute in Washington, D.C., former Federal Trade Commission chairman under President Carter, and among the most important figures associated with the launch of the anti-smoking campaign in the early 1960s. He is currently a leader in efforts to oppose market expansion into developing countries by the transnational tobacco industry. He has written four books on citizen advocacy. And he is eager to see a movement to reestablish the link between nature and future generations of young people.

Unlike the civil rights and labor movements, the tobacco control movement developed top-down, stemming from scientific research and public statements of concern by health authorities; simultaneously, but unconnected at first, the anti-smoking movement was also bottom-up, born out of the pain and shortened lives from passive smoking—breathing the tobacco smoke from others' smoking habits.

"It was only when the science of passive smoking's threat to the lives of involuntary smokers—now scientifically labeled ETS, Environmental Tobacco Smoke—was proved beyond question that these two half-movements came together," says Pertschuk. "And it was only the combination of potent scientific authorities and the passionate outcry of organized community neighbors, in small groups operating out of attics and garages challenging the accepted norms that gave smokers ownership of the air they polluted, that a movement that would radically change social norms took root." National groups, including the lung, heart, and cancer health voluntary associations, joined the movement, organizing and lobbying for laws to create smoke-free environments, backed by massive public education campaigns on the health benefits of smoke-free air. "Just so, the budding movement to reconnect childhood to nature draws potent support from the science of the health risks of nature-parched childhoods, and the growing passion of parents and others who see their children shuttered up on their couches and computer stands." And just so, this movement will rise from the awareness and determination of individuals as well as organized, national networks.

Good works are already taking root. We see the steady if gradual growth of the environment-based education movement, the schoolyard habitat movement, and the simple-living movement; the awakening of environmental organizations and places of worship; the schoolyard greening efforts in the United States and Europe; growing realization that both our physical and mental health are linked to the natural environment. We also see a growing interest in lightening our litigious load by reforming our legal system. Although tort reform is controversial, and its interpretation in the eye of the lawyer, legal reforms must begin to ease the fear of lawsuit felt by so many families. Several national groups are also working for community design changes that connect walking and nature, including the Rails to Trails Conservancy, the Trust for Public Land (TPL), and Active Living by Design. TPL's goal is to ensure a park within reach of every American home. Active Living by Design, a national program of the Robert Wood Johnson Foundation and part of the UNC School of Public Health in Chapel Hill, North Carolina, devises approaches to increase physical activity through community design and public policies; one of its components focuses on nature in the city.

We also see the potential convergence of several trends and campaigns: New Urbanism, Smart Growth, Livable Communities, Green Urbanism, and a neo-agriculture movement. Many of these groups are moving in the same direction. They are pushed by a growing distaste for dependence on Middle East oil, or any fossil fuels, along with concern about global warming and other environmental pressures; they are pulled by a yearning for alternatives to the cities and towns in which they now live. The individuals in these organizations share a sharpened knowledge that our built environment directly affects our physical and emotional health, and a deep sadness at the widening gap between nature and everyday life. When they focus on the young, each of these movements takes on special meaning—and power.

Deeper knowledge will also bring more power. The greatest need is for controlled experimental studies, according to the University of Illinois researchers Taylor and Kuo. Such research could show that nature not only promotes healthy childhood development, but does it more effectively than the methods commonly used in place of nature. Although expensive to gather, such knowledge could have enormous influence in the fight to preserve and ultimately increase the amount of nature available to children, and to us all.

Reasons for Optimism

In West Virginia and Kentucky, where coal is still king, mountain-leveling machines are lowering horizons. Mountaintop removal and valley-fill strip mining have decapitated five hundred square miles of mountains, buried one thousand miles of streams, and destroyed communities. Coal companies maintain that such mining is essential to the local and national economies, but many West Virginians and Kentuckians believe otherwise. Such mining often leaves behind denuded lunar-like plateaus. Coal slurry, composed of mountain debris and chemicals used in coal washing and processing, mixes with rain in these impoundments.

On October 11, 2000, one impoundment near Inez, Kentucky, failed, spilling 250 million gallons of slurry and waste-water (more than twenty times the amount of oil lost by the *Exxon Valdez* in the nation's worst oil-tanker spill) to pollute and kill all aquatic life in more than seventy miles of West Virginia and Kentucky streams. My friend Janet Fout, one of the leaders of the Ohio Valley Environmental Coalition (OVEC), is fighting mountaintop removal. She is hopeful about the future of the environment, because of both some recent OVEC successes and evidence of growing concern—as expressed by so many people in this book—about the connection of children to nature. She points to the adults she knows "who aren't afraid to get a little mud on their shoes—new back-to-the-landers who have chosen to tread lightly on their own little piece of earth." They live in very rural areas where they home-school their children. "The kids learn about the web of life because it's tied to their own well-being. It's not an occasional hike in the woods with these folks—it's their life. The children are taught to value and care for the earth as though their very lives depend on it, because that is the truth of their lives."

Most encouraging to her is that her daughter, like many of her generation, is also being exposed, "in a way that I never dreamed possible," to global society. "Young people are traveling far beyond this country's boundaries, being exposed to not only different cultures, but also, they are learning how our lavish, throw-away lifestyles in the United States are wreaking havoc outside our borders. These firsthand experiences, at the height of their youthful idealism, will undoubtedly spark new leaders, who will not only do battle to save more of our natural world, but also take a stand for greater justice for all people.

"While my personal social and environmental consciousness was fueled by experiences in the natural world and reading biographies of people who made a difference, I believe that a passion to save the Earth and its people will spring from these global experiences. Young people are connecting more and more with others across the globe. My daughter can already speak directly to a young person in Buenos Aires or Katmandu via the Internet—without intermediation. She can get the truth straight from the horse's mouth in a matter of seconds. So, I'm hopeful."

I hope Janet is right, but I believe that her optimism will prove valid only with a far greater societal commitment to the bond between our young and the natural world—a commitment that goes beyond today's environmentalism. While she fights mountaintop removal in West Virginia, strip miners of a different sort are at work in my backyard. Mammoth, rumbling graders slice away the natural curves of the land; this is, in effect, the strip-mining of San Diego. In larger building projects, several earthmovers typically remove ninety thousand cubic yards in a day. Stack this dirt, in cubic yards, and the result would be a tower reaching fifty-one miles into the air; all in a day's work, all for one development. This stripping of the landscape is the first stage in the creation of a new kind of urban place in which *everything* is graded and riveted by human hands. Unless a different road is chosen, these are the neighborhoods in which generations of American children will grow up.

Speaking with college students during the research for this book did give me hope. When the issue of nature's role in health—physical, mental, and spiritual—was introduced into the conversation, the tone changed; what often began as a fatalistic, intellectual discussion about the hole in the ozone layer quickly turned personal. Some students approached me to say they had never thought about the fate of the environment in such a personalized, direct way. I sense that these young people, who belong to what could be considered the first de-natured generation, hunger for a greater purpose. Some of these students wrote me later to describe how the conversation with their classmates about children and nature had moved them. Even dormant, the seed of nature grows with just a little water.

Perhaps, as the years go by, these young people will realize their sense of purpose in this cause, and dedicate their career skills to it. Not just as a matter of ideology, or even survival, but because they see the potential joy that they and their own children could share someday, as could many of us—if we act quickly.

23. While It Lasts

IT SEEMS LIKE just the other day . . .

The boys are small. We're staying in a three-room cabin beside the Owens River on the east slope of the Sierras. We can hear the October wind move down from the mountains. Jason and Matthew are in their beds, and I read to them from the 1955 juvenile novel *Lion Hound*, by Jim Kjelgaard. I have had this book since junior high. I read: "When Johnny Torrington awoke, the autumn dawn was still two hours away.

"For five luxurious minutes he stretched in his warm bed, the covers pulled up to his chin while he listened to the wind blowing through the bedroom's open window. Though the wind was no colder than it had been yesterday, it seemed to have a quality now that had been lacking then." My younger son's eyes, made larger by strong, round glasses, widen. The older boy, Jason, tucks his face under the blanket, where he can surely see the lion circling.

The next evening, after Matthew goes into town with his mother, Jason and I walk a stretch of the Owens to fish with barbless flies. As we fish, we watch a great blue heron lift effortlessly, and I recall another heron rising above a pond in woods long ago, and I feel the awe that I felt then. I watch my son lift the fly line in a long loop above his head. Under the cottonwoods, he tells me with firmness that he wants to tie his own leader. And I understand that it is time for me to put some distance between us on the river.

When it is too dark to see into the water, we walk toward home in the cold. We hear a noise in the bushes and look up to see seven mule deer watching us. Their heads and long ears are silhouetted against the dark lavender sky. We hear other sounds in the bushes. We reach the gravel road, and an Oldsmobile rolls up behind us and an old man cranks down his window and asks, "Do you need a ride or are you almost there?"

"We're almost there," I say.

We can see the light in our cabin. Matthew and his mother are waiting, and tonight I'll read a few more pages of *Lion Hound* before they sleep.

JASON IS A MAN NOW. He graduated from college last spring. Matthew has two years left of high school. I feel a sense of pride and relief that they have grown well, and a deep grief that my years as a parent of young children is over, except in memory. And I am thankful. The times I spent with my children in nature are among my most meaningful memories—and I hope theirs.

We have such a brief opportunity to pass on to our children our love for this Earth, and to tell our stories. These are the moments when the world is made whole. In my children's memories, the adventures we've had together in nature will always exist. These will be their turtle tales.

Notes

1. Gifts of Nature

8 *We attach two meanings to the word nature*   Gary Snyder, *The Practice of the Wild* (Washington, D.C.: Shoemaker & Hoard, 2004), 8.

2. The Third Frontier

15 *"The smallest boys can build . . . simple shelters"*   Daniel C. Beard, *Shelters, Shacks and Shanties* (Berkeley, CA: Ten Speed Press, 1992), xv.

17 *The passing, and importance, of the first frontier*   Frederick Jackson Turner, "The Problem of the West," *Atlantic Monthly*, September 1896.

18 *The federal government dropped its long-standing annual survey of farm residents*   Barbara Vobejda, "Agriculture No Longer Counts," *Washington Post*, October 9, 1993.

20 *"When Nick's children were small"*   Richard Louv, *The Web of Life: Weaving the Values That Sustain Us* (York Beach, ME: Conari Press, 1996), 57.

23 *how some nonhuman animals compose music*   Patricia M. Gray, Bernie Krause, Jelle Atema, Roger Payne, Carol Krumhansl, and Luis Baptista, "The Music of Nature and the Nature of Music," *Science*, January 5, 2001, p. 52.

24 *new dialectic between the 'wild' and 'urban'*   Mike Davis, *The Ecology of Fear: Los Angeles and the Imagination of Disaster* (New York: Henry Holt, 1998), 202.

25 *"An important lesson from many of these European cities"*   Timothy Beatley, *Green Urbanism: Learning from European Cities* (Washington, D.C.: Island Press, 2000).

3. The Criminalization of Natural Play

30 *Each year, 53,000 acres of land are developed in the Chesapeake Bay watershed*   Natural Resources Inventory Report, U.S. Department of Agriculture, 2002.

33 *in 1986, Robin Moore . . . charted the shrinkage of natural play spaces*   Robin C. Moore, "The Need for Nature: A Childhood Right," *Social Justice* 24, no. 3 (fall 1997): 203.

4. Climbing the Tree of Health

43 *"biophilia," the hypothesis of Harvard University scientist*   Edward O. Wilson, *Biophilia* (Cambridge, MA: Harvard University Press, 1984).

44 *modern psychology has split the inner life from the outer life*   Theodore Roszak, *Psychology Today* (January/February, 1996).

44 *"Psychotherapists have exhaustively analyzed every form of dysfunctional family"*   Lisa Kocian, "Exploring the Link Between Mind, Nature," *Boston Globe*, May 30, 2002.

45 *significant decreases in blood pressure simply by watching fish*   Peter H. Kahn, Jr., *The Human Relationship with Nature* (Cambridge, MA: MIT Press, 1999), 15; citing Aaron Katcher, Erika Freidmann, Alan M. Beck, and James J. Lynch, "Looking, Talking, and Blood Pressure: The Physiological Consequences of Interaction with the Living Environment" in Aaron Katcher and A. Beck, eds., *New Perspectives on Our Lives with Companion Animals* (Philadelphia: University of Philadelphia Press, 1983).

45 *The mortality rate of heart-disease patients*   Peter H. Kahn, Jr., *The Human Relationship with Nature* (Cambridge, MA: MIT Press, 1999), 16; citing Alan M. Beck and Aaron Katcher, *Between Pets and People: The Importance of Animal Companionship* (West Lafayette, IN: Purdue University Press, 1996).

46 *ten-year study of gallbladder surgery patients*   Howard Frumkin, "Beyond Toxicity: Human Health and the Natural Environment," *American Journal of Preventive Medicine* (April 2001): 234–240.

46 *people who watch images of natural landscape . . . calm markedly*   Roger S. Ulrich, "Human Experiences with Architecture," *Science*, April 1984.

46 *our visual environment profoundly affects our physical and mental well-being*   Gordon Orians and Judith Heerwagen, "Evolved Responses to Landscapes," in Jerome Barkow, Leda Cosmides, and John Tooby, eds., *The Adapted Mind: Evolutionary Psychology and the Generation of Culture* (Oxford: Oxford University Press, 1992), vol. 7, no. 1: 555–579.

47 *the rate at which American children are prescribed antidepressants*   Thomas Delate, Alan J. Gelenberg, Valarie A. Simmons, and Brenda R. Motheral, "Trends in the Use of Anitidepressants in a National Sample of Commercially Insured Pediatric Patients, 1998 to 2002," *Psychiatric Services* 55 (April 2004): 387–391.

48 *spending on such drugs . . . surpassed spending on antibiotics*   Linda A. Johnson, "Behavior Drugs Top Kids' Prescriptions," *Associated Press*, May 17, 2004.

49 *one of the main benefits of spending time in nature is stress reduction*   Peter H. Kahn, Jr., *The Human Relationship with Nature* (Cambridge, MA: MIT Press, 1999), 13; citing R. S. Ulrich, "Biophilia, Biophobia, and Natural Landscapes," in S. R. Kellert and E. O. Wilson, eds., *The Biophilia Hypothesis* (Washington, D.C.: Island Press, 1993), 73–137.

49 *a room with a view of nature can help protect children against stress*   Nancy Wells and Gary Evans, "Nearby Nature: A Buffer of Life Stress among Rural Children," *Environment and Behavior* 35 (2003): 311–330.

49 *children and parents who live in places that allow for outdoor access*   M. Huttenmoser, "Children and Their Living Surroundings: Empirical Investigations into the Significance of Living Surrounds for the Everyday Life and Development of Children," *Children's Environments Quarterly* 12 (1995): 403–413.

51 *"We have a small hill, a mound"*   From an interview in the online professional journal *The Massachusetts Psychologist*, http://www.masspsy.com (1999).

5. A Life of the Senses

57 *"Superficially, the world has become small and known"*   Tony Hillerman, ed., *The Spell of New Mexico* (Albuquerque, NM: University of New Mexico Press, 1976), 29–30; citing *Phoenix: The Posthumous Papers of D. H. Lawrence*, ed. Edward D. McDonald (New York: Viking, 1978).

60 *Such design emphasis now permeates malls*   John Beardsley, "Kiss Nature Goodbye," *Harvard Design Magazine* 10 (winter/spring 2000).

61 *"countless possibilities for moving ads out of the virtual world"*   Matt Richtel, "Nature, Brought to You by . . . " *New York Times*, August 11, 2002.

65 *"Children live through their senses"*   Robin C. Moore, "The Need for Nature: A Childhood Right," *Social Justice* 24, no. 3 (fall 1997): 203.

65 *Little is known about the impact of new technologies*   Robert Kraut, Vicki Lundmark, Michael Patterson, Sara Kiesler, Tridas Mukopadhyay, and William Scherlis, "Internet Paradox: A

Social Technology That Reduces Social Involvement and Psychological Well-Being?" *American Psychologist* 53, no. 9 (September 1998): 1017–1031.

6. The "Eighth Intelligence"

70   *Ben Franklin lived a block from Boston Harbor*   H. W. Brands, *The First American: The Life and Times of Benjamin Franklin* (New York: Doubleday, 2000), 17.

71   *"The core of the naturalist intelligence"*   Ronnie Durie, "An Interview with Howard Gardner, *Mindshift Connection* (Saint Paul, MN: Zephyr Press, 1996).

72   *"Were I granted another lifetime or two"*   Howard Gardner, "Multiple Intelligences after Twenty Years" (paper presented at the American Educational Research Association, Chicago, Illinois, April 2003). © Howard Gardner: Harvard Graduate School of Education, Cambridge, MA.

76   *"Noses seem to make perfectly good perches"*   Robert Michael Pyle, *The Thunder Tree: Lessons from an Urban Wildland* (New York: Houghton Mifflin, 1993), 147.

83   *Ben and his friends liked to hunt small fish*   Brands, *The First American*, 18.

7. The Genius of Childhood

85   *"the natural genius of childhood and the 'spirit of place' "*   Bernard Berenson, *Sketch for a Self-Portrait* (Toronto: Pantheon Books, 1949), 18.

86   *"Natural spaces and materials stimulate children's limitless imaginations"*   Robin C. Moore and Herb H. Hong, *Natural Learning: Creating Environments for Rediscovering Nature's Way of Teaching* (Berkeley, CA: MIG Communications, 1997).

86   *Early theoretical work in this field was done by . . . Simon Nicholson*   Simon Nicholson, "The Theory of Loose Parts," *Landscape Architecture* 62, no. 1 (1971): 30–34.

86   *A typical list of loose parts for a natural play area*   Simon Nicholson, "How Not to Cheat Children: The Theory of Loose Parts," *Landscape Architecture* 62, no. 1 (1971): 30–34.

87   *Researchers have also observed that when children played*   Among the studies of creative play mentioned:

> Mary Ann Kirkby, "Nature as Refuge in Children's Environments," *Children's Environments Quarterly* 6, no. 1 (1989): 7–12.

> Patrik Grahn, Fredrika Martensson, Bodil Lindblad, Paula Nilsson, and Anna Ekman, *Ute pa Dagis. Stad & Land, Nr. 145*, (Outdoor daycare. City and country), Hasselholm, Sweden: Norra Skane Offset, 1997.

> Karen Malone and Paul J. Tranter, "School Grounds as Sites for Learning: Making the Most of Environmental Opportunities," *Environmental Education Research* 9, no. 3 (2003): 283–303.

> Andrea Faber Taylor, Angela Wiley, Frances Kuo, William Sullivan, "Growing Up in the Inner City: Green Spaces as Places to Grow," *Environment and Behavior* 30, no. 1 (1998): 3–27.

> Susan Herrington and Kenneth Studtmann, "Landscape Interventions: New Directions for the Design of Children's Outdoor Play Environments," *Landscape and Urban Planning* 42, no. 2–4 (1998): 191–205.

87   *children were self-selecting the spaces in which they played*   Andrea Faber Taylor, Frances Kuo. From a paper prior to publication, used with permission from the authors.

88   *"During the winter months [Clarke] often cycled home"*   Neil McAleer, *Arthur C. Clarke: The Authorized Biography* (Chicago: Contemporary Books, 1992), 4, 10.

89   *"I saw baby chickens come out of the eggs"*   Neil Baldwin, *Edison: Inventing the Century* (1995; reprint, Chicago: University of Chicago Press, 2001), 18–19.

90   *"The changes of the seasons, the play of the light"*   Joseph P. Lash, *Eleanor and Franklin* (New York: Signet Press, 1971), 64, 66.

91   The two siblings *"smuggled home innumerable beetles"*   Margaret Lane, *The Tale of Beatrix Potter: A Biography* (London: Penguin Books, 2001).

93   *inventiveness and imagination . . . was rooted in their early experiences of nature*   Edith Cobb, *The Ecology of Imagination in Childhood* (New York: Columbia University Press, 1977).

93   *Cobb's theory must be amended to allow for different degrees of experience*   Louise Chawla, "Ecstatic Places," *Children's Environments Quarterly* 3, no. 4 (winter 1986); and Louise Chawla, "Life Paths into Effective Environmental Action," *Journal of Environmental Education* 31, no. 1 (1990): 15–26.

95   *"the question of a speculative, unmarveling adult"*   Phyllis Theroux, *California and Other States of Grace: A Memoir* (New York: William Morrow, 1980), 55.

8. Nature-Deficit Disorder and the Restorative Environment

98   *40 percent of five- to eight-year-olds suffer cardiac risk factors*   Mike Bowler, "To Play, or Not to Play," *Baltimore Sun*, June 20, 2001, sec. 2B.

100   *Between 2000 and 2003, spending on ADHD for preschoolers increased 369 percent*   Linda A. Johnson, "Behavior Drugs Top Kids' Prescriptions," *Associated Press*, May 17, 2004.

100   *Both boys and girls are diagnosed with ADHD*   "Methylphenidate (A Background Paper)," October 1995, Drug and Chemical Evaluation Section, Office of Diversion Control, Drug Enforcement Administration.

100   *each hour of TV watched per day by preschoolers increases . . . concentration problems*   J. M. Healey, "Early Television Exposure and Subsequent Attention Problems in Children," *Pediatrics* 113, no. 4 (April 1, 2004): 917–918.

102   *"an environment where the attention is automatic"*   Rebecca A. Clay, "Green Is Good for You," *Monitor on Psychology* 32, no. 4 (April 2001).

102   *Those with a window view of trees . . . experienced significantly less frustration*   Rachel Kaplan, Stephen Kaplan, and Robert L. Ryan, "With People in Mind: Design and Management for Everyday Nature" (Washington, D.C.,: Island Press, 1998).

103   *Hartig asked participants to complete a forty-minute sequence of tasks*   Clay, "Green Is Good for You."

104   *within two daycare settings*   Patrik Grahn, Fredrika Martensson, Bodil Lindblad, Paula Nilsson, and Anna Ekman, *Ute pa Dagis. Stad & Land, Nr. 145* (Outdoor daycare. City and country), Hasselholm, Sweden: Norra Skane Offset, 1997.

105   *"the aftereffects of play in paved outdoor or indoor areas"*   Andrea Faber Taylor, Frances E. Kuo, and William C. Sullivan, "Coping with ADD: The Surprising Connection to Green Play Settings," *Environment and Behavior* 33, no. 1 (January 2001): 54–77.

105   *the positive influence of near-home nature on concentration*   Andrea Faber Taylor, Frances E. Kuo, and William C. Sullivan, "Views of Nature and Self-Discipline: Evidence from Inner City Children," *Journal of Environmental Psychology* (February 2002): 46–63.

106 *"Participants were asked if they had had any experiences"* Andrea Faber Taylor, Frances E. Kuo, and William C. Sullivan, "Coping with ADD: The Surprising Connection to Green Play Settings," *Environment and Behavior* 33, no. 1 (January 2001): 54–77.

107 *medications can also have unpleasant side effects* Victoria Stagg Elliott, "Think Beyond Drug Therapy for Treating ADHD," *AMA News*, April 19, 2004.

108 *"intuition empathetically asserts that nature is good for children"* Andrea Faber Taylor and Frances Kuo. From a paper prior to publication, used with permission from the authors.

9. Time and Fear

116 *When did playing catch in a park become a form of killing time* Richard Louv, *Childhood's Future* (Boston: Houghton Mifflin, 1990), 109.

116 *Eighty percent of Americans live in metropolitan areas* Paul M. Sherer, "Why America Needs More City Parks and Open Space" (San Francisco: Trust for Public Land, 2003). Available on the Web at http://tpl.org.

116 *parks increasingly favor . . . "commercialization of play"* J. Evans, "Where Have All the Players Gone?" *International Play Journal* 3, no. 1 (1995): 3–19.

117 *the amount of time children spent in organized sports increased by 27 percent* The U.S. Youth Soccer Association, Richardson, Texas, http://www.usyouthsoccer.org.

118 *"I don't really have much time to play at all"* Richard Louv, *Childhood's Future* (Boston: Houghton Mifflin, 1990), 109.

119 *the amount of time children . . . spent studying increased by 20 percent* David Brooks, "The Organization Kid," *Atlantic Monthly*, April 2001, 40.

119 *as Internet use grows, Americans spend less time with friends and family* Norman Nie and Lutz Erbring, "Stanford Online Report," Stanford Institute for the Quantitative Study of Society, February 16, 2000.

119 *we are just busy* Linda Dong, Gladys Block, Shelly Mandel, "Activities Contributing to Total Energy Expenditure in the United States: Results from the NHAPS Study," *International Journal of Behavioral Nutrition and Physical Activity* 1, no. 4 (2004).

120 *both parents cut back on sleep* Nancy Zukewich, "Work, Parenthood and the Experience of Time Scarcity," Statistics Canada—Housing, Family and Social Statistics Division, no. 1, 1998.

10. The Bogeyman Syndrome Redux

123 *the radius around the home where children were allowed to roam* Sanford Gaster, "Urban Children's Access to Their Neighbourhoods: Changes Over Three Generations," *Environment and Behavior* (January 1991): 70–85.

124 *"When I was a little kid"* Three quotes: Richard Louv, *Childhood's Future* (Boston: Houghton Mifflin, 1990), 26.

130 *Worried about lions, tigers, and bears* Sandra G. Davis, Amy M. Corbitt, Virginia M. Everton, Catherine A. Grano, Pamela A. Kiefner, Angela S. Wilson, and Mark Gray, "Are Ball Pits the Playground for Potentially Harmful Bacteria?" *Pediatric Nursing* 25, no. 2 (March 1, 1999): 151.

131 *the word "accident"* Ronald Davis and Barry Pless, "BMJ Bans 'Accidents': Accidents Are Not Unpredictable," *British Medical Journal* 322 (2001): 1320–1321.

11. Don't Know Much about Natural History

133 *"Just as ethnobotanists are descending on tropical forests"* David Sobel, *Beyond Ecophobia: Reclaiming the Heart in Nature Education,* Orion Society Nature Literacy Series, vol. 1 (Great Barrington, MA: Orion Society, 1996).

136 *In 2001, the Alliance for Childhood* Colleen Cordes and Edward Miller, eds., "Fools Gold: A Critical Look at Children and Computers" (a Web-published report by Alliance for Childhood, 2001). For more information, see http://www.allianceforchildhood.net/projects/computers/computers_reports_fools_gold_download.htm.

137 *public school districts continue to shortchange the arts* William Symond, "Wired Schools," *BusinessWeek,* September 25, 2000.

138 *"Ten Years of before-and-after photos"* Richard Louv, *The Web of Life: Weaving the Values That Sustain Us* (Berkeley, CA: Conari Press, 1996), 137.

142 *"The last century has seen enormous environmental degradation"* Paul K. Drayton, "The Importance of the Natural Sciences to Conservation," an American Society of Naturalists Symposium Paper, *The American Naturalist* (June 27, 2003): 1–13.

12. Where Will Future Stewards of Nature Come From?

146 *"Environmentalists, by and large, are deeply invested"* Theodore Roszak, as interviewed in *Adbusters.* Roszak is the author of *The Voice of the Earth: An Exploration of Ecopsychology* (New York: Simon & Schuster, 1993).

147 *"Statisticians predict further declines"* Michael Milstein, "Fewer Families Choose National Park Vacations," *The Oregonian,* June 15, 2003.

150 *"Most children have a bug period"* E. O. Wilson, *Naturalist* (New York: Warner Books, 1994), 56.

150 *"the bookish 'Teedie'"* Edmund Morris, *The Rise of Theodore Roosevelt* (New York: Putnam, 1979), 19.

150 *Wallace Stegner filled his childhood with collected critters* Wallace Stegner, "Personality, Play, and a Sense of Place," *Amicus Journal* (renamed *OnEarth*), 1997.

13. Bringing Nature Home

165 *"They were on an island in a sea of trees"* Kathryn Kramer, "Writers on Writing," *New York Times,* December 30, 2002.

166 *the word wasn't in anyone's vocabulary until the nineteenth century* Patricia Meyer Spacks, *Boredom: The Literary History of a State of Mind* (Chicago: University of Chicago Press, 1995).

171 *"Your job isn't to hit them with another Fine Educational Opportunity"* Deborah Churchman, "How to Turn Kids Green; Reinstilling the Love for Nature Among Children," *American Forests* 98, no. 9–10 (September 1992): 28.

171 *"Almost everyone who cares deeply about the outdoors can identify"* Robert Michael Pyle, *The Thunder Tree: Lessons from an Urban Wildland* (New York: Houghton Mifflin, 1993), xv, xvi.

172 *"The kid who yawns when you say 'let's go outside'"* Churchman, "How to Turn Kids Green," 28.

173 *the sunflower house* Sharon Lovejoy, *Sunflower Houses: Inspiration from the Garden—A Book for Children and Their Grown-Ups* (New York: Workman, 2001). For more information, see http://www.rain.org/~philfear/sunflowerhouse.html.

175 *"Our son was overstressed"*   Richard Louv, *Childhood's Future* (Boston: Houghton Mifflin, 1990), 40–41.

14. Scared Smart

183 *"trying to teach personal safety to children"*   Quoted in Richard Louv, *Childhood's Future* (Boston: Houghton Mifflin, 1990), 39.

15. Telling Turtle Tales

194 *Americans participating in traditional forms of recreational wildlife watching decreased*   From a paper by Responsive Management, a public opinion and attitude survey research firm specializing in natural resource and outdoor recreation issues, http:// www.responsivemanagement .com.

195 *For a child who is primarily an audile learner*   Tina Kelley, "A Sight for Sensitive Ears: A New Generation of Audio Technology Is Opening Up the Wonders of Birding to the Visually Impaired—and the Sighted, Too," *Audubon* 104 (January/February 2002): 76–81.

195 *"Don't rush to the library for a book"*   Linda Batt, "All Hail Our Fair Feathered Friends: A Backyard Birdfeeder Makes Science Fun!" *Mothering*, January/February 2000, 58.

196 *For more than 150 years, New England anglers have been keeping fishing logs*   Richard Louv, *Fly-Fishing for Sharks* (New York: Simon & Schuster, 2000), 220.

196 *Outdoor journaling is something a family can do together*   Linda Chorice, "Nature Journaling— the Art of Seeing Nature," *Missouri Conservationist*, July 1997.

198 *"We're part of nature"*   Quoted in Richard Louv, *Fly-Fishing for Sharks* (New York: Simon & Schuster, 2000), 466.

16. Natural School Reform

201 *experiential education teaches through the senses*   John A. Hattie, Herbert W. Marsh, James T. Neill, and Garry E. Richards. "Adventure Education and Outward Bound: Out-of-Class Experiences That Make a Lasting Difference," *Review of Educational Research* (1997): 43–87.

202 *"Finland's recipe is both complex and unabashedly basic"*   Lezette Alvarez, "Suutarila Journal: Educators Flocking to Finland, Land of Literate Children," *New York Times*, April 9, 2004.

205 *David Sobel . . . describes place-based education*   David Sobel, *Place-Based Education: Connecting Classrooms and Communities* (Great Barrington, MA: The Orion Society and the Myrin Institute, 2004).

207 *"I used to take student groups on trips to the California deserts"*   Will Nixon, "Letting Nature Shape Childhood," *Amicus Journal*, National Resources Defense Council, distributed by The Los Angeles Times Syndicate, December 24, 1997.

210 *At Torrey Pines Elementary*   Richard Louv, *The Web of Life: Weaving the Values That Sustain Us* (Berkeley, CA: Conari Press, 1996), 148.

211 *seventh-graders attended four hundred trout fingerlings*   Richard Louv, *Fly-Fishing for Sharks* (New York: Simon & Schuster, 2000), 393.

216 *Mary Rivkin, a professor of early childhood education*   Mary Rivkin, "The Schoolyard Habitat Movement: What It Is and Why Children Need It," *Early Childhood Education Journal* 25, no. 1 (1997).

220 *The dominant form of education today "alienates us from life"*   David Orr, *Earth in Mind: On Education, Environment, and the Human Prospect* (Washington, D.C.: Island Press, 1994).

220 *"ecological design intelligence"*   David Orr, "What Is Education For? Six Myths about the Foundations of Modern Education, and Six New Principles to Replace Them," *Context: A Quarterly of Human Sustainable Culture*, Context Institute (winter 1991): 52.

222 *"Without a sound formation on natural history"*   Paul K. Dayton and Enric Sala, "Natural History: The Sense of Wonder, Creativity, and Progress in Ecology," *Scientia Marina* (2001): 196–206.

17. Camp Revival

225 *"Some of the most exciting findings"*   Andrea Faber Taylor and Frances E. Kuo. From a paper prior to publication, used with permission from the authors.

225 *participants in adventure-therapy programs made gains in self-esteem*   John A. Hattie, Herbert W. Marsh, James T. Neill, and Garry E. Richards, "Adventure Education and Outward Bound: Out-of-Class Experiences That Make a Lasting Difference," *Review of Educational Research* (1997): 43–87.

226 *Outward Bound programs stimulate the development of interpersonal competencies*   John A. Hattie, Herbert W. Marsh, James T. Neill, and Garry E. Richards, "Adventure Education and Outward Bound," *Review of Educational Research* 67 (1997): 43–87.

226 *the National Survey of Recreation and the Environment*   Leo McAvoy, "Outdoors for Everyone: Opportunities That Include People with Disabilities," *Parks and Recreation*, National Recreation and Park Association 36, no. 8 (2001): 24.

226 *people with disabilities gain enhanced body image*   Alan Ewert and Leo McAvoy, "The Effects of Wilderness Settings on Organized Groups," *Therapeutic Recreation Journal* 22, no. 1 (1987): 53–69.

227 *Puget Sound Environmental Learning Center*   Debera Carlton Harrell, "Away from the Tube and into Nature, Children Find a New World," *Seattle Post-Intelligencer,* April 5, 2002.

19. Cities Gone Wild

241 *"We need to hold out for healthy ecosystems in the city"*   John Beardsley, "Kiss Nature Goodbye, Marketing the Great Outdoors," *Harvard Design Magazine*, no. 10 (winter/spring 2000).

242 *As recently as 1990, you could barely comprehend that most people spent most of their lives in cities*   John Balzar, "True Nature: Author Jennifer Price Hopes City-Dwellers Will Learn to See, to Love and to Nurture What's Wild and Wonderful in Their Midst, *Los Angeles Times*, May 31, 2003.

243 *remnants of virgin forests still stand in the Bronx and Queens*   Ben Breedlove, online interview, "E Design Online interview," September 24, 1996, http://www.state.fl.us/fdi/edesign/news/9609/breedluv.htm.

243 *"The fast-expanding metropolitan edge brings a wide range of species"*   Andrea L. Gullo, Unna I. Lassiter, and Jennifer Wolch, "The Cougar's Tale," *Animal Geographies: Place, Politics, and Identity in the Nature-Culture Borderlands*, ed. Jennifer Wolch and Jody Emel (London, New York: Verso Books, 1998).

246 *A similar Dutch development called Het Groene Dak*   Timothy Beatley, *Green Urbanism: Learning from European Cities* (Washington, D.C.: Island Press, 2000), 212.

253 *"Flowers calm people down"* George F. Will, "The Greening of Chicago," *Newsweek*, August 4, 2003, 64.

254 *The 1909 Plan of Chicago called for "wild forests"* Nancy Seeger, "Greening Chicago," *Planning* 68, no. 1 (January 1, 2002): 25.

255 *research related to urban design and the environment of childhood* Robin C. Moore, "The Need for Nature: A Childhood Right," *Social Justice* 24, no. 3 (fall 1997): 203.

258 *municipal land-use practices would appear to minimize environmental damage* William B. Honachefsky, *Ecologically Based Municipal Land Use Planning* (Boca Raton, FL: Lewis Publishers, CRC Press, 1999).

259 *A 2001 report by the Centers for Disease Control and Prevention* Richard J. Jackson and Chris Kochtitzky, "Creating a Healthy Environment: The Impact of the Built Environment on Public Health," Sprawl Watch Clearinghouse Monograph Series (Washington, D.C.: Sprawl Watch Clearinghouse, 2001).

259 *students are four times more likely to walk* Mike Snyder, "Sprawl Damages Our Health, CDC Says," *Houston Chronicle*, November 9, 2001, sec. A-45.

20. Where the Wild Things Will Be

268 *"something quite extraordinary happened"* Dirk Johnson, "The Great Plains: Plains, While Still Bleak, Offer a Chance to the Few," *New York Times*, December 12, 1993, sec. 1, p. 1.

271 *a paradigm shift in "design intelligence"* David Orr, *Earth in Mind: On Education, Environment, and the Human Prospect* (Washington, D.C.: Island Press, 1994).

275 *the median age of residents is already creeping into the sixties* John G. Mitchell, "Change of Heartland," *National Geographic*, May 2004.

279 *Bayside Village, in Tsawwassen, British Columbia* CIVITAS, Vancouver, B.C. http://www.civitasdesign.com/newcomm.html.

21. The Spiritual Necessity of Nature for the Young

287 *"Late in Jung's career"* Edward Hoffman, *Visions of Innocence: Spiritual and Inspirational Experiences of Childhood* (Boston: Shambhala, 1992).

291 *a companion different from any offered by human exchange* John Berger, *About Looking* (New York: Pantheon Books, 1980), 20.

297 *"Science is the human endeavor in which we are frequently reminded how wrong we can be"* Gretel H. Schueller, "Scientists, Religious Groups Come to the Aid of Nature," *Environmental News Network, Knight Ridder/Tribune Business News*, September 3, 2001.

297 *how Americans really think about environmental issues* Willett Kempton, James S. Boster, and Jennifer A. Hartley, *Environmental Values in American Culture* (Cambridge, MA: MIT Press, 1997).

Suggested Reading

A partial listing of an expanding literature

Bartholomew, Mel. *Square Foot Gardening*. Emmaus, PA: Rodale Press, 1981.

Beatley, Timothy. *Green Urbanism: Learning from European Cities*. Washington, D.C.: Island Press, 2000.

Berry, Thomas. *The Dream of the Earth*. San Francisco: Sierra Club Books, 1988.

Bice, Barbara, et. al. *Conserving and Enhancing the Natural Environment: A Guide for Planning, Design, Construction, and Maintenance on New and Existing School Sites*. Baltimore: Maryland State Dept. of Education, 1999.

Blakey, Nancy. *Go Outside: Over 130 Activities for Outdoor Adventures*. Berkeley, CA: Tricycle Press, 2002.

Brett, A., and R. Moore. *The Complete Playground Book*. New York: Syracuse University Press, 1993.

Buell, Lawrence. *The Environmental Imagination: Thoreau, Nature Writing, and the Formation of American Culture*. Cambridge, MA: Harvard University Press, 1995.

Carson, Rachel. *The Sense of Wonder*. New York: Harper & Row, 1956.

Chard, Philip Sutton. *The Healing Earth: Nature's Medicine for the Troubled Soul*. Minocqua, WI: NorthWord, 1994.

Chawla, Louise. *In the First Country of Places: Nature, Poetry, and Childhood Memory*. Albany, NY: State University of New York Press, 1994.

———. *Growing Up in an Urbanising World*. London: UNESCO, 2002.

Cobb, Edith. *The Ecology of Imagination in Childhood*. New York: Columbia University Press, 1977.

Corbett, Michael, Judy Corbett, and Robert L. Thayer. *Designing Sustainable Communities: Learning from Village Homes*. Washington, D.C.: Island Press, 2000.

Cornell, Joseph. *Sharing Nature with Children*. Nevada City, CA: Dawn Publications, 1979.

Dannenmaier, M. *A Child's Garden: Enchanting Outdoor Spaces for Children and Parents*. New York: Simon & Schuster, 1998.

Dewey, John. *The Child and the Curriculum*. Chicago: University of Chicago Press, 1902.

Gardner, Howard. *Intelligence Reframed: Multiple Intelligences for the 21st Century*. New York: Basic Books, 1999.

Gil, E. *The Healing Power of Play*. New York: Guilford Press, 1991.

Goldsmity, Edward. *The Way: An Ecology World-View*. Boston: Shambala, 1993.

Grant, Tim, and Gail Littlejohn, eds. *Greening School Grounds: Creating Habitats for Learning*. Gabriola Island, British Columbia: New Society Publishers, 2001.

Guiness, B. *Creating a Family Garden: Magical Outdoor Spaces for All Ages*. New York: Abbeville Press, 1996.

Harrison, George. *Backyard Bird Watching for Kids: How to Attract, Feed, and Provide Homes for Birds*. Minocqua, WI: Willow Creek Press, 1997.

Hart, Roger. *Children's Experience of Place*. New York: Irvington Publishers, 1979.

———. *Children's Participation: The Theory and Practice of Involving Young Citizens in Community Development and Environmental Care*. London: Earthscan, 1997.

Hoffman, Edward. *Visions of Innocence: Spiritual and Inspirational Experiences of Childhood*. Boston and London: Shambhala, 1992.

Jaffe, Roberta, et. al. *The Growing Classroom: Garden-Based Science*. New York: Pearson Learning, 2001.

Johnson, Julie M. "Design for Learning: Values, Qualities and Processes of Enriching School Landscapes." Washington, D.C.: American Society of Landscape Architects, 2000.

Kahn, Peter H., Jr. *The Human Relationship with Nature: Development and Culture*. Cambridge, MA: MIT Press.

Kanner, Allen D., Theodore Roszak, and Mary E. Gomes. *Ecopsychology: Restoring the Earth, Healing the Mind*. San Francisco: Sierra Club Books, 1995.

Kaplan, Rachel, and Stephen Kaplan. *The Experience of Nature: A Psychological Perspective*. New York: Cambridge University Press, 1989.

Kaplan, Rachel, Stephen Kaplan, and Robert L. Ryan. *With People in Mind: Design and Management for Everyday Nature*. Washington, D.C.: Island Press, 1998.

Kellert, Stephen, and Peter Kahn, eds. *Children and Nature*. Cambridge, MA: MIT Press, 2002.

Kellert, S. Introduction in S. R. Kellert and E. O. Wilson, eds., *The Biophilia Hypothesis*. Washington, D.C.: Island Press/Shearwater, 1993.

Kempton, Willett, James S. Boster, and Jennifer A. Hartley. *Environmental Values in American Culture*. Cambridge, MA: MIT Press, 1995.

Lindquist, I. *Therapy Through Play*. London: Arlington Books, 1977.

Lovejoy, Sharon. *Sunflower Houses: Inspiration from the Garden—A Book for Children and Their Grown-Ups*. New York: Workman Publishing Company, 2001.

Martin, Deborah, Bill Lucas, Wendy Titman, and Siobhan Hayward, eds. *The Challenge of the Urban School Site*. Winchester Hants, Great Britain: Learning through Landscapes, 1996.

Metzner, Ralph. *Spirit, Self, and Nature: Essays in Green Psychology*. El Verno, CA: Green Earth, 1993.

Moore, Robin C. *Plants for Play: A Plant Selection Guide for Children's Outdoor Environments*. Berkeley: Mig Communications, 1993.

Moore, Robin C., and Herbert H. Wong. *Natural Learning: The Life of an Environmental Schoolyard*. Berkeley: MIG Communications, 1997.

Nabhan, Gary Paul, and Stephen A. Trimble. *The Geography of Childhood: Why Children Need Wild Places*. Boston: Beacon Press, Concord Library, 1995.

National Wildlife Federation. "Schoolyard Habitats: A How-to Guide for K-12 School Communities." Reston, VA: National Wildlife Federation, 2001.

Nicholson, S. "The Theory of Loose Parts." *Landscape Architecture* 62, no. 1: 30–34.

Orr, David W. *Ecological Literacy: Education and Transition to a Postmodern World*. Albany, NY: State University of New York Press, 1992.

———. *Earth in Mind: On Education, Environment, and the Human Prospect*. Washington, D.C.: Island Press, 1994.

Pyle, Robert Michael. *The Thunder Tree: Lessons from an Urban Wildland*. Boston: Houghton Mifflin, 1993.

Quammen, David. *Natural Acts: A Sidelong View of Science and Nature*. New York: Avon Books, 1985.

Reed, Edward S. *The Necessity of Experience*. New Haven, CT: Yale University Press, 1996.

Reeves, Diane Lindsey. *Career Ideas for Kids Who Like Animals and Nature*. New York: Facts on File, 2000.

Richardson, Beth. *Gardening with Children*. Newtown, CT: Tauton Press, 1998.

Rivkin, R. *The Great Outdoors: Restoring Children's Right to Play Outdoors*. Washington, D.C.: National Association for the Education of Young Children, 1995.

Roszak, Theodore. *The Voice of the Earth: An Exploration of Ecopsychology*. New York: Simon & Schuster, 1992.

Ruth, Linda Cain. *Design Standards for Children's Environments*. New York: McGraw-Hill, 1999.

Schiff, Paul D. *Twenty/Twenty: Projects and Activities for Wild School Sites: An Ohio Project Wild Action Guide*. Columbus, OH: Ohio Division of Wildlife, Education Section, 1996.

Snyder, Gary. *The Practice of the Wild*. Washington, D.C.: Shoemaker & Hoard, 2004.

Sobel, David. *Beyond Ecophobia: Reclaiming the Heart in Nature Education*. Great Barrington, MA: The Orion Society and the Myrin Institute, 1996.

———. *Place-Based Education: Connecting Classrooms and Communities*. Great Barrington, MA: The Orion Society and the Myrin Institute, 2004.

Stine, Sharon. *Landscapes for Learning: Creating Outdoor Environments for Children and Youth*. New York: Wiley, 1997.

Stokes, Donald, and Lillian Stokes. *The Bird Feeder Book*. Boston: Little, Brown, 1987.

Takahashi, Nancy. "Educational Landscapes: Developing School Grounds as Learning Places." Charlottesville, VA: University of Virginia, Thomas Jefferson Center for Educational Design, 1999.

Taylor, Anne P., and George Vlastos. *School Zone: Learning Environments for Children*. New York: School Zone Publishing Company, 1975.

Titman, Wendy. *Special Places; Special People: The Hidden Curriculum of School Grounds*. Surrey, England: World Wide Fund for Nature/Learning through Landscapes; New York: Touchstone, 1994.

United Nations. *The Convention on the Rights of the Child*. New York: UNICEF, 1989.

U.S. Fish and Wildlife Service. "Directory of Schoolyard Habitats Programs." Annapolis, MD: U.S. Fish and Wildlife, 1996.

Wadsworth, Ginger. *Rachel Carson: Voice for the Earth*. Minneapolis: Lerner Publications, 1992.

Wagner, Cheryl. *Planning School Grounds for Outdoor Learning*. Washington, D.C.: National Clearinghouse for Educational Facilities, 2000.

Westland, C., and J. Knight. *Playing, Living, Learning: A Worldwide Perspective on Children's Opportunities to Play*. State College, Pennsylvania: Venture Publishing, 1982.

Wilson, Edward O. *Biophilia*. Cambridge, MA: Harvard University Press, 1986.

Index

About the Author

Richard Louv is the author of seven books about family, nature, and community. A longtime columnist for the *San Diego Union-Tribune*, he has written for the *New York Times*, the *Christian Science Monitor,* and other newspapers and magazines, and he has been a columnist and member of the editoral advisory board for *Parents* magazine. He is also a Visiting Scholar at the Heller School for Social Policy and Management at Brandeis University and serves as an adviser to the National Scientific Council on the Developing Child and the Ford Foundation's Leadership for a Changing World award program. He is also a member of the Citistates Group, an organization of urban observers.

Richard Louv may be reached
by e-mail at rlouv@cts.com
or via www.thefuturesedge.com